Gendered Education

Sociological Reflections on Women, Teaching and Feminism

SANDRA ACKER

OPEN UNIVERSITY PRESS
Buckingham · Philadelphia

Open University Press
Celtic Court
22 Ballmoor
Buckingham
MK18 1XW

and
1900 Frost Road, Suite 101
Bristol, PA 19007, USA

First Published 1994

A catalogue record of this book is available from the British Library

ISBN 0 335 19059 6 (pb)   0 335 19060 X (hb)

Library of Congress Cataloging-in-Publication Data is available

Typeset by Dorwyn Ltd, Rowlands Castle, Hants
Printed in Great Britain by St Edmundsbury Press, Bury St Edmunds, Suffolk

*This book is dedicated to the memory of the women before me:
my mother, Marjorie Mitshkun Acker, and my grandmothers,
Dorothy Mitshkun and Anna Acker*

Contents

Acknowledgements

Chapters 2, 3, 5, 6, 7, 8 and 9 are edited versions of work published earlier. The publishers and journal editors have all graciously given permission to use this material. Publishers and details of the original publications are as follows:

Chapter 2: Blackwell Publishers, Oxford, for 'No-woman's-land: British sociology of education 1960–79'. *Sociological Review*, 1981, *29*(1): 77–104;

Chapter 3: UNESCO Institute for Education, Germany, for 'Feminist theory and the study of gender and education'. *International Review of Education*, 1987, *33*: 419–35;

Chapter 5: Falmer Press (Taylor and Francis), London, for 'Women and teaching: A semi-detached sociology of a semi-profession'. In S. Walker and L. Barton (Eds), *Gender, Class and Education*. Lewes: Falmer Press, 1983.

Chapter 6: Carfax Publishers, Oxford, for 'Teachers, gender and resistance'. *British Journal of Sociology of Education*, 1988, *9*(3): 307–322.

Chapter 7: Blackwell Publishers, Oxford, for 'Creating careers: Women teachers at work'. *Curriculum Inquiry*, 1992, *22*(2): 141–63.

Chapter 8: Carfax Publishers, Oxford, for 'Women, the other academics'. *British Journal of Sociology of Education*, 1980, *1*(1): 81–91.

Chapter 9: Falmer Press (Taylor and Francis), London, for 'Contradictions in terms: women academics in British universities'. In M. Arnot and K. Weiler (Eds), *Feminism and Social Justice in Education*. London: Falmer Press, 1993. Some extracts also appeared in 'New perspectives on an old problem: The position of women academics in British higher education'. *Higher Education*, 1992, *24*: 57–75, and are reproduced here by permission of Kluwer Academic Publishers, the Netherlands.

As the chapters were written over a period of more than a decade, there are many colleagues and friends I could acknowledge here. I found my initial attempts to write this section beginning to look like an invitation list to a large party, and there was the danger of leaving out one or two people inadvertently. Therefore, I decided not to acknowledge all such individuals by name, but to give a general thank you to former colleagues at the University of Bristol;

current colleagues at the Ontario Institute for Studies in Education; people in the wider circles of sociology, education and women's studies who have influenced and supported me; staff of the University of Bristol Education Library who patiently helped me track down references and statistics; students who have listened to my ideas and shared theirs; friends who have been steadfast.

Some of the chapters that follow contain acknowledgements to people who helped with or commented on the particular piece of work. There are also some individuals who must be mentioned by name. Andy Hargreaves, the Series Editor, persuaded me to write this book, continuing his always welcome encouragement for my work. B.J. Cook, Maureen Harvey, Guida Man, Brenda Mignardi, Kristine Pearson, Beth McAuley and the staff of the Open University Press all contributed to the technical production of this book or the manuscripts that preceded it. I owe special gratitude to Maureen Harvey, whose secretarial and caring skills helped me for many years in Bristol, to Beth McAuley, who did the index so capably, and to Kristine Pearson, who made the last stages of the book manageable with her calmness and word-processing ability.

Very special thanks go to David Satterly, whose friendship and wisdom have been invaluable, and to Miriam David, who shares so many of my interests and has always been a supportive friend. Above all I thank my family, especially my father and stepmother, Charles and Mercedes Acker, and my husband and daughter, Geoff and Dorie Millerson. Geoff has provided the domestic and intellectual support so necessary for my development as an academic. Dorie gives me hope for a feminist future.

Critical Introduction: Engendering Education – Feminism and the Sociology of Education

MIRIAM E. DAVID

This book is a very welcome collection of essays, some previously published and presented here in revised and up-to-date form. It spans 20 years of eager and earnest feminist scholarship in the sociology of education and encapsulates all that is excellent about the feminist approach to the sociology of education.

It is an absolute pleasure for me to write this critical introduction, as I have stood on the sidelines and watched the exciting developments in Professor Acker's work over these last 20 years, as both a colleague and friend. I have never failed to be impressed, and indeed astonished, with her facility to collect together an enormously wide-ranging literature, to summarize and impart it to others with clarity and verve and, in addition, to provide both the critical cutting edge and the *bon mot*. Given that, I feel greatly honoured to be invited to provide this critique and yet I also feel somewhat humble about so doing.

Professor Acker must surely be one of the foremost feminist writers in the field of the sociology of education, covering as she does three critical areas – feminist theories and analyses, studies of women as teachers in school and as academics in higher education. Moreover, she always locates her theories and analyses in the wider contexts of educational and social organization, including state policies and practices. In her more recent writings, this has come to include broader theories such as those of post-modernism. In so doing, she does not always embark upon a feminist study but always ends up with an analysis that is gendered. Perhaps this is now inevitable, since she is so thoroughly imbued with a feminist critique.

It is for this reason that I have entitled this introduction 'Engendering Education', as I feel that this is Professor Acker's unique and lasting contribution. Indeed, I hope that this book will be regarded as a textbook on gender and education, the first mature contribution since those early days of feminist approaches in the late 1970s when two important textbooks on gender and education were first published in Britain (Byrne 1978; Deem 1978). There has been little to replace these latter two textbooks, for we have all been largely preoccupied with developing our theories and/or approaches within specific areas, as indeed Sandra Acker has done. However, it is in drawing these areas together to provide such a comprehensive analysis that this new book represents a thorough statement of how education is gendered.

Feminism, gender and the sociology of education

In the Introduction and Part 1 of this book entitled 'Mapping the Field', Acker sets out her approach to feminism and gender analysis in education. She does so in true feminist fashion by starting from where she began and from her own standpoint. She presents her own educational biography and through it we learn about her own understandings of an early feminist approach, drawn partly from involvement in the women's movement and partly from her own feelings of interest and ambivalence about women's roles as teachers and students in education. We hear about her American Jewish origins and her father's career as a teacher, as well as her own graduate studies in a high-status educational institution, though she still intended being a schoolteacher.

We learn about the importance of feelings of marginality in many contexts to the creative urge to comprehend the impact and effects of gender in education. It is important to understand that the driving force behind many feminist approaches is the desire to understand and to try to eradicate what are seen and experienced as injustices. Acker also provides us with a succinct history of the sociology of education in Britain and begins to map its recent demise in the cold political climate of the Right, while pinpointing its limited vision about gender issues in education.

It is this relative exclusion of gender from education or educational studies that leads Acker to explore a variety of possible feminist approaches and analyses as well as different conceptualizations. She pursues her quest with customary vigour and obsessiveness until she finds the suitable theory or method for the occasion.

In this early part of the book, but especially in the Introduction where she also justifies her choice of organization of the chapters of the book, I was often reminded of Acker's other passion – that of music and being a pianist. She does not herself draw the analogy, but the book to me has the feel of a piece of music, perhaps a suite of dances or a theme and variations. I have the sense that there are basic melodies and harmonies, varying in key, rhythm, tempo and dynamic. The two consistent refrains are feminism and gender analysis with an especial emphasis on women; they are played in varying forms and at different levels of intensity.

However, Acker does try, somewhat vainly in my view, to escape what she seems to feel is the growing yoke of being seen only as an academic feminist. There are hints in the book that feminism has become more rather than less burdensome in some respects and in some quarters of academe in the late 1980s and early 1990s, given perhaps the wider political context. She demonstrates this explicitly in Chapter 4, and it is especially clear in her recent analysis of higher education and the position of women academics in Chapter 9. She herself has suffered a great deal from having had to take more responsibility – in true maternal fashion – for keeping alive the feminist credo than any one person in an academy can possibly do. And yet she has shouldered it and weathered it all with great dignity and finesse.

She is, therefore, right to point to the difficulties, blocks, exclusions and marginalizations that feminists experience and yet she perhaps underestimates our relative strengths and influences at least in the academic world and world of educational and sociological research. The backlash may be real – indeed, I am sure it is – but it is a response to a growing and serious influence in the world of educational scholarship to which this book bears witness.

Faludi's (1992) feminist analysis of popular and political cultures and the political 'backlash' against feminism in the USA, provides us with a crucial contextual account of the extent to which there is a dramatic reaction to feminist politics and theories. Coward (1992) also draws our attention to the need for feminists to revise their theories to take account of women's experiences and deeper feelings especially towards motherhood and partnerships with men. So indeed there are the stirrings of a deeper and more mature approach to gender analysis, like the one that Acker herself develops.

As Acker points out, one of her more recent studies, conducted with colleagues, of postgraduate research students, was commenced and carried out without an explicit feminist approach. It was one of her attempts to avoid the constant feminist label and to become more of a mainstream sociological or educational researcher. And to some extent it worked – the research is part of a broader, considered analysis of the state of postgraduate training in Britain today, out of which many conclusions and policy prescriptions have been drawn (Burgess, 1994).

However, she is forced also to acknowledge the importance of applying a feminist analysis to her research materials and evidence. Indeed, almost without explicit consideration the women students 'foreground' themselves, by giving different accounts of their lives, preoccupations and work concerns than the male students. Acker writes in Chapter 4:

> What stood out were categories of family relationships, sense of mission and self-confidence. Interviews with women, especially those over age 25 or so, contained many references to their partners and their children, despite no direct questions being asked about families. For example, when reviewing their past higher education careers, women often integrated into their accounts references to when their children were born, or when they were pregnant, or when they moved because of a partner's job. Men did this very rarely . . .
>   . . . The most arresting theme was what we were calling self-confidence . . . At an extreme we read some transcripts where students appeared to feel they were strangers in the academy . . . More often women seemed to distance themselves from their achievements. (pp. 64–5)

This kind of self-evident gendering of experiences in education, including higher education, and its links with family and family-life experiences, is very powerful indeed. But it requires a sophisticated feminist researcher such as Acker to provide us with the materials and the gloss. It does, however, confirm the continuing salience and importance of feminist studies to ensure that we are constantly alert to such continuing injustices and vigilant in pointing them out.

It also adds to the growing evidence from several studies of the complexities of changing the nature and characteristics of the student population in higher education. I, too, have explored with others some of these thorny questions (David *et al.* 1993). So, too, have Edwards (1993) and Sperling (1991) separately. We have all looked at mature women students who are undergraduates in higher education and who are also mothers, and we have explored the continuities and contrasts between their lives and experiences and those who are not in higher education but may be mothers in adult education or involved in their children's schooling. What is particularly striking is the commonalities in their experiences whatever educational institution they may be attached to; women's experiences of family are more critical for them as preoccupations than are men's. The boundaries between family and education are drawn more tightly and women's experience of them is less easy to avoid.

However, what can and should be done about them remains a thorny problem, as Acker also makes clear in her conclusion. Coward, as I noted above, has also addressed this as a problematic issue and one that is not easily amenable to hasty solutions, such as merely trying to add more women to the academy. Indeed, quite clearly the academy is transformed in fact if not in effect by its gendered nature. Acker properly struggles with these questions for her own conclusion and for future considerations. And in a sense it takes her back to some of her early beginnings – to explore the content of academic curricula and texts and test them for their gender biases.

Chapter 2, 'No-woman's-land', was one of Acker's first contributions to feminist analysis in the sociology of education and still in its updated form it remains for me a *tour de force*. It had, in any event, an immediate and well-deserved reception in the sociology of education. It was taken up and cited not only by feminists but by non-feminists and indeed by antifeminists. It was an intuitively simple approach but, curiously perhaps, no-one had thought to do it before. Acker provided a neat content analysis of three of the journals published in sociology, looking at education articles and looking for gender issues or explicit references to gender and especially women within them. She paints this portrait:

> I noted 184 articles. Of these, the great majority (143) report some kind of empirical work. Their samples were coded as mixed, all male or all female . . .
>
> We might anticipate the details to follow by imagining a Martian coming to Britain and deriving some impressions of the society and its educational system from reading these articles. The Martian would conclude that numerous boys but few girls go to secondary modern schools;

that there are no girls' public schools; that there are almost no adult women influentials of any sort; that most students in higher education study science and engineering; that women rarely make a ritual transition called 'from school to work' and never go into further education colleges. Although some women go to university, most probably enter directly into motherhood, where they are of some interest as transmitters of language codes to their children. And except for a small number of teachers, social workers and nurses, there are almost no adult women workers in the labour market. (pp. 30–1)

The Martian's picture might now be somewhat modified both by the changes in educational organization and political context and by the burgeoning and more explicit gender studies in education. But, as Acker points out, these have not all had a lasting influence and 'malestream' sociology of education remains relatively impervious to such explicit gender analyses.

What is most significant about this chapter is its attention to detail and to very carefully crafted scholarship and content analysis of gender. This method clearly does remain extremely powerful and important to replicate. Perhaps what remains lacking in this approach is an account of why the sociology of education as a whole, then as now, has tended to be relatively impervious to feminist analyses or critiques. This question is not one that concerns Acker greatly, since she is more interested in the mapping of approaches and theories, truly engendering education. Yet for me, through this chapter and others, it remains something of a puzzle which may merit further exploration.

Acker's further exploration is to compare and contrast different feminist theories and explanations, which she tackles in some depth in the next chapter, entitled 'Feminist theory and the study of gender and education'. Originally published at the height of feminist theoretical influence in 1987, here she carefully maps a variety of different feminist theories and shows how they have been used in studies within the sociology of education. This is yet another vital paper for setting out the contextual and conceptual apparatus for a gender analysis. But again Acker fights shy of exploring the reasons for the diversity of approaches, preferring here to present a more pragmatic argument:

Are we moving towards a synthesis of feminist educational approaches? Deep conceptual divides remain. But it seems to me that, with a few exceptions, feminist theoretical writing about education manages to be constructively critical without the vitriol sometimes found in other spheres of feminist commentary. Possibly this can be traced to the tradition of pragmatism in much educational thought: the immediate goal of making conditions better overrides some of the theoretical disputes. Many writers work in educational institutions themselves and thus sustain some commitment to educational change through educational means (p. 53)

Although this chapter, too, has mapped out the diversity of theories from liberal feminist to socialist feminist to radical feminist, this conclusion is implicitly if not explicitly concerned with what I would call a liberal-humanist approach. Acker implies that her own leanings, as those of most educational researchers, are towards the use of scholarship and writing as a means to change, whether social or intellectual.

As an academic and teacher educator – whether or not feminist – she remains throughout thoroughly imbued with her liberal-humanist approach to education and change, which is committed to the idea of scholarship and the development of knowledge. This may, in the end, be as much a weakness as a strength in trying to convince education *institutions* to take serious account of gender. Others have argued for different strategies and stronger solutions, such as transforming the academy through either feminist management and/or the recruitment of more women, particularly non-traditional women students, to study (Sperling 1991; Ruijs 1993).

These stronger political solutions of new styles of academic and educational management may, of course, contribute to the backlash to which I have already alluded against feminism in education and the academy (King 1993; Ozga 1993). Acker may well be right to counsel caution and proper scholarly approaches. On the other hand, she could be accused of being faint-hearted and insufficiently radical, in a political sense, in her solutions to engendering education.

However, she too was involved – and not just on the sidelines – when I published a personal account of becoming a feminist academic manager (David 1989). This essay was included in one of Acker's edited volumes entitled *Teachers, Gender and Careers* (1989). The essay provoked an enormous debate both internally in my educational institution and in print (Harrison and Lyon 1993; Ruijs 1993). To some extent, this debate could be seen as part of a backlash against any forms of unusual educational change or rather precipitate educational change, through feminist politics. It is not, though, dissimilar to the reactions to any kind of change, not only those in education (Marris 1974).

In any event, attempting educational change through feminist management strategies is, with the benefit of hindsight, hazardous and requires a delicate negotiating strategy and political balance. However, professional and senior management pressure groups such as 'Beyond The Glass Ceiling' have recently been formed to develop strategies for women senior academics and/or managers in higher education (King 1993). They may well provide sufficient collective strength to begin to chip away at little, local resistances and help the general processes of transforming management in a feminist direction. But all these solutions and strategies require enormous reserves of strength and energy to keep up the political fight, which may detract from more serious pursuit of knowledge. Researching and working with your students and women colleagues, wherever they are, may prove a far preferable alternative.

This appears to be what Acker has opted for and her passionate interest in their welfare is clearly demonstrated in several chapters, but especially the chapter based on a study of postgraduate research students conducted by Acker and colleagues. The chapter is entitled 'Is research by a feminist always feminist research?' The simple answer to her question appears to be 'yes' as we have already mentioned. However, this chapter sets out clearly and coherently the various approaches to feminist research, demonstrating that feminist research does not necessarily need to be at the stage of conception but may well be equally valid during either gestation or the birth of the project. To take the maternity analogy further, feminist research may well derive from female or maternal 'ways of knowing', rather than more deliberate acts of intervention or involvement.

Interestingly, Acker does not refer to this as one approach to feminist research in this part of the chapter and yet, it seems to me, the idea of different ways of knowing has become an important paradigm in feminist research. Belenky *et al.* (1986) first coined the phrase but the method has been taken up by several researchers, most recently by Gilligan and Brown (1992). Gilligan and Brown explore teenage girls' development into womanhood through a series of in-depth unstructured interviews with girls from two very different locales and high schools in the USA. They concentrate in particular on their method as being crucial to gaining an understanding of how the girls learned relationships. The interviews with postgraduate research students that Acker writes about could merit further detailed analysis to clarify the different ways of knowing between the men and women students. It would add to her repertoire of feminist research and insights.

Feminism, gender and teachers

In Parts 2 and 3 of the book, we are invited first to revisit a number of essays on women teachers at various levels in the educational system – teachers in schools and teachers in higher education – and then to learn more of them from more recent ethnographic or other in-depth research. This approach of setting the scene with her earlier contributions coupled with presenting mature and developing approaches to the subject matter in each of these two parts of the book, yet again leads me to the notion that this book is like a musical arrangement of prose rather than notes. The themes and refrains are here presented in dramatic variations. And Part 2 focuses our attention on the traditional subjects of educational research, whereas Part 3 brings us back to the origins of both the book and feminist research, using personal experience and place as the subject of academic research.

Chapter 5 was also one of Acker's original and exciting pieces of research and scholarship. In analysing 'a semi-detached sociology of a semi-profession', Acker challenged us, then as now, to share her feelings about the various marginalities of women and teaching as a profession. She shared with her audience her own feelings of distance from her subjects and yet, at the same time, her own personal involvements with this. It seems to me that this is a very neat way of conveying mixed feelings of marginality and yet conveying a flavour of their equally rich feelings and experiences. Her use of Etzioni's (1969) theories of 'semi-professions' is inspired, especially in view of his more recent and explicit anti-feminist leanings (Etzioni 1993). However, Acker, as is her wont, is only quietly critical of this theory by reference to a chapter in the book rather than the book's approach as a whole. I quote her:

Semi-professions are schoolteaching, social work, nursing, and librarianship. All are highly 'feminized'. The chapter in the collection that best represents the blame-the-woman approach is 'Women and bureaucracy in the semi-professions' by Richard Simpson and Ida Simpson. It is certainly a caricature and might almost be a parody. Simpson and Simpson (1969) see bureaucratic control . . . as a *consequence* of the presence of women . . . Several pages follow on the harm women do to the professional hopes of these occupations. (pp. 77–8)

In this chapter, she uses her usual method of critical evaluation of the literature on women and teachers to draw her conclusions. Her conclusions were, when this essay was first published, particularly strong for feminist research and its future in engendering education. She wrote:

While we cannot pursue, let alone resolve, all the methodological and epistemological questions that arise from an attempt to develop and apply fundamental and implementary theories, it should be clear that a rapprochement between certain feminist theories and the sociology of teaching could be promising and productive . . . Implementary approaches could result in empirical studies of schools, considering, for example, gender relationships among teachers. (p. 88)

True to her own agenda, she set out to conduct such research, some of which is produced in the following two chapters. In Chapter 6, she again provides us with a fulsome critique and evaluation of the research evidence and literature regarding teachers and gender, especially with respect to the imbalance between the burgeoning academic feminist research and the contrasting limited action on anti-sexist initiatives in schools. Her conclusion is similar to that found in much of the literature on implementing change, as we have already referred to. She does not, however, make much of this problem, preferring to try to convince through her own moral persuasion and intellectual arguments. This is now beginning to appear as her stock-in-trade solution. To quote her:

It could be said that teachers 'resist' such initiatives, in most cases simply by not recognizing or accepting that there is an educational issue involved . . . 'Resistance' appears double-edged, preventing progress but also protecting against illegitimate pressures and impossible demands . . . One gap (indeed, chasm) badly needing filling is the one between feminist and sociological scholarship on gender on the one hand, and teachers' everyday school experience on the other. (p. 103)

In fact, instead of trying to bridge that gap/chasm by action, she sets out, in Chapter 7, to present us with her own fascinatingly rich ethnographic study of two primary schools in England to pinpoint how women's teaching careers develop.

This chapter, which is drawn from her research in the late 1980s and early 1990s, brings out themes and refrains that have come before but in new variations. We are again invited to consider women's marginality, their feelings about family, especially partners and children, their ambivalences to careers and occupational progress, and to feminism itself fraught with dangers as it appears to be. This chapter, however, provides us with rich empirical evidence of these women teachers' feelings, views and values. And as a 'semi-detached sociologist' still looking at a 'semi-profession', Acker enjoins us to sympathize with these dilemmas. She writes:

> It could be argued that women primary school teachers are contributing to the reproduction of gender inequality by their acceptance, unwilling as it may be, of the inequalities in their own lives. My teachers weren't overtly fighting the *status quo* . . . A forcible feminism would have been counterproductive in the circumstances . . . A 'strategic fatalism' . . . seemed much better adapted to the realities of their lives. They remake definitions of careers and commitments to suit their preferences and their possibilities, strategizing for security and maximum flexibility within the particular 'patriarchal bargain' . . . offered by their circumstances. (p. 119–20)

And so in a sense we are back with the original theme, now played more quietly but also far more confidently and assertively – the difficulties and dangers of implementing a feminist analysis, however intuitively appealing it might be.

Now we are invited to return to the stronger rhythms and arguments of earlier feminist analysis, here with one of Acker's first and most powerful critiques. Chapter 8, 'Women, the other academics', in its original version, was published in the *British Journal of Sociology of Education* in its early days. Acker here is at her best with her trenchant critique of how academic life in Britain systematically marginalizes, excludes or discriminates against women but in subtle ways through the themes and operation of family and everyday life. She selects three key issues by which to analyse these processes, concluding with her now familiar but nevertheless strong refrain, expressed most assertively and assuredly:

> What links all three problems . . . is the 'otherness' of women academics . . . Women are marginal to the academic enterprise, because full tribute to greedy institutions is only feasible for persons without competing claims from other greedy institutions; because token status results in invisibility, powerlessness and lack of opportunity; because dominant groups deny the contributions and distort the characteristics of subordinates. (p. 132)

She considers political action but concludes that 'asking feminist questions' is likely to have most impact, 'being in the knowledge business, so to speak'. Here we have an early example of how Acker is so rooted in a liberal-humanist scholarly approach, a truly academic approach.

And so we come full circle, to her academic approach to academic matters in the early 1990s. This is presented in Chapter 9, which is a thorough analysis of the situation of women academics in British universities, seeing the problem as a 'contradiction in terms'. First, we are provided again with a clear and succinct mapping of the facts and problems, of the approaches and theories, including strategies for change. This chapter shows, *par excellence*, just how little progress has been made in the last 10–20 years with engendering higher education. But again Acker counsels caution but not quite despair, giving confidence to others:

> So feminists need not give up just yet. As I have suggested, liberal-feminist analysis is inadequate to explain the persistence of deep gender divisions in academic life. Socialist and radical feminisms go further to explain why the barriers to women are so strong. Yet when considering strategies, we confront something of a paradox. [Socialist feminist and radical feminist strategies] are long term . . . or provocative and likely to arouse opposition or even ridicule . . . [thus] it may be that even those with radical or socialist sympathies need to pursue liberal strategies in the short run . . .
>
> The strategies will need to be adapted to their context: institutions complacent towards certain issues but in flux and crisis. Working through academic unions may provide a relatively 'respectable' base. Feminist academics need to use their skills as scholars to look at their own institutions . . .
>
> . . . Feminist theories help us to understand how serious the situation is, and why change is so frustratingly slow. Accepting this, we can work at deepening the cracks, crevices and contradictions of the patriarchal university. (pp. 149–50)

And so the familiar yet compelling theme returns with quiet confidence and reassurance: to explore a gender analysis and to use this analysis to build new theories and arguments, based on sound scholarship, to whittle away at the traditional structures of patriarchy within education and academe. Here is Acker at her most scholarly liberal best – not the strident feminist, the harridan, the political radical committed only to root and branch change. Acker presents us with *the* most powerful argument, that of voice – giving voice to our theories, our analyses and our passionate dislike of injustice, particularly that based on an irrationality, that of gender.

Acker's volume, then, is indeed the prose equivalent of a musical composition. We read the themes, the variations, the chords, the harmonies, the loud, the soft, the gentle and the almost mute. She has presented us with a veritable feast of ideas, material, information, maps, documents, concepts and theories. We keep being invited to listen to the voices of women – women teachers, women students, women academics, feminist theorists, feminist analysts, feminist methodologists. All tell us, in harmony, of their otherness, their marginality, their exclusion, their preoccupations, their families, their mothers, their sisters, their children, their daughters . . .

And we are urged to listen, to argue, to inform, to build afresh our educational institutions, our universities, through the pursuit of knowledge and scholarly work, through intellectual work as action in itself. And in this way, Acker confidently assures us, education will indeed be engendered.

References

Acker, S. (Ed.) (1989). *Teachers, Gender and Careers.* London: Falmer Press.

Belenky, M., Clinchy, D.M., Goldberger, N.R. and Tarule, J.M. (1986). *Women's Ways of Knowing: The Development of Self, Voice and Mind.* New York: Basic Books.

Burgess, R. (Ed.) (1994). *Postgraduate Education and Training in the Social Sciences.* London: Jessica Kingsley.

Byrne, E. (1978). *Women and Education.* London: Tavistock.

Coward, R. (1992). *Our Treacherous Hearts: Why Women Let Men Get Their Way.* London: Faber and Faber.

David, M.E. (1989). Prima donna inter pares? Women in academic management. In S. Acker (Ed.), *Teachers, Gender and Careers.* London: Falmer Press.

David, M.E., Edwards, R., Hughes, M. and Ribbens, J. (1993). *Mothers and Education Inside Out? Exploring Family Education Experience and Policy.* London: Macmillan.

Deem, R. (1978). *Women and Schooling.* London: Routledge and Kegan Paul.

Edwards, R. (1993). *Mature Women Students: Separating or Connecting Family and Education.* London: Taylor and Francis.

Etzioni, A. (Ed.) (1969). *The Semi-professions and their Organization.* New York: Free Press.

Etzioni, A. (1993). *The Parenting Deficit.* London: Demos.

Faludi, S. (1992). *Backlash: The Undeclared War Against Women.* London: Chatto and Windus.

Gilligan, C. and Brown, L.M. (1992). *Meeting at the Crossroads: Girls' Development.* Cambridge, MA: Harvard University Press.

Harrison, B. and Lyon, E.S. (1993). A note on ethical issues in the use of autobiography in sociological research. *Sociology, 27*(1): 101–110.

King, C. (Ed.) (1993). *Through the Glass Ceiling: Effective Senior Management Development For Women.* Wirral: Tudor.

Marris, P. (1974). *Loss and Change.* London: Routledge and Kegan Paul.

Ozga, J. (Ed.) (1993). *Women in Educational Management.* Buckingham: Open University Press.

Ruijs, A. (1993). *Women Managers in Education: A Worldwide Progress Report.* Coombe Lodge Report Vol. 23, Nos 7–8. Bristol: The Staff College.

Sperling, G. (1991). Can the barrier be breached? Mature women's access to higher education. *Gender and Education, 3*(2): 199–213.

1 Introduction: Finding a Path

This chapter tells the story of how this book came into being, a story that necessitates a look at the biography of its writer – myself – and the intellectual currents that have surrounded me. It also serves as an introduction to the chapters that follow.

The papers in this volume were written in the 1980s and early 1990s. The idea for the book grew out of a conversation with Andy Hargreaves, the editor for the *Modern Educational Thought* series, who encouraged me to collect together my writings on gender and education. In another sense, the origins of the book lie in my interests and inclinations, which go back years before the papers were actually composed. As Mills (1959: 196) tells us: 'You must learn to use your life experience in your intellectual work: continually to examine and interpret it'. My work is influenced by the details of my biography; by the institutional, departmental and subject cultures in which I have participated; and by the national contexts in which I have worked. I cannot do justice to all of these large topics here, but I shall try to sketch some of the most salient features.

Background

My interests in education, in teachers, in careers, in academics and graduate students, and in gender and feminism, all have roots in my personal history. I grew up in Detroit, in a Jewish family, the eldest of three daughters. My parents were teachers, although my mother gave up paid work when I was born. I was successful at school and at the piano and thought for a time I might become a musician. I had a dim awareness of class divisions during school, but not the terminology for it; I had a somewhat higher consciousness of race, both because of Jewish awareness of the catastrophic consequences of racial theories and because Detroit was the site of racial conflict and struggles over territory. I now see gender as having powerful shaping effects, but at the time – the 1950s and early 1960s – we had no means of naming the 'feminine mystique' (Friedan, 1963) or the subordination of women – we simply lived it.

In my junior year (third of four) at Wayne State University, I encountered sociology and psychology for the first time. Sociology, in particular, was a revelation. It provided both intellectual stimulation and social insights. Sociology promised – I thought then – a means of making the world better for its less fortunate inhabitants. I particularly enjoyed a 'School and Society' course, in which we became deeply involved in the problems of disadvantaged children.

But by then I was committed, like most of my female friends, to a school-teaching career. I did my student teaching (in mathematics), taught briefly, and then made the decision to leave home and do a higher degree in Sociology of Education at the University of Chicago. I expected to get a master's degree, concentrating on education and social disadvantage, then return home to teach.

This shift was my first experience of culture shock, certainly socially but even more so intellectually. Even the best courses in my undergraduate degree had served up knowledge in chunks to be memorized and regurgitated for tests. Suddenly, I was handed long reading lists and told they would be the basis of doctoral examinations three years hence. My original ambition was completely outside the department's preferences and snobberies, into which I was gradually inducted: greater prestige derived from theorizing about education systems and abstract schools than from going into real ones; it was better to write about higher education than lower education; above all, it was better to do a doctorate and enter academic life than to stop with the delightfully dubbed 'terminal masters'. But in general the exposure to books, scholarship, ideas and people was exciting and extended my horizons. The one thing that was missing was women academics. Although there were numerous women students, I can only think of four women faculty members anywhere in the university at that time, and only one was tenured.

This was the late 1960s, a time of change and excitement. It was the era of student protest – from Vietnam to university grading practices – and of a taste of countercultural lifestyle in student circles. Most pertinent, there were the stirrings of the women's movement. It became possible, and desirable, to study 'women', and I did so in my doctoral thesis. I could be termed a 'pathfinder', Gumport's (1990) name for the generation of academic feminists who entered graduate school between about 1964 and 1972 and have participated in the construction of feminist scholarship.

My thesis was a survey of over 1000 women and men graduate students at another university. I was looking to see how much they had absorbed the 'graduate school ideology', essentially the one to which I had been painfully converted, that the proper outcome of one's years of study was a desire to be a scholar, an academic, to publish and to conduct research. My study was conceived firmly within what I later saw as a deficit model of women (the dominant model of early women's studies) (see Chapter 8). Why were there so few women academics? Why did women more often do masters degrees than doctorates? Why were women's aspirations and ambitions 'lower' than men's? The framework, typical of its time in the United States, was one of choices and opportunities, and it was rooted in liberal feminism and 'male as norm' common sense. Later, I was to react against such an approach, trying to stop blaming the victim and searching instead for the shapers of action in surrounding structures, while performing the balancing act of allowing individuals to create, interpret and negotiate.

When I moved to Bristol, England, in 1971, I was more culturally stunned than culture-shocked. For quite some time, I was marginalized by not knowing local customs or politics, not grasping the sense of humour and, unexpectedly, barely speaking the language. I was also Jewish in a city without a strong Jewish presence; a woman in a university dominated by men; a feminist where the women's movement was underground in more ways than one (it met in a basement). Even my sociology was all wrong: there were different heroes, different pariahs.

Moreover, I had no networks, mentors or connections in my field. Gradually I became involved, first in sociological circles, and then in the developing networks of the sociology of education and the sociology of women's education. Gumport (1990) notes that many of the 'pathfinders' in her study belonged to informal groups of women academics. Such groups provided a source of moral and intellectual support across disciplines and outside of university departments that might not be hospitable to feminist ideas. The British Sociological Association (BSA) Southwest Women's Caucus functioned in exactly that way in the 1970s and early 1980s. Women social scientists from the Bristol, Bath and Cardiff areas met several times a term to share our research in progress. The standing joke was that only a handful of participants were sociologists and BSA members.[1]*

My experiences of marginality were never as severe as those of many groups different from the dominant society. But they were sufficient to teach me how prevailing ideas are shaped in a social and cultural context, a theme appearing in several of my papers. Chapter 2, which critiques the images of women in sociology of education, Chapter 5, which does the same for studies of the teaching profession, and Chapter 8, which explores the 'otherness' of women academics, all show a concern with the ways in which academic discourses marginalize contributions of particular groups. Similarly, my experiences as a woman and feminist academic in Britain and, since 1991, in Canada frame the discussion in Chapter 4 of what kind of scholarship is possible in particular work settings. Work settings themselves as facilitators or limiting influences for teachers are a theme of Chapters 6 and 7.

Chapters in this volume consider continuities and changes concerning the education of women and gender relations and examine the ways in which scholars have approached these topics. The earliest paper was published in 1980 and the most recent ones were written in 1993. In this time period, we see the rise (and perhaps the start of the fall) of British sociology of education, and the shift of gender from a peripheral to a more central place within the field. The next sections outline these trends.

---

* Superscript numerals refer to numbered notes at the end of each chapter.

Trends in sociology of education

Although the origins of the sociology of education in Britain can be traced to
the efforts of early socialist reformers, or to the demographic studies at the
London School of Economics in the 1930s, it only flourished as an institutionalized discipline in the 1960s, when concern with the effects of home
background upon school performance led to its inclusion in the curriculum of
teacher education. With hindsight, the field's preoccupations in that decade
can be seen as rather narrow. Large areas potentially within the purview of the
field were almost entirely neglected, including the study of processes inside
schools and classrooms, the sociological study of the curriculum, and gender
and race.

The 1970s brought what was dubbed the 'new sociology of education', a
movement particularly associated with the volume *Knowledge and Control*, edited by M.F.D. Young (1971). The book's main contribution was to raise the
question of what counts as knowledge in the school curriculum. Although
some commentators identified the new sociology exclusively with interpretive
approaches, another theme in the volume was that 'what counts' is determined
by a society's economic and political structures. What can be traced to the early
1970s is a two-pronged advance within British sociology of education, with
groupings known in a kind of shorthand as 'the neo-Marxists' and 'the
ethnographers'.

Neo-Marxism was influenced by the 'new sociology' and by certain works
from the United States, especially *Schooling in Capitalist America* (Bowles and
Gintis 1976). The ethnographers developed a British version of Chicago-style
symbolic interactionism and drew upon it to explore processes in schools and
classrooms (see, e.g. Woods 1979; Burgess 1983; Ball and Goodson 1985).
Over time, the neo-Marxists were influenced by Willis (1977), Apple (1979)
and others to move away from rigid reproduction models towards those which
incorporated a notion of resistance. The ethnographers became increasingly
aware of theoretical issues in the production of ethnography.

The two strands were not always as distinct as it might seem; for example,
some of the ethnographers were concerned to locate their work within wider
contexts. By the late 1970s, the two groups had been joined by a third, 'the
feminists', for as Chapter 2 of this volume shows, sociology of education had
paid little attention to gender before that time. Again, in practice, those identifying with the feminist strand usually had affiliations with other approaches,
too. But these three foci together created a dynamic discipline.

A discipline, or even a subdiscipline, has certain identifying symbols: a
textbook, a journal, a professional association or other means of constructing an
intellectual community. Lacking a comfortable home in either the professional
associations of sociology or of education, British sociology of education needed
a new network. Mainly through the efforts of Len Barton, then at Westhill
College of Education and now at Sheffield University, the subdiscipline was
given such a base, first in the annual International Sociology of Education
Conference, which began in 1978 and continues still, and second in the

creation in 1980 of a new flagship journal in the field, the *British Journal of Sociology of Education* (*BJSE*). Many of the same individuals (including myself) were active in both the conferences and the journal. Two of the chapters in this volume (Chapters 6 and 8) were first published in the *BJSE*, and another (Chapter 5) was originally a paper presented at one of the sociology of education conferences.

Sociology of education in North America developed independently of its British cousin. As Jane Gaskell (1992) shows, mainstream sociology in the United States was relatively conservative in the 1960s and 1970s, concerned with order in society and influenced by a functionalist and human capital perspective that saw social arrangements as consequences of society's survival needs. Sociologists of the time regarded education as a largely positive mediator between family and work: The dominant paradigm for linking education and the economy was the status attainment approach, which sought to measure the relative effects on occupational attainment of variables such as family background (including socio-economic status, or 'SES') and educational attainments. The favoured methods were quantitative and statistical. In general, pioneering Canadian research documenting social-class inequality in education took place a few years later than the work in the United States (Synge 1993), although the approach was similar. However, as Synge points out, there are important differences in the political and educational arrangements in the two countries; for example, Canada does not experience the enormous variation in education spending characteristic of the United States.

Despite the strong tradition of 'political arithmetic' in 1960s British empirical work on education and the economy (the calculation of chances of individuals from particular social classes to attain certain educational or occupational outcomes), British sociology of education put less store on the mastery of complex quantitative methods and more emphasis on theory than did American sociology of the same era. Although quantitative work continued in Britain (e.g. Halsey *et al.* 1980), qualitative research techniques became the norm, as the symbolic interactionists and the cultural studies proponents (e.g. Willis, 1977) produced much of the empirical work of the 1970s and 1980s.

Eventually, qualitative research came to prominence in North American educational research, too (Peshkin 1993). One variant, sometimes called critical education theory or critical ethnography (Simon and Dippo 1986), sought to move away from the pessimism and determinism of correspondence theories such as the one outlined in *Schooling in Capitalist America* (Bowles and Gintis 1976). Influenced by Paulo Freire, critical theorists try to retrieve the liberating potential of education and emphasize individual agency as well as (or instead of) structures. Kathleen Weiler (1988) explains how production rather than reproduction of cultures becomes central to the analysis, thus establishing some links with phenomenological or other interpretive perspectives.

Critical education theory, and its classroom counterpart, critical pedagogy, claims to be different from other approaches because it offers an explicit moral commitment to empowerment and emancipation. Examples include: Weiler's (1988) own study of feminist teachers; McLaren's (1989) *Life in Schools*, an account of his year teaching in a Canadian school and his subsequent efforts to theorize it; and Britzman's (1991) *Practice Makes Practice*, a critical ethnography of how student teachers learn to teach. Although British ethnographies also demonstrate commitments to social change, critical education theory remains a largely North American movement and one which straddles curriculum studies and sociology.

British sociology of education, in contrast, appears to be moving away from theory and strongly into educational policy research. This move follows several years of speeches in forums like the British Educational Research Association and the International Sociology of Education Conferences during the 1980s, urging theorists to take their skills into the real world and provide guidance to policy-makers, but does not really result from such exhortations. Instead, the main influence is the long period of Conservative political rule which has been anti-sociology and has failed to provide institutional conditions under which critical scholarship could thrive.

There are several ways in which the shift towards policy studies and away from 'straight' sociology of education has been accomplished. For example, money for educational research has been made available for studies of government initiatives such as the National Curriculum. More important is the way in which teacher training curricula and in-service work have undergone enormous and unsettling changes, with sociological input being squeezed down or out. The right-wing commentators who have apparently had the ear of government were particularly opposed to sociological influences in teacher education, influences that they regarded as irrelevant or subversive (Furlong 1992). Since the mid-1980s, the central government, in part through a body set up to accredit institutions providing teacher training, has been increasingly prescriptive about the shape of the initial teacher education curriculum. As I write, a new agency, with even greater control over teacher education and educational research, is being proposed. In-service teacher education has also been altered by providing funds targeted only to government priorities. Money for in-service education has been delegated to the schools and efforts have been made to shift responsibility for initial teacher education, too, towards schools and away from institutions of higher education.

These trends have been harmful – possibly catastrophic – for the sociology of education. Furlong (1992: 172) tells us that in teacher education, 'disciplinary teaching as such is now virtually extinct', while Dale (1992: 202) notes the 'almost total disappearance of the sociology of education as a separate teaching subject from the syllabus of courses of teacher education'. British sociology of education's traditionally close affiliation with teacher education (Bernbaum 1977), once its ticket to influence, now seems a serious weakness. Shilling (1993), in a review of *Voicing Concerns* (Arnot and Barton, 1992), the book containing the Furlong and Dale chapters referenced above, takes the field to task for moving so far away from its parent discipline of sociology and for substituting atheoretical policy studies for intellectual contributions. His review is titled 'The demise of sociology of education in Britain?'

Certainly, sociology of education in Britain can no longer be said to be flourishing. To my knowledge, no comprehensive textbooks have been published since 1986 (Burgess 1986; Meighan 1986; Reid 1986). *Voicing Concerns* (Arnot and Barton 1992) comes closest to a volume of key readings for the subject and it is, as Shilling notes, forced to be defensive about the value of the field. Like myself, certain key figures have left the country, including Ivor Goodson, Andy Hargreaves and Roger Dale. About half of the articles published in the *BJSE* come from outside the UK, although that could be seen as a welcome attempt to internationalize, rather than harm, the discipline. The combination of financial squeezes and the lack of demand for sociology of education meant that when I left my university position in Britain, I was not replaced.

My view, however, is that it is the institutional and political factors, rather than the mistakes of its practitioners, that account for the perilous position of the field. 'Demand' for courses has been engineered in the manner described above. There is a certain irony in the continuing popularity of sociology at A-level. For sociologists of education, teacher education had provided an audience for its teaching, a market for its books, jobs for its scholars. Although the successful institutionalization of a conference and a journal in the field could be said to have deepened the split between the subdiscipline and sociology proper, there is no evidence that the parent discipline especially wanted education in its fold. The last BSA Annual Conference with education as its theme was in 1970.

It must also be remembered that universities have been in constant crisis and contraction since the early 1980s (Walford 1992). Working conditions have worsened and even the cash to travel to multiple conferences is just not available. There has been a major shift towards casualized labour (see Chapter 9) in the academic labour market. Sociology of education is only one of the many academic fields that will be faced with problems of reproduction, as its adherents grow older and the younger generation (if there is one) fail to find secure jobs.

Schools of Education have had to face *both* the incursions into academic freedom and security suffered by higher education generally *and* the fallout from the government's educational reforms in the schools and alterations of teacher education. The survival strategies (moving into applied and policy areas) criticized by Dale (1992) and Shilling (1993) do not seem so unreasonable to me; they may at least ensure there is a core of the field to be regenerated in better times. Largely ignored in the debate over the future of the field is the feminist input, to which I now turn more explicitly.

The sociology of women's education[2]

Creating a focus

Education was an issue in the early second-wave American women's movement (Friedan 1963), and publications in the 1970s frequently concerned 'sex roles', thought to be learned through socialization and formal education. Chapter 2 of this volume shows that gender was almost entirely absent from British sociological work on education during the 1960s and 1970s, even when other sociologists were beginning to study 'sexual divisions', the topic of an important BSA conference in the early 1970s. Two collections of articles emanating from that conference were published, and within the BSA, a Women's Caucus, a Study Group on Sexual Divisions, and later a Standing Committee on the Equality of the Sexes developed.

The impact of feminism on the subdisciplines of education was uneven. For some areas, like child development, women had always played a visible role, and 'sex differences' had long been a respectable subject of study. For others, such as the study of higher education, women were scarce and feminist influence minimal. By the late 1970s, 'women and education' seemed to be emerging as a subfield in its own right. Several important textbooks, edited collections and monographs were published then and in the early 1980s in Britain by writers including Madeleine Arnot, Eileen Byrne, Miriam David, Rosemary Deem, Sara Delamont and Dale Spender. The stances taken by these writers were diverse, but it was clear there was a market for their work. By the mid-1980s, the visibility of what Arnot (1985) has called the sociology of women's education had increased still further. One of the sociology of education conferences was devoted to questions of race and gender and its papers were published (Barton and Walker 1983; Walker and Barton 1983). Other collections with sociological content included Acker *et al.* (1984), Weiner (1985), Whyte *et al.* (1985), Arnot and Weiner (1987b) and Weiner and Arnot (1987). The culmination of many of these efforts to carve out a new scholarly field was the founding of the journal *Gender and Education* by June Purvis in 1989.

Student demand and access to a body of scholarship made it possible to deliver courses on women and education; the University of Sussex, and later the Open University, offered an MA on the topic. Initial teacher education usually featured some input on gender issues in education, although it was frequently marginalized (Coffey and Acker 1991). A recent text with a largely sociological approach is, however, directed at the teacher education market (Measor and Sikes 1992). The sociology of women's education is more than a British innovation; it can be seen developing in various forms in Canada (Gaskell and McLaren 1991), the United States (Wrigley 1992), Australia (Yates 1987; Kenway 1990; Kenway and Willis 1990), New Zealand (Middleton and Jones 1992) and elsewhere.

It seems to me that the sociology of women's education escapes some of the criticisms which have been directed towards the sociology of education as a whole. Like the main field, it does have a 'redemptive view' of education (Dale 1992), the hope that education can make a difference and the subsequent effort to identify barriers to the successful accomplishment of progressive change. Dale (1992) and Shilling (1993) point out that in an era where our confidence in progress has been shaken, and given that there was always a tension between the belief in barriers and the belief in education's potential, sociologists have retreated into interpreting the effects of educational policies on individuals and have given up theoretical development (Shilling 1993).

However, their observations do not apply all that well to feminist work in the field. Certainly much of the scholarship on women and education has not been theoretically sophisticated, but it could be seen to be politically driven instead. Writers have been concerned to make their work accessible to teachers and others who might 'make a difference', not just to write for other scholars. Much of the work clearly under the rubric of 'sociology of women's education' or 'gender issues in education' is theoretical, although perhaps drawing upon a different body of theory than do other sociologists. What I have in mind is feminist theory, the body of literature concerned with understanding the origins and nature of gender divisions and hierarchies. Writing on feminist theory has reached a voluminous output, and some of it is very sophisticated indeed! A recent volume on issues of feminism and education (Arnot and Weiler 1993) demonstrates my point. There is certainly a preoccupation with educational policy that runs throughout the book, but most of the authors are also concerned to locate their writing within feminist theory.

New directions

Until recently, feminist theory was often divided into 'types', such as liberal, socialist and radical. Chapter 3 takes this approach. In the last few years, however, post-modern and post-structuralist influences, as well as developments in feminism generally, have made it more difficult to identify a typology.[3] Post-structuralism tells us to see grand theories as competing discourses, rather than as repositories of truths, and feminist theories are no exception. It also criticizes the humanist conception of the 'self' (Weedon 1987). Instead of a stable self, people have 'subjectivities', which fluctuate according to positioning in a network of social relations and access to particular discourses. These subjectivities can't help but be gendered; the struggle is over what gender is to mean.

Particularly relevant is the calling into question of the very concept of 'woman', once it is recognized that women are possessors of multiple subjectivities based on race, class, age, sexual orientation, religion, and so forth. Different affiliations may come to prominence in different circumstances, perhaps according to political priorities (Alcoff 1988). Not without its shortcomings, such as the relativizing and problematic political implications for the women's movement, this post-structuralist tendency in scholarship does shed some light on certain puzzles in women's education, among them the difficulty of accomplishing reforms based on gender equity and non-sexist teaching.

Examples can be found in the work of Weiler (1988), Gilbert and Taylor (1991), Davies (1989a, 1989b) and Walkerdine (1981, 1986a). For instance, Gilbert and Taylor (1991) are concerned with the role played by cultural texts in constructions of femininity and how the texts relate to the lived experiences of teenage girls. Cultural texts include representational forms such as television soap operas or teenage magazines, as well as ways groups of people actually live and interrelate. In trying to understand femininity, adolescent girls are exposed to discourses (systems of representation which circulate a set of meanings) that limit the ways in which young women typically see the world. These discourses create pressures on them to get a boyfriend, to focus on marriage and motherhood, and to give 'romance' centre stage, whatever they know about 'real' families breaking up and economic pressures. Consequently, even when feminist teachers explicitly encourage pre-teen or adolescent girls to move away from standard, stereotyped plots in their writing, the girls find it difficult to do so. An example of a girl trying to write about a young woman's adventures in Italy shows how she ends up falling back on formulaic romantic patterns:

> She has no speaking position of authority available to her, no alternative discourses which offer her other ways of constructing gendered subjects . . . positioned by discourses other than romantic ideology.
> (Gilbert and Taylor 1991: 119)

Although one can see reproductive processes at work in the outcomes here, the approach stresses contradiction and potential for change and alternative readings. Girls *can* 'position themselves' otherwise (see also Wolffensperger 1993), but it is not easy because 'the power of gender ideologies lies in the fact that they work at an unconscious level, through the structuring of desires, as well as at a conscious or rational level' (Gilbert and Taylor 1991: 135).

Classroom studies, too, are beginning to reflect a post-structuralist approach, stressing multiple subjectivities and multiple notions of femininity and ways in which it is simplistic to see all girls as alike and all girls as equally subordinate (Jones 1993). Weiler's (1988) classroom observations document pupil resistance to feminist efforts. The white middle-class teacher finds it harder to empathize with students of different colour or class, who in turn appear to reject the alternative discourse she is trying to put into place. Bird (1992, cited in Jones 1993) shows that one available 'subject positioning' for girls in New Zealand primary classrooms is a kind of derivative power based on their identification with the female teacher. In the United States, Grant (1992) saw 6- and 7-year-old African-American girls encouraged to demonstrate social competence and sometimes acting as go-betweens (between teacher and class) or enforcers, helping teachers with control of the class. In contrast, white girls in the same classrooms were expected to stay close to the teacher, to conform to the rules, and to demonstrate greater cognitive maturity than other pupils.

We can also use the approach to consider why teachers sometimes appear so resistant to feminist ideas, a topic that arises in Chapters 6 and 7. Although feminist discourse is available to teachers, it is one that is not familiar or comfortable, and that may carry risks of alienating colleagues (Chapter 7). It is also challenging to a teacher's very notion of pedagogy; instead of seeing children as genderless individuals with talents to be developed, she is being asked to see them (and herself) as privileged or otherwise by gender, engaged in power struggles in the classroom over which discourse will prevail (Walkerdine 1981, 1986b).

Not everyone is convinced that post-structuralism makes potentially valuable contributions to educational research and theory (Measor and Sikes 1992; Maynard 1993). I have given it some serious discussion here in part because it is an approach missing from my discussion of feminist theory in Chapter 3. It is certainly becoming more difficult to talk in terms of three feminisms (although I would maintain that the separate strands have historical justification and heuristic utility). But it is equally difficult to see how post-structuralist feminism can translate into practical educational strategies. It does, however, illuminate the difficulties apparent in deploying any strategies that depend on simple notions of 'women' or 'girls'. Moreover, it makes sense of findings such as the way teachers in Chapter 7 talk about their concepts of 'career'. Unlike many previous conceptions of teachers' careers as pathways or ladders, the teachers in my study talked about their careers as a series of accidents and chance encounters. Such a finding is perfectly compatible with a theoretical approach that does not expect grand theories and all-embracing concepts to have much validity. Similarly, the experiences of persons who have responsible, important jobs in the 'outside world', and yet are full of doubt and uncertainty when they arrive on university terrain as part-time research students (Chapter 4) can also be conceptualized in terms of available discourses and subject positioning.

I do not think we can ignore the post-structuralist position, whether or not we like it much – it has too many implications for our pedagogy and our understandings of the very possibility of feminist theory (Middleton 1993). Perhaps the sociology of women's education will not share in the so-called 'demise' of British sociology of education as long as it takes part in the lively, international debates on the influence of post-structuralism, while not surrendering its traditional focus on social justice (Arnot and Weiler 1993).

Plan of the book

This work falls into three sections, plus introductory and concluding chapters. Each section moves from critiques of previous work and conceptualizations to newer feminist approaches and possibilities for improved understandings. In all three sections, I move chronologically from a paper written in the early 1980s to one written in 1992 or 1993. In this chapter, the Introduction, I explain how aspects of my biography, in conjunction with developments in the sociology of education and the sociology of women's education, provided the context for the book.

Part 1 includes chapters whose purpose it is to map aspects of the field of the sociology of women's education. Chapter 2, 'No-woman's-land', from 1981, is primarily a critique of the neglect of women within British sociology of education prior to the 1980s. It rests on an empirical base, a content analysis of journal articles in the three main British sociology journals over 20 years, plus a reading of textbooks and edited collections used in the field. The other chapters in this section show a move away from critique to establishing the parameters of study in the developing scholarship on gender and education.

Chapter 3, 'Feminist theory and the study of gender and education', published in 1987, explores how varieties of feminist theory attempt to explain women's educational experiences, in part by considering actual research, in part by extrapolating to the educational implications and strategies that follow logically from each position. Chapter 4, 'Is research by a feminist always feminist research?', is newly written for this book. It questions some of the rigidities that have crept into definitions of feminist research and presents an example of research on graduate students that was not initially conceptualized as feminist research, in order to consider whether a feminist framework can be effectively used in the analysis rather than the design stage in research.

The second and third parts apply the general insights of the earlier chapters to more specific topics concerning teachers and academics, respectively. Part 2, on 'Women and Teaching', opens in Chapter 5 with 'Women and teaching', a 1983 critique of conventional approaches to the sociology of the teaching occupation. For many years, scholars relied on commonsense sexism, blaming women for compromising teaching's efforts to become a 'real' profession. Chapter 6, 'Teachers, gender and resistance', from the mid-1980s, makes use of literature on the implementation of educational innovation to question why feminist reform efforts apparently meet with little enthusiasm in the schools. Both this chapter and Chapter 7 raise questions about the influence of teachers' working conditions and cultures on their outlooks. Chapter 7, 'Creating careers: Women teachers at work', was written in the early 1990s and draws upon my ethnographic work in two primary schools in considering what influences teachers' understandings about careers.

Part 3 turns to a topic even closer to my own life, the experiences of women in universities. Chapter 8, 'Women, the other academics', was one of my earliest publications in 1980. I explored the difficulties of being a token woman academic in a man's world, where women are 'other'. The companion piece that appears in Chapter 9, 'Contradictions in terms: Women academics in British universities', is very recent, a more searching attempt to understand why women's position in British academic life remains so disadvantaged compared with men's, despite all the advances in other professions and in scholarship on women. As in other chapters, I ask where feminist theories lead us in attempting to account for this phenomenon.

The concluding chapter, Chapter 10, picks up the issue of social change and considers how women's place in education has developed throughout the years represented by the chapters in this book. Despite the apparent resistance to feminist influence on the part of the central government and the population at large, improvements can be noted. I question whether feminists in education are in danger of being regarded as out of date, despite our perceptions that there is a lot left to do.

I have edited and made revisions to all the chapters originally published elsewhere. Usually the purpose was to improve readability, strengthen coherence or reduce overlap among the chapters. Some of my early publications were rather heavy with footnotes and references, and I have deleted those I now regard as unnecessary to the main argument. I have also deleted some references or statistics that are now out of date, and updated others, but I have not tried to update the actual arguments and theories used in the older chapters. My reasoning was that such efforts might destroy the impact of the pieces, simply adding bits that might appear to be grafted on. Instead, I have used endnotes, the new chapters (1, 4 and 10) and the chapters recently published (7 and 9) to introduce contemporary material. The book as a whole represents my contribution and my tribute to the sociology of women's education.

Notes

1. Further biographical details can be found in Chapter 4.
2. I chose the subheading 'sociology of women's education' for this section because it describes well most of the research and emphasizes the link with 'women's studies' on the one hand, and a nesting within the sociology of education on the other. However, there is a problematic side to the phrase, to the extent that it might appear to mean exclusively the study of women, rather than something like the study of gender relations while making women's perspectives central. See Chapter 4 for a discussion of the allied issue of what is feminist research.
3. Lather (1991) makes a distinction between post-modern, applying to shifts in society, and post-structural, referring to theoretical efforts within that context, but then uses the terms interchangeably. I generally use the term 'post-structuralism' but have not attempted to tackle any definitional problems that might arise.

PART 1

Mapping the Field

2 No-Woman's-Land: British Sociology of Education 1960–79

In the 1970s, there appeared a number of feminist critiques of aspects of sociological work. While sociologists were taken to task for their treatment of deviance, the family and stratification, the sociology of education remained surprisingly free from attack, and largely impervious to those attacks it did sustain. This neglect is surprising given that the sociology of education was particularly reflexive in that decade. This chapter[1] considers British sociology of education from a feminist perspective, an approach rather different from those found in conventional accounts of the field. At the very least, a feminist perspective challenges assumptions and stereotypes about women; at most, it provides a new creative edge for revitalizing the sociology of education.

I begin with a discussion of feminist criticism of sociology, before turning to the question of what we find when we examine British sociology of education in the 1960s and 1970s from such a vantage point. I then discuss some specific areas where a feminist perspective is providing new directions as well as questioning the old, and conclude by suggesting reasons why this perspective has had difficulty making inroads on mainstream sociology of education. Readers should keep in mind that the observations to follow were written in the early 1980s; the sociology of education has of course changed since then, as documented in Chapter 1 and elsewhere in this volume. Thus some of the features criticized here, such as the unreflective use of male pronouns, are much less in evidence in the 1990s.

Feminist consciousness, men's models

It is no doubt impossible to find a definition of feminism that pleases everyone. Richards (1980) provides us with a reasonable working definition with the virtue of simplicity. She regards a feminist as someone who believes that 'women suffer from systematic social injustice because of their sex'. Feminism is the movement opposed to such injustice. Such a broad definition is desirable, she argues, because it creates more rather than fewer feminists and because it ensures that the survival of feminism is not dependent on the appeal of any particular set of theories about women.

Feminist sociologists analyse and oppose systematic social injustice by pointing to taken-for-granted biases deeply imbedded within their own discipline. 'Men's models' (E. Ardener 1975; S. Ardener 1975) have influenced sociology in both obvious and subtle ways. Most obvious has been the frequent reliance on all-male samples. As Lofland (1975) observes about studies of street-corner communities, women are 'just there', like the scenery, while happenings in the 'boys' world' receive a 'fine textured, closed-grained, empirically loving portrayal . . . we see the world through their eyes, watch them in the process of defining, coping, interacting'.

Moreover, distortions and stereotypes are introduced into sociology whenever sociologists operate with a perspective laced with commonsense notions about the nature of women. A double standard exists. Writing of men, sociologists show an acute awareness of the social constraints upon their actions. Writing of women, or of sex differences, they frequently switch to psychological or biological levels of explanation. Examples might be the equating of teacher non-militancy with conservatism of women teachers, or explaining the under-representation of women in school headships by women's lack of ambition. One is reminded of Durkheim's (1895/1938) warnings not to explain social life by invoking psychological phenomena. But even Durkheim (1897/1952: 215) could write:

> When a widow is seen to endure her condition much better than a widower and desires marriage less passionately, one is led to consider this ease in dispensing with the family a mark of superiority . . . Actually, if this is her privilege it is because her sensibility is rudimentary rather than highly developed. As she lives outside of community existence more than man, she is less penetrated by it; society is less necessary to her because she is less impregnated with sociability. She has few needs in this direction and satisfies them easily. With a few devotional practices and some animals to care for, the unmarried woman's life is full . . . it is because these very simple social forms satisfy all her needs.[2]

Beyond the attack on neglect, distortion and stereotyping of women in social science, a critique at an epistemological level is emerging in sociology, perhaps best represented by the work of Dorothy Smith (1974, 1975, 1979). At issue here is the very legitimacy of our accepted ways of recognizing, organizing, justifying and 'doing' sociology. Targets for criticism include the hierarchical and usually male-directed organization of research (Hanmer and Leonard 1980), and the centrality to the field of men's conventional concerns rather than women's (Bernard 1973). Bernard (1973) writes of a 'machismo factor' in sociological research, which ensures the dominance of research methods that are 'agentic' (implying powerful distant manipulation of variables) rather than 'communal' (implying naturalistic observation of people). Consequently, we study 'sex as a variable' more often than 'women as people'. Others have questioned the necessity for persistently dichotomizing categories like rational *vs* emotional, hard data *vs* soft data, objective *vs* subjective (Spender 1978). These dichotomies are of feminist interest because of their parallel with cultural beliefs about 'masculine *vs* feminine' and the relative prestige in sociology of the 'masculine' (rational, hard, objective, etc.) pole. Abandoning or modifying such dichotomies would enlarge the scope of sociology. Hochschild (1975b), for example, has shown how our preference for rationality over emotion has led us to ignore the possibilities in a sociological theory of emotion. Feminists join with certain other sociologists to note the artificiality of the objective/ subjective dichotomy in traditional sociological research methodology. They stress instead the insights possible when women sociologists call upon their own experience to understand, intersubjectively, that of other women. Such an approach could mean that 'women's models' become central rather than peripheral to sociology.

Westcott (1979: 426) elaborates some of these ideas:

> The idea of grounding inquiry in concrete experience rather than in abstract categories is reflected in women's historical identification with the concrete, everyday life of people and their survival needs. The idea of knowledge as an unpredictable discovery rather than a controlled outcome is reflected in women's historical exclusions from institutions, where planned rational control is the mode of operation, and in women's historical identification with domestic spheres which have been less rationally controlled or predictable. And finally, the idea of knowledge emerging from a self–other dialectic is reflected both in the historical exclusion of women from educational institutions where knowledge has been transmitted through books and lectures and in women's participation in societies and friendships where social knowledge has emerged from dialogue, a practice recently exemplified by women's consciousness-raising and support groups.

The key point made by Smith (1979), Westcott (1979) and others is that 'man-made sociology' is not merely neglectful but seriously debilitated. We cannot legitimately claim even to understand the experiences of men and boys if we have excluded or distorted the experiences of women and ignored the interactions and inequalities between the sexes. There is not space here to consider further these important challenges to the nature of conventional sociological knowledge. Instead, I turn to a practical demonstration of the potential of feminist criticism, an examination of 'women's place' in the literature of two decades of British sociology of education.

The place of women in sociology of education

Most of the evidence for my arguments in this section comes from a systematic review of articles on education published between 1960 and 1979 in the three major British sociology journals: *British Journal of Sociology*, *Sociological Review* and *Sociology* (*Sociology* since 1967 when it began publication). The emphasis is on identifying themes rather than on providing quantitative detail. Supporting evidence is drawn from introductory textbooks, collections of readings, and articles on the nature of sociology of education, as well as the ideas and opinions derived from teaching, reading and researching in the subject area for many years. It is intended that this analysis provide some documentation of the images of women that prevail in sociology of education as well as point to directions for 'remedial sociology' (Mackie 1977).

The journal study

Before 1980, when the *British Journal of Sociology of Education* began publication, articles coming under the compass of sociology of education were scattered in a wide variety of journals. In deciding to analyse the articles in the three sociology journals, I chose only a particular slice of the sociological cake and clearly cannot claim that it represents all work done in the field. It may be that rather different sociological articles find their way into education journals. Education journals were not considered because it was more difficult to find articles that were clearly sociological in education journals than it was to identify educational articles in sociology journals. Numerous other decisions had to be made. Articles on socialization and language of children, on professional or occupational socialization in educational settings and on the social and educational backgrounds of persons in particular adult roles were included. Articles on non-educational topics that might have mentioned education in passing, comments on other people's articles and authors' replies to these comments, and articles about the teaching of sociology were excluded.

I noted 184 articles. Of these, the great majority (143) reported some kind of empirical work. Their samples were coded as mixed, all male or all female. Writers were surprisingly cavalier about giving the social characteristics of their samples. Those studies that did not specify sex of sample but referred, for example, to 'children' were coded as mixed, as were those based on populations with only a small representation of women such as studies of university teachers or chemistry students. Even giving the benefit of the doubt, so to speak, to difficult cases and calling them 'mixed', a large minority – 37 per cent – of these studies had all-male samples. Mixed samples were most common (58 per cent) and all-female samples rare (5 per cent).

We might anticipate the details to follow by imagining a Martian coming to Britain and deriving some impressions of its educational system from reading these articles. The Martian would conclude that numerous boys but few girls go to secondary modern schools; that there are no girls' public schools; that there are almost no adult women influentials of any sort; that most students in higher education study science and engineering; that women rarely make a ritual transition called 'from school to work' and never go into further education colleges. Although some women go to university, most probably enter directly into motherhood, where they are of some interest as transmitters of language codes to their children. And except for a small number of teachers, social workers and nurses, there are almost no adult women workers in the labour market.

Invisible women

Men's work and elite schooling

Certain favourite themes nearly always exclude women. One such category is studies about work, including the transition from school to work, occupational aspirations, occupational or professional self-concept, and further education as a 'second chance' opportunity for working-class children (boys). A second category of near-exclusive male samples is studies of the social and educational background of elites. Choosing a sample in these cases does not mean intentionally excluding women, but the effect is the same when one studies army and navy officers, Anglican bishops, vice-chancellors or directors of firms. A third category with close links to the second is studies about public (i.e. elite private) schools and their clientele. None explicitly states that the public schools were for boys only, but it is clear from the context.

Most writers on these subjects give no reason for confining attention to males. A few explain that the concentration is a function of the social characteristics of the group. Thus Collison and Millen (1969) take care to point out that only 10 of 116 vice-chancellors and college principals and 6 of 43 chancellors were women (the women principals all heading women's colleges and 5 of the 6 women chancellors from the Royal Family). Some of the other apologies appeal to convention. Looking at trends in career mobility of school leavers, Lee (1968: 310) states (in an endnote):

> Throughout the paper the discussion has been confined to the experience of males on the grounds that the occupation of the (male) head of household is usually used to assess the original social position of both males and females.

The choice of male samples in studies of this sort reflects both the over-representation of men among elites in society and the assumption that men's work (and consequently their occupational socialization and schooling) is of more interest and importance than women's. Researchers could have studied the education and occupational socialization of hairdressers just as easily as that of printing apprentices. Or the social and educational backgrounds of nurses or social workers or actresses. Or the workings of university departments of French or technical college departments of catering. Or the role of further education in mobility chances of working-class girls. But no-one did.

Controlling boys and variables

Those studies concentrating on work and elites are not the only ones to restrict the universe to males. First, there is a 'trouble' or social control theme. Researchers are drawn to study youth-culture groups, delinquent adolescents, anti-school subcultures and other groups regarded as potential control problems. Presumably, male investigators have gravitated towards male versions of these phenomena (thereby also reinforcing the impression that only boys are troublesome). In another set of studies, it seems the researchers are looking for a convenient way to 'control' for extraneous variables, usually in order to focus on class differences in some educational outcome or linguistic practice. For example, Bernstein's (1960) famous contrast of the speech of post office messengers (working class) and public school boys (middle class) states that the two groups of boys were 'matched for age and sex'. Matched for sex meant in this case, and a number of others, all male. This would not seem so unreasonable if anyone chose two all-female groups for comparisons on some other variable, but none of the journal authors does this. Studies that include sex as an independent variable run the risk that the data on females will destroy the theory, as we shall see shortly.

In some other studies, I can see no 'good' reason whatsoever for the choice of an all-male sample. In a couple of cases, data for both sexes are collected, but most of the discussion centres on the boys. Nash (1973), for example, after some discussion of sex differences in educational aspirations among primary school children, then considers a first-year secondary school group including both boys and girls. He states: 'At this point it may be worthwhile to describe in detail the pattern of friendships among the boys in their first year at secondary school' and goes on to do so. He does not say why he singles out boys and never mentions the girls again.

He embraces she

Sexist bias in the English language is the subject of several books (Thorne and Henley 1975; Miller and Swift 1977; Spender 1980). I could find no examples of overtly sexist writing about women, although irritating phrases like 'the fairer sex' turn up occasionally. What tends to happen instead is that the terminology used in the articles contributes to the invisibility of women.

While in the journals it is conventional to use 'he' for 'he and she' and (less often) 'men' for 'humanity', on occasion this practice is so overused as to suggest women are literally non-existent or not relevant to the argument. It is impossible in these cases to be really sure whether the writer is talking about people or just about males – a confusion common among young children, according to studies cited by Miller and Swift (1977). An example is Lane's (1972) critique of models of class and educational choice. Nowhere does he say 'women are excluded'. In two consecutive paragraphs, he writes that 'men possess relatively systematic maps or pictures of the world . . . Such models of the world provide men generally with a handbook for behaviour . . . Men's models of the world are . . . Men's market situations remain . . . ' (pp. 257–8), and so on throughout. Other hints in the article imply he is himself working with a 'picture of the world' composed of one sex only.

Particularly interesting is the tendency of many studies to make tacit equations of non-sex-specific categories (public schools, adolescents) with boys or men, the equation becoming clear with the content of the article. As already mentioned, 'public school' inevitably means 'boys' public school'. Other studies with all-male samples discuss the results in terms of 'young people' and 'adolescents' as if all young people were male. One writer (Startup 1972) points out that despite university students' wishes for more contact with lecturers, 'staff are subject to competing claims from their wives . . . ' (all lecturers are not only male, but married).

Visible women

Sex differences[3]

If we turn now to 'visible women' in the journals, we recall that the majority of the empirical studies have mixed samples, although sometimes women were in the minority within these. Writers do not always analyse data for sex differences, even when it would seem a relevant dimension. Frequently, only a small proportion of the data is presented separately for the sexes. It is not usually clear whether this limitation is because sex differences did not occur on other variables or because the researcher did not look beyond those reported. The modal approach seems to be the presentation of at least some of the data cross-tabulated by sex, with little or no attempt to interpret the sex differences that emerge. For example, we learn that men students are more likely to feel staff had 'poor attitudes' (Startup 1972), and that comprehensive school girls have a higher commitment to school activities than boys despite leaving school at an earlier age (Holly 1965). In neither case do we learn why the phenomenon occurs.

Timperley and Gregory (1971) provide a good example of a study that carefully documents sex differences but fails to go further. They follow a fairly detailed description of sex-differentiated aspirations and A-level subject choice among sixth-formers not with a search for causes but with a value judgement:

> The problem of the lack of science teachers would therefore appear to be
> even more specific to male science teachers and the excessive proportion
> of potential women arts and language teachers must give some cause for
> concern.
>
> (Timperley and Gregory 1971: 103)

Most of the studies that report sex differences do not conceptualize sex as a major independent variable influencing an education-related outcome as dependent variable. Such a strategy would require an examination of the relationship of sex to the dependent variable, controlling for a series of other variables that might interpret or specify the original relationship or render it spurious (Rosenberg 1968). The logic in nearly all these studies is different. The focus of interest is the relationship between some other independent variable (often, but not always, social class) and an educational outcome. The researcher reasons that the relationship might look different for boys and girls, and sex becomes one of the necessary controls rather than a major independent variable in its own right (not even equal among variables).

The odd women

Those writers who do consider sex differences often seem puzzled by the results for women. This situation happens when results for boys or men confirm some hypothesis but those for girls or women are inconsistent or contrary. A famous example of this kind of occurrence in psychology is the research on achievement motivation, where early studies showed predicted results for boys but confusing ones for girls. Rather than modify their theories, researchers thereafter excluded girls from their samples. Among studies examined here, Witkin (1971: 184) is puzzled, as 'the findings for girls in secondary modern schools were not anticipated'. For Synge (1973: 107), the high educational aspirations of rural girls were 'contrary to our expectations'. Robinson and Rackstraw (1978: 279) admit 'at present we have no supportable explanations to offer for these occasional sex differences in performance'. Liversidge (1962) is surprised that working-class girls' occupational aspirations don't differ much between those in grammar schools and in secondary modern schools, unlike those of boys. And Robertson and Kapur (1972: 471) go so far as to say their results for women students are 'bizarre'.

Focus on women
Only a handful of the articles are centrally concerned with women. Although seven feature all-female samples, only one (Joseph 1961) focuses specifically on women as women. It examines the attitudes to work and marriage of a large sample of adolescent girls. Girls were asked various questions about intentions to return to work after marriage and to write an essay imagining they were near the end of their lives looking back on events after they had left school. Although 90 per cent wrote essays that included marriage, it is interesting to note that 31 per cent of these reported the demise of the husband, usually well before he made it to old age, frequently through a gory accident. Of the others, one is a study of the effects of a particular admissions practice in a training scheme for nurses. The other five are all surveys of mothers, one asking about attitudes towards adolescents, the four others by Bernstein and/or colleagues considering class, language and socialization. I think it is fair to say that the real interest here seems to be in the young children, not in the mothers themselves, except in so far as they are vehicles for transmission of language codes and similar.

Some of the mixed-sample studies give sexual inequality a prominent place, although they usually conceptualize it as a competing inequality with other (more important?) kinds.[4] Only a half dozen or so articles have sexual inequality as their major focus. This set includes studies on university teachers, changing attitudes to marriage and family in West Africa, and careers of sociology graduates. Two small-scale classroom studies look specifically at gender as an influence on teacher perception of pupils (Ingleby and Cooper 1974; Evans, 1979).

Purvis' (1973) discussion of school teaching as a career is the only theoretical article to discuss women in any detail. She examines the implications for the teaching profession of its relatively high proportion of women members. While going along with the other writers on this subject who equate high proportions of women fairly automatically with lower professional commitments (see Chapter 5), she is careful to 'blame' cultural ideas about the role of women rather than deficient motivation of women themselves. Not one theoretical

article on education in the entire 20 years takes as its topic educational inequality for women.

Other sociology of education

Of course, the particular themes identified in the journal review may not apply
without modification to British sociology of education as a whole. I consulted
some other 1960–79 sources (less intensively) to judge whether these journals
presented a representative picture.

Accounts of the field

Except for Olive Banks' (1977) bibliography, which includes two sections
relevant to the education of women, I could find no general review or critique
of 'trends in the field' that singled out issues of gender and education as of
concern (among 12 consulted).[5] Karabel and Halsey's (1977) lengthy account
of research in Britain and in the United States is typical in its low level of
consciousness in this respect. Women are only given the briefest of mentions-
in-passing, for example 'blacks, women, and other subordinated groups' (p.
21), and there is no discussion of any relevant research. Five pages are devoted
to a discussion of Jencks and co-workers' (1972) *Inequality* without pointing
out anywhere that their analysis pertains only to men.

Readers

Edited collections became a popular outlet for work in the sociology of education during the period under examination. I looked at 29 of these, including
the more general collections and those that specialized in some fairly central
area such as classroom interaction.[6] Compared with the journals, the readers
had more speculative, theoretical and review articles and fewer straight research
reports. The type of journal article that reported 'sex differences' was thus less
likely to appear, but so were those with all-male samples. As most of the readers
were published in the 1970s, many provided forums for the 'new sociology of
education' (Young 1971), which was not as well represented in the journals.

Women were not more visible in the readers than in the journals, however.
There were occasional minor mentions, for example of women's position as
teachers or of the paucity of research on the education of women. Although
some studies took place in girls' schools and others in mixed ones, only a few
articles intentionally investigated aspects of the educational experiences of
women or girls.

Textbooks

The four major introductory textbooks of the 1970s (Banks 1976; Morrish
1978; Reid 1978; Musgrave 1979) were, with one exception, generally more

sensitive than the edited collections to issues relevant to women and education. The exception is the 1978 edition of Morrish's text (supposedly revised from the 1972 version, but not where women are mentioned). He notes that inequality occurs due not only to social class but to sex 'for a variety of reasons' (p. 134), but does not elaborate. Elsewhere he points out that married women are increasingly undertaking paid employment and adds this comment:

> Where mothers who have young children are absent from the home there always arises the problem of children left unattended, or left to their own devices in streets or playing-fields, or deposited in, perhaps, a third-rate nursery.
>
> (Morrish 1978: 169)

Except for a couple of sentences on co-education, the only other point at which women enter Morrish's text is in a 1960s-style discussion of problems of wastage in teaching. Although 'there is no question but that young women at the end of their present three-year college of education course are better prepared for the responsibilities of life and motherhood, as well as for teaching itself', their tendency to leave teaching is a 'serious', 'considerable and increasing' problem. The solution he favours is to make it more difficult to qualify as a teacher and then only the really committed women would embark on such a career. If teaching could recruit larger numbers of 'well qualified and professionally minded men', he adds, it might give men in teaching 'a greater equality with women' and improve the status of teachers, as 'much of the sense of a second-rate profession . . . has been the fact that it was predominantly female in membership' (Morrish 1978: 234).

The textbooks of Banks (1976), Reid (1978) and Musgrave (1979) do not contain such gratuitous sexism. Their coverage of work on women reflects the availability of research in the field, but they often choose different aspects to highlight. All discuss sex differences in examination performance and the under-representation of women in higher education. All mention women in considering relations of education to the economy: Reid gives extensive statistics; Musgrave points out problems of measuring social class for women; Banks discusses girls' avoidance of science. With respect to links between family socialization and educational aspirations or achievements, Musgrave several times focuses attention on socialization into sex roles via family, media and peer group; Banks devotes a few pages to 'women: a special case'; Reid says little. Looking at processes within schools, Reid points to 'sexist curricula' but does not develop a discussion; Musgrave notes a few relevant aspects of the hidden curriculum including images in textbooks; Banks cites work on differential resource provision in boys' and girls' schools. All mention differentiated teacher expectations for boys and girls. Musgrave is the only one to consider specifically girls' part in 'youth culture'. Finally, the various implications of high numbers of women in the teaching profession are commented upon in some detail by Banks, less so by Musgrave and not at all by Reid.

To sum up the trends in these three introductory textbooks, while the writers, especially Banks, are clearly aware of the education of girls and women as an issue, the extent to which the issue surfaces varies from one subtopic to the next. Treatment remains patchy and often superficial. No writer explores thoroughly the links between family, school and the economy as these affect women. None provides any historical material on the struggle of British women to gain access to education. Ways in which hidden and overt curricula or teacher–pupil interaction affect girls are barely explored. No-one discusses the historical role of domestic science education in preparing girls for their future lives or the recommendations about girls' schooling contained in government reports.

Towards a feminist sociology of education

Rather than succumb to pessimism based on what is, I turn now to what might be.[7] Increasingly, we are seeing a body of feminist theory and research that derives some of its impetus from the feminist critique of sociology. Feminist theorists have been particularly concerned to elucidate the material basis and ideological supports for the oppression of women. They seek to analyse the impacts and interactions of capitalism and patriarchy on gender relations. There have also been attempts to develop a feminist methodology. Although there is no universal consensus about what is to qualify as feminist work, I think most would agree that feminist work will be characterized by a clear influence of feminist criticism and theory on choice of research topic, definition of concepts and interpretation of data.

How might a feminist approach contribute to the sociology of education? We might think in terms of a number of tasks. These include:

1. Filling gaps in our knowledge about the education of girls and women.
2. Reassessing and reinterpreting data and findings from past studies that contain some information on women or sex differences.
3. Asking questions through making problematic those commonsense assumptions about women and women's education that have so far passed for fact.
4. Uncovering and replacing what I have called elsewhere 'deficit models of women' – essentially, approaches that blame the victim for her lack of some quality that is defined as desirable because it is normally associated with men (see Chapter 8).
5. Discovering exactly why and how schooling shapes the lives of women in particular ways.

Although I have phrased these tasks in terms of research on women, that is to indicate the prevailing direction such work would take, not its boundaries. Such work could easily encompass studies of, for example, the interaction of boys and girls, and it would typically encourage reassessment of the one-sided view we have so often had of the 'boys' world'.

In the next sections, I discuss two linked topics usually regarded as within sociology of education in order to give some indication of the directions in which sociology of education might go: the aspirations of adolescent girls and the sociology of the school.

Occupational and educational aspirations of girls

What we have had in the past tends to be either exclusion of girls from samples or a conceptualization of their options as simply 'marriage or career'. We know little about the processes by which girls in school make school subject choices or occupational decisions. Ways in which the experiences of women in further education serve to widen or narrow aspirations and opportunities are virtually unstudied. Some of these potential research problems have hitherto been seen as 'non-problems'. Roberts (1968: 181–2) studied the entry into employment for young men only, but felt able to assert: 'For girls work does not possess such a central socio-psychological significance, and unemployment consequently does not bring such deleterious effects'.

Not all work has been so dismissive, and there are interesting hints in the journal articles and elsewhere that the processes shaping aspirations may differ for girls and boys. Girls' aspirations are influenced not only by sex but also by variables such as social class, region, ethnicity and type of school attended. Byrne (1978) reminds us of the cumulative disadvantages suffered by those who are female, working class, rural and non-academic; we need to inquire more closely into the experiences of people in various such categories and also to be alert to cases where characteristics thought to be disadvantageous may combine in unexpected ways. How do schools influence these aspirations, expectations and outcomes? Can action research change girls' and teachers' attitudes to conventional careers for girls?

Researchers must guard against any temptation to regard the relatively low aspirations of girls compared with boys as resulting from girls' short-sighted perceptions or sluggish motivation. This is the kind of psychological reductionism pointed to earlier in this chapter. Such arguments often blame the victim, without appreciating that such decisions are made by rational individuals who may well make the best of a particular situation or even opt for a future that despite its devaluation by society, allows the pursuit of important values. Moreover, they fail to see that it is not just individual girls' preferences for particular types of work that account for high proportions of women workers in these occupations. An emerging feminist critique suggests that girls' aspirations should not simply be seen as consequent upon the workings of individual choice or of sex-typed socialization. The shaping of such aspirations within schools and colleges can be seen as an integral, not incidental, part of the reproduction of the sexual and social division of labour (David 1980).

Sociology of the school

Considerable feminist work is under way on social processes within school, and an understanding of ways in which schooling contributes to the reproduction of gender relations is beginning to emerge. MacDonald (1980b) suggests that schools transmit a *gender code*, usually with 'strong classification which reproduces the power relations of male–female hierarchy and strong framing where teachers play a large part in determining gender definitions and control'.

Several British sociologists have documented the existence of patriarchal structures within school staff hierarchies and suggested that powerful messages about male dominance are thereby transmitted (e.g. Davies and Meighan 1975). Sex appears to provide a pervasive basis for differentiation throughout school life. Children become 'boys' and 'girls' for registration, seating, queuing; are conventionally addressed as such by teachers and set to compete against each other; are timetabled and 'optioned' into what sometimes amounts to single-sex schooling within mixed secondary schools.

Content analyses of school textbooks show biases, stereotypes and neglect of women across a wide range of subjects (e.g. Lobban 1975). The ideologies of some subjects taught mostly to girls – especially domestic science – have been shown both historically and currently to be heavily saturated with appeals to domesticity as a sacred calling, an aim for the education of girls broadly sanctioned by official government reports (Dyhouse 1977; Delamont 1978).

Teacher expectations and preferences often seem to be sex-specific, although it is not yet clear under what circumstances particular expectations are produced and operationalized in classrooms. Fuller (1978) interprets the (mostly American) research as meaning teachers prefer girls throughout primary school but boys in secondary school, but Clarricoates (1978), in a British study, finds that although primary teachers do regard boys as difficult to control, they also see them as the source of their most rewarding interactions. Most of the studies suggest boys get more attention, both in terms of praise and punishment, and that the content of the classroom work is often chosen with boys in mind. These outcomes seem to be more than an expression of teacher biases, although both Clarricoates (1980b) and Davies (1979) find that teachers tend to dismiss girls' academic achievements as due to hard work rather than talent.

Gearing lesson content and discussion to boys may also be a teacher strategy to deal with greater demands from boys for attention and greater difficulties in controlling their behaviour. One hopes that order will prevail in class if the project appeals to the boys; the girls will grumble but go along anyway. The control of girls becomes more difficult at secondary school level, especially when schools discourage physical punishment for girls, and several studies (Davies 1979; Llewellyn 1980) suggest one technique used almost exclusively for girls is calling their morality or sexual appeal publicly into question in embarrassing ways. On the pupil side, adolescent girls' subcultures appear to differ from those of boys' subcultures, both in the criteria used to judge peers and teachers and in the forms of resistance to school (Sharpe, 1976; McRobbie, 1978).

Finally, there are some interesting suggestions in the literature that space in and around schools is divided up into girls' and boys' territories. In the school Wolpe (1977) studied, there was a mixed-sex playground, in which boys played football and girls chatted around the edges, and a girls' 'quiet' playground, with ball playing not allowed. Clarricoates (1980b) notes that boys dominated space inside and outside all the primary schools she studied; in one, girls organized themselves into groups to protect themselves from persecution by the boys in the nooks and crannies of the school where teacher supervision was absent. Some American research on pre-school classes found teachers gave girls more attention when they stayed physically close to a teacher, while for boys proximity made no difference (Serbin *et al.* 1973).

Behind these studies lie implicit questions about the relationships of gender, education and work. We need to understand the social forces that shape the life chances of women and also the sources of resistance and change. Events within schools may play a key role in these processes. What may also be evident to readers is that this picture of schools is unlike the one often found in the sociology of education. In the 1960s, studies of pupil subcultures told us what schools were like – but only for boys; in the 1970s, we zeroed in on the intricacies of pupil–teacher interaction, but as 'pupils' and 'teachers' without important latent identities (Becker and Geer 1960; Olesen and Whittaker 1968). If pupils were girls, it was irrelevant; but the research reviewed above suggests it is surely more than that.

Conclusion

I have devoted much of this chapter to unearthing images of women in two decades of British sociology of education. I have also discussed briefly some feminist work on education in order to show promising directions for the field. As of 1981, mainstream sociology of education and feminist studies on women's education were like the proverbial ships that pass in the night. Although we can perhaps be charitable about the biases of 1960s sociology of education, when the status of women was only just re-emerging from a long slumber to become a significant social concern, no such excuse exists for the work of the 1970s. One might have expected research on classroom interaction or the processing of knowledge in the curriculum to have been sensitive to the differentiation of boys and girls in the classroom or to the way in which girls' experiences of schooling prepared them for their place in the secondary labour market and for marriage and homemaking. But the groups of sociologists who forged ahead in the study of classroom processes and curriculum appear to have had no appreciation of sex differentiation as problematic.

On the other hand, the sort of feminist-influenced research described in the previous sections of this chapter remains, I suspect, largely undiscovered by most sociologists of education. In the mid-1970s, studies by Marks (1976), Sharpe (1976), Shaw (1976) and Wolpe (1977) began to raise important issues about women and education from a feminist perspective. Other feminist textbooks (Byrne 1978; Deem 1978) and edited collections (Deem 1980; Spender and Sarah 1980) promised changes in the 1980s. But as of 1981, most sociological work on women and education has not been in the mainstream outlets for sociology of education. Instead, it has appeared in special editions of journals, or has been presented at specialist conferences (often remaining unpublished), or has been conducted as part of research theses with their usual limited circulation, or appeared in feminist journals or in collections of writings on women.

This situation reflects both demand and supply aspects of the field. The policies of publishers and the expectations of teachers and researchers in sociology of education probably affect the demand side. On the supply side, two points are relevant. First, informal, feminist audiences are likely to be more receptive and encouraging to such work than sociologists at large, and it is understandable if such audiences are preferred. Second, the recent outpouring of edited collections in the sociology of education seems to have worked in such a way as to exclude feminist concerns, indeed women, from their production. It is probably relevant that women writers were poorly represented among writers in edited collections, more so, it appeared, than in the journals. (At a guess, about 10 per cent of articles in readers were by women, about 20 per cent in the journals.) Journal articles, whatever their shortcomings, are reviewed by independent referees and presumably provide a more meritocratic forum for sociologists. In contrast, one has to be invited to contribute to a collection of readings, and thus the under-representation of women in these collections could well reflect their exclusion from social and intellectual networks.[8]

At least two consequences follow from the combined effects of these demand and supply factors. To the extent that work is unpublished or in limited circulation, many interested individuals will not hear of it. And, second, mainstream sociology of education remains untransformed by feminist thinking. Consequently, generations of students, especially teachers in initial training or in-service programmes, are not encouraged to be alert to issues of sexual inequality in school and society.

It would require considerable additional effort to expose the deepest-level reasons for patterns reported here and to assess prospects for change. One would have to consider systematically the influences of: (1) social characteristics (such as sex) of researchers and writers: (2) sites where ideas are produced and disseminated, especially the university; (3) attitudes about women (and their education) prevalent in the wider society; (4) aspects of the wider social structure (demographic, economic, political, etc.) that affect the status of women. Here I shall only discuss one point, the question of whether the sex of sociologists influences the work produced. I think it does, but not in a simple manner. There are reasons of access and consciousness involved.

Male researchers clearly have greater access to boys' groups and boys' schools than women do, and thus our sociology of schools is about boys' schools and our sociology of youth cultures about boys' youth cultures. Consciousness is just as important. First, membership in or identification with a social group shapes conceptions of what is problematic. Many sociologists study aspects of their autobiographies partially disguised as a 'detached choice of an interesting problem'. It is unlikely that a male sociologist would have a burning personal interest in girls' schools or subcultures. Thus women sociologists are likely to be the only ones with sufficient motivation and access to illuminate these areas and to be able to unearth submerged 'women's models'.

Women are still very much a minority in universities, especially at higher levels (see Chapters 8 and 9). 'Tokens' in a university department may be highly visible as a symbol of what their group can or cannot do, but may not be fully encouraged, sponsored or integrated into informal networks. Also, the consequence of being at low-status ranks may be continued low status, as resources and approbation go disproportionately to those already in a higher-status position. Moreover, it is likely that many women sociologists of education work in colleges of higher education or other non-university positions. Compared with university academics, they have heavier teacher loads and fewer research resources and it is less likely that their ideas will reach a wide audience.

Such considerations may explain in part why so much feminist work in sociology of education is, as of 1981, not yet evident in the mainstream of the field. I am not arguing that women sociologists will automatically utilize a feminist perspective. While their specific experiences of postgraduate education and of academic life may differ from those of men, women, too, have been exposed to prevailing features of 'professional socialization' that shape our conceptions of what it is to do sociology. Women, too, have participated in work that has focused exclusively on men or introduced biases about women. However, I would venture that were there more women in academic settings, especially in influential positions, the chances of feminist consciousness becoming widespread would be greater, and 'women's models' would have correspondingly greater credence within sociology and sociology of education.

Notes

1. Geoff Millerson, Gill Blunden and members of the British Sociological Association Southwest Women's Caucus gave helpful comments on an early version of this chapter presented at the BSA Annual Conference, Lancaster, 8 April 1980. It was subsequently published in 1981 in *Sociological Review* (see the Acknowledgements for details).
2. I am grateful to Mary Lou Finley for bringing this passage to my attention.
3. Current conventions tend to replace 'sex' with 'gender'. I have retained the use of 'sex' and 'sex differences' in the chapter, however, as terminology typical of the time when the original version was written.
4. The original article version of this chapter (Acker 1981) has detailed citations to back up generalizations such as those made in this paragraph. They have not been included here in order to aid ease of reading.
5. The full list appears in Acker (1981).
6. The full list also appears in Acker (1981).
7. Other chapters in this volume update this review. See especially Chapters 1, 3, 6 and 10.
8. Of the shorter collections of readings – those with 5–19 articles – 4 had no women contributors, 9 had 1, 1 had 3, and 1 had 4. Of collections with 20 or more articles (the largest with 58), 1 had 1 woman contributor, 3 had 2, 2 had 3, 3 had 4, and 3 had 6. It was usually clear whether the writer was male or female, and only a few educated guesses were made. A corresponding count could not be made for journals, as too many writers were only identified by initials and surname, and their identity was not well enough known to me to make even educated guesses practical. It also appeared that certain groups of writers published disproportionately in the edited collections; some names appeared again and again.

3 Feminist Theory and the Study of Gender and Education

'What is feminism?' (Mitchell and Oakley 1986) is a question of deceptive simplicity. Feminist theory, like feminism itself, is multifaceted and complex. My aim in this chapter[1] is to draw out the implications of certain feminist frameworks for the analysis of education. I begin by outlining the three major forms taken by contemporary Western feminist theory.[2] The main part of the chapter makes connections between each of the three forms and educational perspectives and research. In each case I consider the typical educational objectives, the conceptual base, strategies for change and criticisms of the approach. The conclusion looks at prospects for synthesis among approaches and at some underlying tensions in all the feminist frameworks.

I focus on British approaches, plus work from other countries that is reasonably well known in Britain, especially studies from Australia, New Zealand, Canada and the United States. Most of the discussion thus refers to Western forms of feminism, which may differ from those found elsewhere (see Acker *et al.* 1984; Jayawardena 1986).

Feminist theory

By 'theory' I mean the construction of sets of interrelated statements about how some aspect of the world operates. Traditional textbook definitions insist that theories lead to testable hypotheses. I should like to use the term 'theory' more broadly here, to refer to perspectives that guide the search for answers to a central series of questions and dilemmas about sex and gender. Feminist theoretical frameworks address, above all, the question of women's subordination to men: how it arose, how and why it is perpetuated, how it might be changed and (sometimes) what life would be like without it. 'Middle range' theories may be less dramatic and consider particular aspects of gender relations and specific sectors of social life such as education, the family or politics. Feminist theories serve a dual purpose, as guides to understanding gender inequality and as guides to action. There are disagreements among theorists about who is to be counted as a feminist and how to accomplish social change.

Most accounts of feminist theory identify at least two or three divisions within contemporary Western feminism. Eisenstein (1984: xix–xx) provides a capsule portrait of the three major approaches:

> . . . recent analysts seem to agree on the distinction between radical feminism, which holds that gender oppression is the oldest and most profound form of exploitation, which predates and underlies all other forms including those of race and class; and socialist feminism, which argues that class, race and gender oppression interact in a complex way, that class oppression stems from capitalism, and that capitalism must be eliminated for women to be liberated. Both of these, in turn, would be distinguished from a liberal or bourgeois feminist view, which would argue that women's liberation can be fully achieved without any major alterations to the economic and political structures of contemporary capitalist democracies.

There is considerable mutual criticism among theoretical perspectives. Liberal feminism is accused of elitism: while liberal strategies may enable a few token women to 'have careers' and join the ranks of the powerful, the structures of oppression survive untouched. Liberal feminists are also criticized for converting the concept of equality of outcome to equality of opportunity (O'Brien 1983).

Liberal feminists tend to believe sex differences (biological) are really gender differences (cultural). But some radical feminists stress the validity of sex differences – accepting and celebrating women's capacity for nurture, cooperation, passionate attachment to peace in the face of men's persistent attempts at war. Eisenstein (1984) is sharply critical of the tendencies within radical feminism that imply female superiority is physiological, that reject rationality and logic as devices of men, that portray women as the inevitable victims of evil men.

In turn, socialist feminists have been criticized by radicals for their eagerness to make alliances with men (in which the women's interests are bound to be subordinate) and for the linguistic and logical contortions required to reconcile Marxism with feminism. Radical feminists charge that the socialist focus on capitalism fails to do justice to the myriad ways in which men hold power over women through control of sexuality and the threat of violence (MacKinnon 1982).

All three 'traditional' types of feminism have been challenged by those who argue that feminism has been unduly preoccupied with privileged Western, white women's concerns. One strand of this critique argues for the need to understand imperialism and to inject an international perspective into Western feminism (Amos and Parmar 1984). There are also heated debates within individual countries. For example, Britain's *Feminist Review*, a journal of socialist-feminist thought, has published a series of articles about feminism and racism. On similar lines, radical feminism has been attacked by Murphy and

Livingstone (1985), who object to what they see as its mistaken prioritizing of sexual oppression over that based on race and class. Bryan *et al.* (1985) suggest that rather than reject feminism simply as white ideology, black women should redefine and reclaim the term.

'Hyphenated feminism' (O'Brien 1983) has its limitations. Delmar (1986) suggests that this urge to subdivide feminism may mean feminism degenerating into a 'naming of the parts'. Nevertheless, the tripartite classification provides a useful heuristic device, which I use to construct 'ideal type' descriptions of how each feminist framework approaches the task of conceptualizing and reforming education.

Liberal feminism and education

Securing equal opportunities for the sexes is the main aim of liberal feminism. The intent of liberal feminists in education is to remove barriers that prevent girls reaching their full potential, whether such barriers are located in the school, the individual psyche or discriminatory labour practices. What is the conceptual foundation for liberal-feminist education scholarship? There are three major themes: (1) equal opportunities; (2) socialization and sex stereo-typing; (3) sex discrimination.

Equal opportunities rhetoric is almost the *sine qua non* by which liberal-feminist perspectives are recognized as such. 'Equal means the same' claims Eileen Byrne (1978: 19), arguing that separate educational provision for girls has usually meant inferior facilities and restricted features. Yet the *same* treatment may produce unequal outcomes if, for example, prior socialization en-sures the sexes typically have differential initial competence or interest in a given subject; or labour market practices mean employers will welcome equally qualified boys and girls with differential enthusiasm. The failure of schools to accomplish 'equality of educational opportunity' in social-class terms is widely acknowledged, and consequently the phrase has nearly disappeared from socio-logical studies of class inequality, yet its meaning has been revised to be some-thing of a code phrase for inequalities based on race and/or sex (and occasionally disability). Some local education authorities (LEAs) in Britain have appointed 'equal opportunities advisers', and universities, companies and local governments proclaim themselves 'equal opportunity employers'. In Australia, Yates (1986) suggests that the rhetoric, in this transformed way, may persist because class differences apart, the provision of educational resources on a gender-neutral basis still seems attainable.

In Britain, the discourse of equal opportunity, however flawed, is virtually the only one acceptable to the general public. It is the language of central government and its quasi-governmental agencies and research teams; it is also to a large extent the choice of local government, trade unions and political parties. Terms like 'sexism', 'oppression' and 'patriarchy' are staples of feminist writing, but official documents and projects still employ them gingerly if at all. Prudent efforts to introduce feminist perspectives into the teacher training

curriculum tend to use phrases like 'equal opportunities for the sexes in education' or, increasingly, 'gender and education'.

A second major concern of liberal feminists in education focuses on socialization, sex roles and sex stereotyping. Girls (and boys) are thought to be socialized (by the family, the school, the media) into traditional attitudes and
orientations that limit their futures unnecessarily to sex-stereotyped occupational and family roles. At the same time, socialization encourages patterns of
interpersonal relationships between the sexes that disadvantage females, who
are placed in a position of dependency and deference, and also males, who are
forced to suppress their emotional and caring potential. DuBois *et al.* (1985)
argue that 'sex differences' have always been a concern within American educational research; the problem is 'to analyze sex differences where research
indicates they exist and not to invoke them artificially as explanations where
they do not' (p. 28). In contrast, British educational work on 'sex differences'
has been unevenly spread through the subdisciplines of education; in sociology
of education, for example, virtually no attention was paid to the topic before
the late 1970s, as I showed in Chapter 2. 'Gender' has taken over from 'sex' in
much British educational scholarship, but more as a token of good faith than as
a result of a clearly understood distinction between the terms.

The sex-role socialization framework is thought of as particularly characteristic of the United States and has been criticized by Arnot (1981) in Britain,
Connell (1985) in Australia and Middleton (1984) in New Zealand. There is a
third theme within liberal feminism, centring on notions of discrimination,
rights, justice and fairness. Those who use these terms come much closer to
admitting an impact of 'structures' than those confined to a 'sex-role' or 'sex-
differences' approach. As Arnot (1981) points out, Byrne (1978) recognized the
impact of policies as well as attitudes in creating a structure of disadvantage for
girls, especially for those from rural or working-class origins. Rendel's (1980,
1984) work on British academics (and similar work in other countries) also
demonstrates the point. She argues that the fact women university teachers, a
select group, fail to be promoted to professorships is unlikely to be due solely to
the women's limitations (Rendel 1984).

Whyte and her co-editors' (1985) collection illustrates the merging of the
three liberal-feminist themes. Attitudes figure prominently, but they are generally attitudes of teachers, seen as contributing to sex-stereotyped subject
choices within schools and eventually to sex-stereotyped occupations for
school leavers. The concern with access to science and technology is strong.
Reports from government-sponsored projects and equal opportunities personnel are featured, and feminist rhetoric is conspicuously absent. The tone of the
book is polite rather than outraged. But neither is there recourse to arguments
that assert that girls' own attitudes (however derived) prevent them recognizing their own best interests. Instead, there is attention paid to LEA re-
calcitrance, limits of equal opportunity legislation, and vagaries of industrial
tribunal proceedings in cases of women teachers charging discrimination.

Strategies for educational change emanating from liberal feminism follow
from the conceptual base. In general, there is an attempt to alter socialization

practices, change attitudes, use legal processes. The gathering and disseminating of information and evidence is important (Middleton 1984). Whyte (1986) notes that science teachers involved in the 'Girls into Science and Technology' project were noticeably more impressed with 'facts and figures' than with social science terminology. The promotion of 'good practice' in schools is an aim of the Equal Opportunities Commission (EOC) in Britain, and a number of booklets have been prepared and distributed with that objective. The EOC puts informal pressure on schools and LEAs acting illegally or against the spirit of the Sex Discrimination Act. Legal remedies are used where possible, although the limits of Britain's sex discrimination legislation in the education field are oft-noted. Weiner (1986) provides a list of liberal-feminist strategies aimed at changing the attitudes of teachers and children. The strategies include reviewing aspects of school organization such as the timetable, analysing curriculum materials for stereotyping, persuading girls not to drop science and technology subjects, and establishing teacher working parties on the issues. There has also been increasing interest in assertiveness training for women teachers wishing promotion. Another strategy is providing teachers in training and those on in-service courses with ideas for combating sexism.

The liberal-feminist stance on education has attracted fierce criticism from other feminists, so much so that it is hard to find an extended defence of the position in Britain. The critics generally point to the limitations of the conceptual framework, especially ideas about equality of opportunity and the reliance on socialization and sex-role models. The emphasis on individual attitudes in these approaches is seen as a kind of psychological reductionism, blaming the victim for her (socialized) lack of perception or confidence. *Why* socialization proceeds as it does, with such apparently deleterious consequences, is unexplained (Connell 1985). It is charged that sex equality is mistakenly approached as if solutions might be wholly educational (Arnot 1981); that the labour market process and capitalism are regarded uncritically; that change is conceptualized as if it were merely a matter of appealing to good will (Acker 1984b); that male frameworks such as 'career' remain unchallenged by attempts to make a few women assertive enough to succeed in them (Weiner 1986). Liberal feminism is accused, above all, of ignoring the impact of patriarchy, power and the systematic subordination of women by men (O'Brien 1983; Weiner 1986), as well as the effects of racism and class hegemony (Arnot 1981, 1982). It is striking that in the 'official' British equal opportunity literature (e.g. from the EOC) girls are simply girls: the differential potential impacts of class, ethnicity or other attributes upon their life chances appear a taboo topic. This avoidance would not seem, however, to be a necessary characteristic of liberal-feminist educational thought, as Byrne's (1978) approach shows.

Socialist feminism and education

The socialist-feminist work I am considering analyses Western capitalist states. In the long run, the aim is to remove oppression (in part by abolishing capitalism), but the immediate task is to elucidate the processes involved. Most socialist-feminist theoreticians have focused on women's position within the economy and the family. For those concerned with education, the key question is 'how is education related to the reproduction of gender divisions within capitalism?' (Arnot and Weiner 1987a).

The development of socialist-feminist perspectives within education has been strongly influenced by neo-Marxist trends within the sociology of education (see Chapter 1). A major concept used in this body of literature is 'reproduction'. Theorists have analysed how schooling, by a variety of mechanisms, perpetuates (reproduces) class divisions within the work force. Socialist-feminist sociologists of education have used these theories as a starting point for a 'political economy perspective' (Arnot 1981), calling attention to the schools' role in reproducing a sexual as well as a social division of labour in the family and the workplace.

For example, in Canada, Jane Gaskell (1986), looks critically at the notion of 'skill', often seen as a consequence of formal education and as a determinant of occupational placement and its rewards. Yet 'skill' is a socially constructed category. Apprenticeships for 'skilled' trades have been mostly held by males who have been sufficiently organized to limit others' access to training and practice. In contrast, the skills of office work, arguably no less difficult to learn, are defined as part of every woman's 'natural' equipment, easy and taken for granted. According to Gaskell, training for office work, but not for 'male crafts', is extensive in the Canadian high school, supplemented by easy access through evening classes at schools and colleges. Entry is uncontrolled and the result is a large pool of labour trained at no cost to the employers. Curriculum differentiation processes within the school are important not only because girls are trained in office skills such as word processing, but because they are not trained in allied areas such as computer science or management that might allow entry into alternative careers. In this analysis, the partnership between education and the economy operates to confirm large numbers of girls and women in restricted, low-paid sectors of employment.

Other socialist-feminist analyses have explored the links between school and motherhood. Miriam David (1984), for example, notes multiple ways in which British primary schools operate with the expectation of *mothers'* participation in school activities. Even before children start school, mothers, especially those of the middle classes, are expected to educate their children – give them cultural capital – if they are to benefit fully from schooling itself. Schools, especially in situations of declining resources and in socially advantaged areas, rely on unpaid help from mothers (some of whom are themselves trained teachers), ranging from repairing books to assisting with classroom routines. School hours and holidays in Britain (including the convention of a week off in the middle of each term, known as 'half-term holiday') place dramatic restrictions on the kinds of paid employment mothers of young children can pursue. So schools make use of, and simultaneously perpetuate, a sexual division of labour in the home.

Much of the socialist-feminist work in education consists of theoretical arguments, historical research or policy analysis. There have been comparatively few empirical studies of school processes. In part, this neglect is due to the difficulty of subjecting 'reproduction theory' to the kind of hypothesis-testing that makes up the classic scientific method. Thus socialist-feminist research, along with neo-Marxist research in sociology of education generally, can be accused of substituting the 'apt illustration' for rigorous testing (Hargreaves 1982). The most promising concept to guide empirical work is probably the 'gender code' (MacDonald 1980b). A few ethnographic studies are beginning to show the operation of class and gender codes (e.g. Connell *et al.* 1982; Russell 1986), especially in career guidance or subject choice exercises, whereby schools and the labour market can be most obviously linked. But there is still difficulty with the macrosociological nature of the theory and the microsociological level of most school-based research. The extent to which any such school practices actually are required for the reproduction of the sexual and social division of labour is probably undemonstrable.

A category of empirical research sometimes called 'cultural studies' comes partially and rather uneasily under the socialist-feminist wing. In recent years, sociologists of education have sought to give greater weight to ways in which individuals and groups resist or contest dominant ideologies and processes of social control. In this vein, several studies have begun to chart girls' cultures. Some are explicitly concerned with class and ethnic variations (e.g. Fuller 1983; Griffin 1985). Yet not all of these studies can be placed clearly within the socialist-feminist framework, despite the resistance theme. Arnot (1981) has pointed out that although the studies of girls' *culture* moved the focus beyond the liberal-feminist one on individual girls' *attitudes*, the roots of gender differentiation remain buried.

It is in strategies for educational action that socialist-feminist writing appears most underdeveloped. This situation is demonstrated indirectly by Weiner's (1986) comparison of equal opportunities (liberal) and anti-sexist (radical) educational strategies. She has no separate category of socialist-feminist strategies. Weiner remarks in passing that Marxist analyses have been theoretical and academic rather than classroom-oriented. Although reproduction theories can sometimes appear to forestall any social change, socialist-feminist writers at least gesture towards 'an education praxis, a radical pedagogy' (Middleton 1984: 49). This may mean (eventually) the potential development, with teachers and pupils, of strategies of resistance or moves towards a curriculum that challenges the dominant hegemony.

Theorizing itself, of course, can be regarded as a strategy that calls attention to the role of schooling in mediating and reproducing gender, class and other divisions. Yet if this strategy is to be effective, theorists will have to develop ways of talking to the teachers rather than to each other (Yates 1986: 128). I have found that although teachers in training (and to a lesser extent those on in-service courses) will repeat socialist-feminist statements in essays, they are far more excited by radical feminists' appeal to personal experience or liberal feminists' to equity.

After a series of critiques from black British women (e.g. Amos and Parmar 1981; Carby 1982), socialist-feminist writings on education show increasing awareness that gender, race and class interact in complex ways to shape girls' lives in and out of school (Brah and Minhas 1985; Brah and Deem, 1986). Some of the generalizations in the feminist literature about marriages and the family, or the descriptions of girls' conformity and resistance in schools, or the arguments about single-sex schools, may need reworking in so far as they have in the past taken middle-class white British experience as an unquestioned departure point.

Another line of criticism points to the social determinism implied in 'reproduction' accounts. Capitalism becomes reified; society is seen as a 'field of play of pre-given and essential interests or needs' (Culley and Demaine 1983: 170). Culley and Demaine argue that if any attempt by the state to improve matters can be dismissed as 'really' for control purposes and ultimately reproductive, constructive political action becomes impossible. Connell (1985) recommends moving towards a theory of practice that would avoid voluntarism and pluralism (as in liberal feminism) on the one hand, and over-determinism by 'categories' on the other. Culley and Demaine suggest concentrating on specific struggles and practices in schools and local education authorities where outcomes depend on an array of influences, some under teacher control, rather than on external forces alone.

Radical feminism and education

Like socialist feminists, radical feminists want to see a fundamental change in the social structure, one that will eliminate male dominance and patriarchal structures. 'The goal of a feminist education', writes Mary O'Brien (1983: 13), 'is not equality in knowledge, power and wealth, but the abolition of gender as an oppressive cultural reality'. Unlike socialist feminists and liberal feminists writing about education, radical feminists have made few attempts to relate school life to the economy or to the family. Their analyses do sometimes use a concept of 'reproduction' (Mahony 1985: 66), but what is being reproduced is the domination of men over women, denying girls and women full access to knowledge, resources, self-esteem and freedom from fear and harassment.

Two major concerns characterize this body of literature: (1) the male monopolization of culture and knowledge; and (2) the sexual politics of everyday life in schools. The major exponent of the first of these concerns is Dale Spender (1980, 1981, 1982; see also Spender and Sarah 1980). Spender argues that what we 'know' is dangerously deficient, for it is the record of decisions and activities of men, presented in the guise of *human* knowledge. For centuries, women's contributions and understandings have been ignored or disparaged, notwithstanding female resistance. Spender wishes to uncover the logic of male dominance and the contribution schools make towards it; ways in which gatekeeping processes silence women and allow men to dominate decision-making in educational (and other) contexts; and the role of language in controlling the ways in which women conceptualize themselves and their world. There are obvious implications here for the school curriculum and also for women teachers' and girls' access to power and policy-making within education. Women's studies courses in higher education also build on (although not exclusively) the radical-feminist analysis of knowledge. Radical-feminist perspectives have been extended into the adult education field by Jane Thompson (1983).

The second main theme concerns the sexual politics of daily life in educational institutions. Here, too, Spender has made a significant contribution by delineating two aspects of the problem: teacher attention unequally divided between the sexes to the advantage of boys (Spender 1982); and the potential, although not unmixed, benefits of single-sex schooling for girls (Spender and Sarah 1980; Spender 1982). Both of these issues have been approached from other perspectives as well, but they are most closely associated with radical-feminist ones, as the basic reason for concern is the dominance of males over females in mixed-sex settings; moreover, they are examples of the radical-feminist dictum that 'the personal is political'.

In the 1980s, British radical-feminist writing became more insistent about the extent to which boys (sometimes aided by male teachers) oppress, demean and harass girls (and sometimes women teachers). These accounts are painful to read. Schools, especially mixed secondary schools, appear as amplifiers of male tendencies towards violence. According to Mahony (1985), it is not simply that girls receive less teacher time, but that their classroom contributions are met with systematic ridicule from boys and their existence outside classrooms is filled with verbal and non-verbal abuse and physical molestation. Carol Jones (1985) describes one London secondary school that was covered with woman-hating graffiti and pornographic drawings, populated by boys boasting of watching videos of violence towards women, and characterized by a stream of abuse from boys to girls. 'Male violence – visual, verbal and physical harassment – was part of daily school life' (p. 30). Jones adds that girls and teachers had developed some strategies for resistance. Sexual harassment and abuse can take different forms when combined with racism (Suleiman and Suleiman 1985) or directed against those (of both sexes) who breach norms of heterosexuality.

Exposing these practices through publications is clearly one radical-feminist strategy. Weiner (1986) points out that radical feminists have successfully legitimated discussions of sexuality and sexual harassment in schools, topics that were formerly ignored. Anti-sexist strategies for teachers or girls are recommended or summarized in Jones (1985), Mahony (1985) and Weiner (1986). What runs through these works is a commitment to place girls and women at the centre of concern. This accomplishment means believing their complaints and according validity to their perspectives. Revisions of curricula, texts and the extension of scholarship on gender have a similar rationale. There are also attempts at pedagogical change, especially in higher and adult education, intended to develop non-hierarchical, less competitive, participatory teaching methods. A number of proposed strategies involve (sometimes temporary) separation of the sexes: single-sex schools, colleges, classes, discussion groups and youth clubs. A central unresolved problem with these ideas is how to educate and re-educate the boys and who should do it (Mahony 1985: 91).

Radical feminism attracts considerable criticism. Middleton (1984) argues that radical feminism is the least articulated of the three perspectives with regard to education, and that it is descriptive rather than explanatory. Radical feminists would reply that there is a clear explanation – the universality of patriarchy or male dominance – and that male power and control over women is not simply ideological but material (Mahony 1985: 68). The critics' response is to accuse radical feminism of biological reductionism or essentialism. The problem here lies in answering in non-biological terms the question of *why* men wish to dominate women. A number of critics (e.g. Connell 1985; Murphy and Livingstone 1985) charge that radical-feminist analyses with their generalizations about (all) women and (all) men direct attention away from divisions that cut across or complicate women/men categories, such as class, race, nationality and age. There is an issue here to which I shall return in the conclusion to this chapter: the similarity yet diversity of women. However, radical-feminist educational accounts are increasingly trying to consider racism along with sexism (e.g. Bunch and Pollack 1983; Weiner 1985).

Certainly some radical feminists in education, including Spender, make sweeping statements about 'men' and 'women', and studies like Mahony's (1985) or Jones' (1985) stress particularly unpleasant aspects of masculinity. Mahony (1985: 71) attempts to counter charges of essentialism by developing a concept of the social (rather than biological) construction of masculinity ('social maleness'). In one sense, this effort returns us to a socialization approach (with its defects): boys behave badly because they have learned to do so. Why has socialization encouraged this pattern? Mahony (1985) suggests it persists because men benefit from being powerful. But why should 'being powerful' automatically be a rewarding experience unless one has been socialized to believe this?

British radical-feminist writing on education *is* accessible and popular. It avoids the dullness of some liberal-feminist research and the opacity of some socialist-feminist analysis. Perhaps its impact stems from a belief that 'change is possible and teachers and pupils can make it happen' (Mahony 1985: 93), even when such a hope appears to contradict the conception of patriarchy as pandemic and powerful.

Radical-feminist scholarship is also open to criticism on methodological grounds. Feminist methodology tries to break free from the male biases in research paradigms criticized by Spender and others (Stanley and Wise 1983), and it opens up important new possibilities and unearths data ignored by conventional approaches, such as the evidence of sexual harassment in schools. But I believe that some standards have to be set beyond personal validation of data (see Chapter 4). It is unlikely that all teachers favour boys all of the time, or that all schools are as riddled by sexism as the one in Jones' (1985) study or the worst of Mahony's (1985) examples. The dilemma of the 'apt example' surfaces, just as it did for reproduction and resistance research. Mahony (1985: 36) deliberately uses this technique to ring an 'alarm bell' – and we hear it – but it is still necessary to know under what conditions such findings will and will not obtain, if oppression is to be fought most effectively.

Feminist theoretical frameworks: Problems and prospects

Are we moving towards a synthesis of feminist educational approaches? Deep conceptual divides remain. But it seems to me that, with a few exceptions, feminist theoretical writing about education manages to be constructively critical without the vitriol sometimes found in other spheres of feminist commentary. Possibly this can be traced to the tradition of pragmatism in much educational thought: the immediate goal of making conditions better overrides some of the theoretical disputes. Many writers work in educational institutions themselves and thus sustain some commitment to educational change through educational means (directly through their teaching, indirectly through the teaching of teachers and prospective teachers and the production of scholarship). The tension between education-as-reproductive and education-as-liberating is encountered daily. Additionally, in Britain, education has been rather peripheral to feminist theory. Mitchell and Oakley's (1986) book, for example, has no separate chapter on education and barely a mention of it elsewhere; Segal's (1987) lengthy critique of Dale Spender's work totally ignores all Spender's books and articles on education. Possibly pragmatism and marginality encourage educational scholars and activists into alliances across theoretical divides. As Sally Miller Gearhart (1983) points out, alliances may be built on the coincidence of the goals of liberal feminists with the strategies of radical (or socialist) feminists. The preference for equal opportunities discourse in British public policy means that under an equal opportunities cloak, a socialist or radical feminist heart may beat!

For educational theorists as well as for other feminists, certain dilemmas remain. One of these dilemmas is the relationship between *structure* and *agency*. Should women be seen as immobilized by reproductive social and economic structures, by tradition-bound institutions, by discrimination, by men? Or are they active agents, struggling to control and change their lives? Even more problematic is the issue of *universality and diversity*, one of the 'paradoxes of feminism':

> . . . rooted in women's actual situation, being the same (in a species sense) as men; being different, with respect to reproductive biology and gender construction, from men. In another complication, all women may be said to be 'the same', as distinct from all men with respect to reproductive biology, and yet 'not the same', with respect to the variance of gender construction. Both theory and practice in feminism historically have had to deal with the fact that women are the same as and different from men, and the fact that women's gender identity is not separable from the other factors that make up our selves: race, religion, culture, class, age.
>
> (Cott 1986: 49)

The history of struggles for women's education shows the tensions between strategies emphasizing sameness or difference, structures or agency. The contemporary arguments I have reviewed again show these tensions. But tensions can be productive as well as destructive. It is through these very dilemmas, through attempts to solve the unsolvable, through exchanges among feminist frameworks that feminist theory moves ahead.

Notes

1. The original article version of this chapter was published in 1987 (see Acknowledgements for details).
2. A discussion of post-structural or post-modern feminism and its educational implications can be found in Chapter 1.

4 Is Research by a Feminist Always Feminist Research?

This chapter approaches the question of 'what is feminist research' in an unusual way, by discussing an example of research that did not start out to be feminist.[1] I argue that feminist research, like other research, is shaped by its surroundings, and that in certain circumstances the best that can be expected is work that is *covertly* feminist. The implication is that rather than following a list of criteria at the design stage in order to determine what is authentic feminist research, we might think of feminist work as that which is informed at any point by a feminist framework.

I begin the chapter with a review of the arguments for the development of feminist scholarship and research. I also identify some of the problems arising from overly rigid prescriptions for doing 'proper' feminist research. I then argue that the social conditions under which research is conducted play a major role in determining what research does, and does not, get done. I illustrate this point by an extended example drawn from my own work. I describe the events that led up to devising a particular research project and why gender was relatively neglected in that project. I consider why gender issues rarely surfaced in the fieldwork and did not feature significantly in the early analysis. Then I describe steps taken to probe for gender aspects in the data once I had moved to a different work setting, and show how a general knowledge of feminist scholarship could be applied at that point. In the conclusion, I return to the question of what consequences work context has for the production of feminist research.

This story shows the extent to which research – my research in this case – is a social construction. I was an 'agent', choosing to do certain things and not to do others, but my decisions were influenced by factors such as the reward system in my workplace culture and the opportunities to gain funds for research. My concern is that potential contributions to feminist scholarship may never be made, if researchers are squeezed between feminist pre-scriptions on the one hand, and workplace or disciplinary conventions on the other.

Feminist research

Feminist writers have been fruitful in the production of scholarship and research; moreover, they have engaged in unusually extensive reflection about what it is they do. Thus we do not simply have a body of feminist research, we have a body of questions about the epistemological assumptions and preferred techniques within feminist research (e.g. Roberts 1981; Stanley and Wise 1983; Cook and Fonow 1986; Harding 1986, 1991; Collins 1990; Nielsen 1990; Stanley 1990; Gluck and Patai 1991; Lather 1991; Reinharz 1992). Moreover, perhaps because of women's historical positioning as teachers, we have a body of literature about teaching *about* feminist research and scholarship (e.g. Bowles and Klein 1983; Bunch and Pollack 1983; Aiken *et al.* 1988; hooks 1988; Laird 1988; Aaron and Walby 1991; Briskin and Coulter 1992; Luke and Gore 1992b). Such teaching is usually labelled 'women's studies' or 'feminist pedagogy', although a distinction can be made between the former as an umbrella term for the institutional programmes for scholarship on women, and the latter as the appropriate teaching and learning styles and strategies for the communication of feminist scholarship.

The origins of such work lie in the second-wave women's movement starting in the 1960s, and the gradual recognition among those who felt its influence that what they had imbibed as the received wisdom of their respective fields was produced mostly by males and based on male experience. Later, the fact that only certain males (white, middle-class, etc.) were in such privileged positions and that their critics, too, were generally operating out of a shared white, Western, middle-class position became much better understood (e.g. Baca Zinn *et al.* 1986), and some of the righteous certainty of feminists began to give way to a deeper level of reflection, concerned with the effect that positionality has on all conceptions of knowledge (Alcoff 1988).

However, in the early stages of feminist critique, it was demonstrated for field after field that women had been left out of the production of knowledge, and it was claimed that the result was a distortion of human experience. Chapter 2 makes this argument about the sociology of education in the 1960s and 1970s.

Dale Spender (1982: 24) delivers a scathing attack on the notions of knowledge embodied in the various curricula of higher education:

> Women have been kept 'off the record' in most, if not all, branches of knowledge by the simple process of men naming the world as it appears to them. They have taken themselves as the starting point, defined themselves as central, and then proceeded to describe the rest of the world in relation to themselves. They have assumed their experience is universal, that it is representative of humanity, and that it constitutes a basis for generalising about *all* human beings. Whenever the experience of women is different from men, therefore, it stays 'off the record', for there is no way of entering it into the record when the experience is not shared by men, and men are the ones who write the record.

Many feminists would distance themselves from Spender's sweeping generalities and hints of conspiracy, but she does vividly capture the starting point of feminist scholarship: the desire to remedy a history of exclusion and distortion. With the development of critiques and the attempts to do research that no longer distorts or omits, came the efforts to delineate the field(s). When is research authentically feminist? Does its feminism reside in its content or its method or both? Is it to be found in the intent of its practitioners? As feminism itself splits ever further (Delmar 1986), the questions become ever more difficult.

Culled from a number of sources, core assumptions in feminist research go something like this:

1. Feminist research involves an acute state of awareness of the injustice women suffer because of their sex.
2. The purpose of this research is to improve women's lives.
3. Feminist research asserts the centrality of women and of gender to all aspects of human existence.
4. It rests on the belief that existing knowledge and techniques are deficient and need revision and replacing.
5. Women's experience in patriarchal society is the starting point for research: the personal is political and valid.
6. The researcher should enter into the same space as her subject, rather than taking up a powerful or detached position.

These assumptions are contentious, perhaps especially the last two. If research starts with women's experience in patriarchal society, does this mean that only women can do feminist research because only women can have that experience for themselves (Stanley and Wise 1983)? How could feminist research go beyond the individual experience of the researcher? Can men do feminist research? If not, what is their role to be and what incentives are there for men (the gatekeepers) to read and reflect on the new scholarship? Must feminist research be *about* women? Does it apply to all disciplines (Morrell 1991)? Do the attempts to collaborate with rather than to control the research subjects lead to just another form of duplicity (Stacey 1991)? If a researcher should bond with her subjects, can she retain the capacity to do critical research (Reinharz 1992)? How can feminist research avoid essentialism (the unproblematic construction of 'woman' as homogeneous) and speak to the diversity found among women? Finally, what standards are to replace patriarchal ones for the evaluation of feminist scholarship?

The influence of post-modern or post-structuralist thinking has added even greater urgency to such questioning (Hare-Mustin and Marecek 1990; Lather 1991). Grand theories and 'master narratives' are no longer desirable constructions, when knowledge is recognized as provisional, grounded and uncertain. In one sense, this is good news for feminists, because it parallels what their critique has been asserting; in another, it is destabilizing, for surely the feminist alternatives are just as provisional and uncertain.

In line with this turn towards questioning of the questioning, it may be time to redirect the debate over what is feminist research, or at least tone down its ferocity. Most typifications of feminist research assume that such research must be designed from a feminist perspective and must conform to a set of rules such as those listed above. One might consider this a trait theory of feminist research, analogous to the efforts to decide 'what is a profession' by listing criteria (Millerson 1963). It is a constraining approach that fails to allow for growth and change and that builds in an assumption that new gatekeepers are to replace the old ones in determining what is proper research. One reason I make this argument is my awareness that many feminists do not work in conditions conducive to doing openly feminist research.

Contexts and conditions

We are beginning to understand that scholarship is produced in particular contexts. Several writers have linked the production of feminist scholarship (and the fate of feminist scholars, or, more broadly, women academics) to the settings in which they operate (Spender 1981; McRobbie 1982; Stanley 1984, 1990; Smith 1987; Aisenberg and Harrington 1988; Acker 1990a; Gumport 1990; Bannerji et al. 1991; Ng 1991; Wilkinson 1991; Luke and Gore 1992a), and it is a point taken up in Chapters 8 and 9 of this volume. Additionally, Maher and Tetreault (1993) remind us that even a construct like 'feminist pedagogy' takes very different forms in different institutions. Such approaches deserve more attention if only because they provide a counterweight to the flood of psychological explanations of women's experiences.

For example, Luke and Gore (1992a) distinguish three forms of control in academic settings, which they label sexist, patriarchal and phallocentric discourse, roughly equivalent, respectively, to everyday encounters, institutionalized structures whereby men hold decision-making and gatekeeping power, and the privileging and universalizing of male experience in texts. Liz Stanley (1984) categorizes the 'discrimination' (even in its neutral sense) involved in professional practices as: *overt discrimination*, the rules and codes intended to guard and protect standards; *covert discrimination*, the shared, but informal ideas about what is correct and valid scholarship and behaviour; and *self-discrimination*, the monitoring we learn to do to ensure we stay within the parameters set by the first two forms. In a later publication, Stanley (1990) elaborates upon the 'academic mode of production', whereby 'knowledge' is produced in the complex operations of gatekeepers, organizational structures, divisions of labour, techniques and symbols (see also Bannerji et al. 1991).

Gumport (1990) interviewed women academics in philosophy, sociology and history, and her results show how disciplinary conventions influence women's chances of doing feminist research and having it recognized and rewarded. 'Women's history' has gained some status as a specialty, while philosophy has shown a reluctance to regard feminist work as real philosophy. Feminists in philosophy either developed two lines of work, 'straight philosophy' and feminist analysis, or moved into women's studies programmes.

Wilkinson (1991) provides a gripping account of processes of exclusion in her description of efforts of feminists to gain a base within the discipline of psychology in Britain. She argues that when feminism presents a perceived challenge to traditional epistemologies as well as hierarchies of power, strenuous efforts are made to defend against it. Control is exercised by definition (feminism is inappropriate), by tactics (denial of platforms) and by rhetoric (appeal to democracy, meritocracy). She goes on to give concrete examples, including the rejection in official circles and refereed journals of Celia Kitzinger's work on lesbianism, and the formidable efforts required to set up a 'Psychology of Women' section within the British Psychological Society. One of the most interesting responses of the BPS was the resort to equal opportunities rhetoric to *oppose* special consideration for women.

The next sections of this chapter describe a research project that I devised when I was working as an academic in Britain. I explain what features of my particular work context discouraged my constructing this study as a feminist one.

Background to the research: My work context

The study I shall describe was conceived while I was a lecturer in a university school of education in Britain, a post I held from 1972 until 1990. As I indicate in Chapter 9, the lectureship is the 'career grade' in British universities. Internal promotions to readerships and senior lectureships are possible. Few British academics become professors, and most departments have only one or two.

In Chapter 1, I outlined the early stages of my career in the United States and Britain. My interest in gender issues can be traced back to my graduate school days. When I began working in the school of education, I integrated this concern into my teaching and publications and political activity. Because I also taught about class and race, one student dubbed me 'the oppression tutor'. I came close to having the monopoly on such issues in the school, which perhaps gave me an image as somewhat eccentric. One colleague said I had 'an American instinct for democracy'.

Nevertheless, I received tenure and moved 'through the salary bar' (a marker halfway through the lecturer salary scale) without difficulty. All I had to do at both points was to produce a curriculum vitae (CV). The three professors in the department simply made the recommendation. I was told at one of these junctures that a professor had questioned whether I might 'be one of those people who only do one thing' in their careers. I was unsure whether he meant that I would not do further research after my dissertation or that I would not move beyond 'women and education'. I doubt if he realized how varied that field could be!

When I approached age 40, I received for the first time information about promotion criteria in the university. This was standard practice, probably because the average age of promotion, at least to senior lecturer, was somewhere in one's forties. I entered the 'competition' in the same year I turned 40.[2] The procedure required support from one's senior colleagues in order to be recommended to a Committee of Professors in the Social Sciences. That committee – all but one male – drew up a shortlist of recommended candidates on the basis of CVs and recommendations of heads of departments. It was only after being placed on the shortlist that candidates were able to get selections from their work read (by those same professors). No other evidence (e.g. student evaluations) was collected. For the senior lecturer route, there was no use of outside appraisers.

From my colleagues' experiences, I knew that my chances would not be good until I had gone through the exercise several times. Several of my older male colleagues and ex-colleagues had become quite bitter about the amount of time it had taken them to achieve promotion. After several years trying to reach the magic shortlist, I was ready to join them.

Moreover, I was aware, both through my research and through looking around me, that women were a distinct minority among academics in Britain, and very scarce in the upper ranks (see Chapter 9 for more detail). Toren (1993), using data from Israel and the United States, demonstrates that women indeed stay longer at each rank before promotion. She argues that publication rates are not causing the differential; on the contrary, the extended duration means that 'women "pay" more in terms of number of publications for promotion and tenure' (p. 445). I wondered how much my chances were influenced by my being a *woman* academic (Evans 1993; Toren 1993), and how much by my involvement in feminist scholarship (Gumport 1990).

Looking back, I see an absence of mentoring or sponsorship, although there was no shortage of friends and supportive colleagues. With no formal appraisal system until my last year in the school of education, and a promotion system that was competitive, rested heavily on sponsorship, gave little guidance as to appropriate endeavours, and did not kick in until relatively late in one's career, I had found myself doing the work that interested me rather than satisfying a set of requirements.

Certainly, no-one ever discouraged me from doing research on gender. However, it had become apparent to me that none of the decision-makers was going to be an expert in this area, and some of them would be likely not to consider it proper scholarship at all. So I had a strong motivation for developing new directions in my research. I needed to do the kind of work that would receive some recognition and comprehension, not just in my wider reference groups of sociologists of education and feminist scholars, but in my home institution. Gumport (1990: 241) puts it well when she says that for feminists the tension of being simultaneously inside and outside a discipline 'entails a burden of dual loyalties, shifting audiences, and multiple sets of criteria for evaluating one's work'.

A turning point was the summer of 1986, which I spent doing research for a chapter on primary teaching as an occupation (Acker 1987) for an edited collection. I was amazed to find how much literature there was on 'teachers' and how interesting it all was. Our daughter was in primary school and I began to think about doing some empirical research on primary school teachers. I began research on teachers' work in a primary school in April 1987.[3] I saw a chance here not to study women, or do feminist research, but to study 'teachers', an interest shared by a number of colleagues in my department.

The following year another 'opportunity' for non-feminist research presented itself. This opportunity was a call for research proposals on 'research training in the social sciences'. It came from the Economic and Social Research Council (ESRC), the main source of public funding for social science researchers and doctoral students in the UK. My dissertation research had left me familiar with a body of knowledge I could draw upon, and I had kept up with some of the literature out of interest in the topic. I thought: now or never. Below I describe the project that resulted from that decision.[4]

Designing the research

The ESRC was interested in the topic of graduate study, not only for reasons of adding to knowledge, but as a consequence of the era of accountability and value for money that prevailed in Thatcher's Britain. 'Education' had metamorphosed into 'training'. It had been deemed (not unreasonably) unacceptable to spend vast quantities of money on graduate students who never finished their degrees. Policies were put in place to penalize departments with poor submission rates, and eventually research was commissioned on the topic itself.

Proposals were to be based on the short document announcing the initiative (ESRC 1988), which identified two 'pressing' areas for long-term research and a series of possible short-term projects. The first of the pressing areas was labelled 'The contribution of social science research training to the labour market, to the academic and professional community, and to the careers of individuals', and the second 'The research training process'. A number of sub-questions were posed under each heading, most policy-oriented; for example, under 'Contribution to the individual career', sub-questions included 'How important are the skills individuals acquire during research training to their subsequent jobs and careers?' and 'Which skills are particularly valuable?' The 'key question' under the research training process category was 'How do the characteristics of the participants affect the nature of the outcomes?' 'Characteristics' were then elaborated upon, to include skills, aptitudes, student isolation, supervisor's track record, status granted to supervision by institutions. The recommended shorter term research projects involved collecting data on the characteristics and distribution of doctoral students, the responses of institutions to ESRC policy and the strengths and weaknesses of different modes of training.

It should be apparent that none of the topics featured – nor even mentioned – gender or gender issues. 'Characteristics' might have been defined in terms of gender, race, class, and so forth, but was not. One of the short-term projects proposed mentioned 'demographic data', but only in terms of collecting baseline statistics. There was some acknowledgement that student experience might vary, but not according to social divisions.

It was logical, and strategic, for would-be researchers to follow the drift of the call for proposals rather than their own inclinations, or at least to compromise. My proposal focused on thesis supervision as an element of the research process. It conceptualized supervision as a teaching–learning process embedded in particular disciplinary and departmental structures and cultures. It went through several versions, eventually becoming an interview-based study of supervisors and students in three departments of psychology and three of education.

Gender was mentioned in my proposal, but only in passing, and mostly in the context of selecting a sample. In retrospect, I think I was responding to the absence of gender in the call for proposals, and my increasing sense that I needed to do research on something *other than* gender if I wanted to be promoted. The prevailing assumption seemed to be that gender research, and certainly feminist research, was 'other'. It was not research on teachers, administrators, curriculum, learning, students, or whatever, it was 'research on women'. As such, it was not of interest to the people studying teachers, administrators, curriculum, and so forth.

There seemed no way around this pattern of exclusion and ignoring, apart from coming in from the cold. Now I was no longer doing 'just' research on women. I was doing research on graduate students and, from my other project, research on teachers. Although I continued to write papers, teach and do other professional work concerned with gender, I was pleased that (perhaps) I had dispelled the image that I was an academic with only one string to my bow.

In the field

The early stages of the project were focused on modifying the research design, selecting the departments and gaining access, developing the interview schedule and coping with various crises. Initial contacts with potential departments were made, and heads of department and individuals in charge of research student matters were interviewed.[5]

The main phase of the study involved interviews with supervisors and students. The project team (myself, my co-director Tim Hill, and a full-time research officer, Edith Black) had decided to make sure that women supervisors were included among those interviewed, if necessary by oversampling women, and expected that we would have equal numbers of male and female students. Nearly all of the women supervisors in the six departments were interviewed. The numbers were not very large (14 out of 61 interviews), reflecting the low proportion of women in mainstream positions in British universities. In both disciplines, women students were commonplace and comprised over half of our student sample.

Our commitment was to qualitative research, and the interviews were semi-structured. While some questions were 'closed', most were 'open', allowing the interviewees to expand at length in their answers. The interview schedule was also sufficiently flexible to allow the interviewer to follow up and probe any interesting or unexpected issues that arose during the interview. No direct questions were asked about gender issues. The interview schedule was already lengthy and, as is usually the case, not everything of interest could be included. We followed the priorities identified in the proposal in constructing the schedule. Our expectation was that if gender issues were important, they would 'emerge'. There were plenty of questions about relationships with the supervisor and supervisor style, use of departmental facilities, encouragement and sponsorship, integration into social networks. Any of these topics might have produced observations about differential treatment for women and men, or about problems women students experienced with male supervisors, or any of a number of possibilities.

Only a few supervisors made statements about women students as opposed to men; far more discussed overseas students as a special (problematic) category. The women supervisors sometimes made reference to their experience *as women*, but not at length. In one case, the interviewer's attempt to question the supervisor (after the formal interview) about her experiences as a woman in a male-dominated academic world met with a rebuff, the gist of which was that she was no different than any other academic in her field.

At first glance, the students seemed no more aware of gender than the academics were. There were exceptions. One woman interviewed made repeated references to gender. She stated that she had chosen her specialty within psychology for various reasons, including: 'It was a very male-dominated thing and, almost for political reasons, I thought, you know, I want to be in on this as a woman and see what's happening'.

Her career had been influenced by moves with her partner and the birth of her children and she was critical of the maternity leave policy of the research council that funded her study:

> My grant was put in abeyance, like I could have been going off to jolly round the world or something, so I had basically a six-month period, then a nine-month period of abeyance when I wasn't paid anything . . . in terms of completion rates I got a letter that implied that these two periods of abeyance actually counted towards . . . the amount of time I have taken to do my PhD so far.

She also noted the difficulty of participating in departmental activities:

> Seminars, I think, yes I did occasionally go to a few. One point I'd like to make about the seminars was that they were all set at a very anti-social time for people who have got children. So quite often I couldn't, on a regular basis I couldn't make them because it was just too difficult.

Her pregnancies may have influenced her relationship with her supervisor in the early stages of the research:

> I mean men always find pregnant women very difficult I think. I think he was just, I mean he was very sort of caring and concerned but he just didn't really, we weren't as connected, I suppose, as people.

This student's responses were what might have been expected from a reading of the literature on women students in higher education. The influence of gender has been studied to a small extent in Britain, notably by Taylorson (1984), who depicted the marginality experienced by many women graduate students. Early works in North America also stressed the problems women faced in graduate school, including relationships with male faculty who felt more comfortable with and tended to sponsor male rather than female students (Adler 1976). Although there is still some concern with mentoring (Grant *et al.* 1993), much recent work (Vartuli 1982; Filteau 1989; Pearson *et al.* 1989) downplays such questions and asks instead how higher education might be altered to introduce communal and caring rather than competitive and individualistic styles of learning and working. Presumably, supervisory relationships might also change in the same direction.

However, what was remarkable about the student quoted above was her singularity. She was one of only a few students to express any awareness of gender issues and to give it such centrality. Gender issues were not emerging in the field, at least not in any obvious manner. It would take a feat of analysis to find them, it seemed.

The final report for this project was submitted to the funding body in March 1992. Time constraints, especially after the research officer was no longer paid by the project, limited what aspects of the data received extended analysis. The main focus has been on elucidating the nature of the supervisory process. Our final report noted our intention to consider gender issues at a later date.

Looking for gender

That later date arrived in the autumn of 1992, when I was in a new job in Canada and was able to secure the help of two graduate students who were interested in working with me to investigate gender issues in the data (Si Transken and Kelly McDowell). These two students were 'graduate assistants', that is, full-time students paid for part-time work on projects for faculty members, a common scheme in North American social science departments but not British ones.

We struggled with the odd problem of how to analyse something apparently 'not there'. We decided to concentrate on the student transcripts first, and divided up the data so that each of us had responsibility for two departments, one in each discipline. Then we began a process of reading interviews with male and female students, initially looking in a very general way for any differences between the sexes.

What stood out were categories of family relationships, sense of mission and self-confidence. Interviews with women, especially those over age 25 or so, contained many references to their partners and children, despite no direct questions being asked about families. For example, when reviewing their past higher education careers, women often integrated into their accounts references to when their children were born, or when they were pregnant, or when they moved because of a partner's job. Men did this very rarely, more often making oblique references to having roots in the local community, or sometimes noting problems of finding time for family when their dissertation work was pressing.

'Sense of mission' referred to the reasons students gave for pursuing their research. Not all wanted to be academics. Some with a deep sense of purpose wanted to discover something of burning interest to themselves, or do work that would be of use to the school system, special needs children, or some other cause. 'Mission' students are more often female and more likely to be in education than psychology.

The most arresting theme was what we were calling 'self-confidence'. Gradually it seemed that a more encompassing term might be necessary, as we were detecting differences in how students understood their whole experience and their place (relative to a supervisor) in it. At an extreme, we read some transcripts where students appeared to feel they were strangers in the academy, barely entitled to supervisor time and constantly aware of their own shortcomings. All three quotations below come from 'mature' (late forties and up) women students in education departments:

> For the first degree, of course, I used the main one [university library] although I was frightened of that and I used the central [city] library for the first year because I didn't understand the university library system and I was too ashamed to ask. But once I got my mind around that I used that a lot . . . I still don't quite understand the microfiche system, although it's been explained to me at least three times, but they're terribly kind . . .

> But I think, I think I still would like that PhD but at times I feel competent and feel 'oh yes, yes, I'll go ahead' and other times I think 'oh I'll never do that, I don't know why I'm worrying about it and why don't I throw the whole thing over and what do I want it for' because I'm not going to get any sort of career advancement or whatever out of it, at my time of life I'm not really concerned, so I ask myself 'what do I want it for?' I think in a way it's just to prove something to myself, and this is how I've done all my studies, because not having had what I call the foundations of education, which is the grammar school education, I feel very, almost as if I'm proving . . . you can still get where you want to get, even if you haven't made the grade at school, as it were.

> . . . and I find [supervisor] a bit intimidating, I don't know whether it's just that he's, you know, his stature. And I think also having been at home for 12 years, I mean I'm just frightened of everybody because they've been using their brains for all that time and I haven't and I think I've always felt intellectually intimidated by others actually. But it sounds ever so wet and feeble, doesn't it, you know, sort of with feminist leanings and everything you should be more assertive but I'm not.

More often, women seemed to distance themselves from their achievements, for example coupling a discussion of a successful paper given at a conference with a monologue about how frightened they had been or how they had never done anything like it before. This woman student in psychology seems to be getting on very successfully with her doctoral research, but here she speaks about her fears:

> And I'm giving a paper on it at a conference here . . . I mean it fills me with dread. I hate, I've never given a paper at a big conference . . . I've talked about this research to the [research group in the department] but I've never given a paper at a conference. I just feel very nervous about it.

Or in making reference to a setback, they might indicate its justice: 'then I tried to get into ------ University and quite wisely they said no'.

Certainly, women can be confident students and we also have transcripts that demonstrate this fact. For example, this young woman in a psychology department, who has written four papers and a book chapter together with her supervisor, derives an advantage from her background:

> I think I made the right decision in terms of doing a PhD. I can't remember a time when I didn't really expect to do it, partly because I come from an academic family . . . So I came in perhaps a bit more knowledgeable about the whole set up. Obviously there are times when it's going badly and you get fed up and you haven't got any money. As I said, I can't think of anything else I'd rather be doing and as I said it's not too much of a struggle to get myself into the department most days.

Conversely, we have some interviews with men that register their uncertainty. This education student is finding it difficult to finish his MPhil after his full-time registration has ended and he is back in a teaching job. He also believes he doesn't write in the appropriate manner:

> And if I'd have read somebody else's MPhil paper that had been written like that I wouldn't have been very happy with it. And at other times I felt unhappy because I knew, no matter how hard I'd tried, I hadn't been able to do it the way that I, and I knew it was going to be wrong, and I knew he'd criticize it.

Another male education student also identified shortcomings in his preparation but was better at problem-solving:

> And I wasn't sure actually, at that point, how it would be analysed. I knew what I wanted but one of my main problems is that I'm not mathematically inclined and don't really know about stats. So it was when I came back again to [where he works] I was able to find out there who were the stats people and who would have a knowledge of how to handle the data, and a couple of colleagues were particularly helpful. And we again just explored it together and I also went to the university, to the computing department there to find out . . .

The transcripts which show few doubts and high self-confidence are often those of young men. This young male psychology student refers to the same conference mentioned in the extract from the woman who described her fears about giving a paper:

Well obviously this is the first year of the hopefully three year PhD that I'm doing, so it's getting to the stage now where I'm just pulling together certain experimentation that I've done. I've got a couple of, well I'm giving a departmental seminar in a fortnight, and then, hopefully, it will get rehashed into a conference paper, which is to be given at this year's international conference on [topic], then hopefully that gets rehashed again a few times over the summer to get ready for submission for publication. That's the grand plan anyway.

The researcher comments on what sounds like excellent progress for six months' registration and he replies: 'Well my ambition is to hopefully get out roughly somewhere in the region of one paper per year and to write my thesis more or less as I go along in the summer of each year . . .'.

Having realized we had something of interest here, we moved to concentrate on this topic, named for the time being 'confidence'. Si Transken developed a provisional coding scheme, with examples, which contained sub-categories of confidence issues. We are now at the point where we can begin to analyse 'confidence' in more depth. We believe we have found a dimension (whatever we end up calling it) that may tend to differ for men and women, although not inevitably so. We can make comparisons according to age, part-time/full-time status, discipline, department. What we also need is an explanatory framework for the dimension.

Feminist frameworks

It is at this point that our 'feminist framework' becomes especially relevant. In Chapter 2, I described a review of articles on education in the three main British sociology journals. At that time, gender was almost never an intentional focus in this body of research. However, some articles did report 'sex differences'. It was notable that in such cases the analysis very rarely proceeded any further, as if there were an unstated agreement that there could be no other variables that might explain the 'sex difference'. Presumably, the biological bedrock had been reached and there was no reason to explore differential experiences that might have accounted for the differences found.

Now, thanks to several decades of feminist scholarship, we are less likely to see things this way. If men and women students adopt different presentations of self in these interviews, we are obliged to speculate or investigate *why*. We are not just including women in our sample, nor simply adding gender to our analysis. We are drawing upon our immersion in feminist thinking to give us the perspective we need and a set of possible explanations for our findings.

At this point, several possibilities can be noted. First, there are methodological considerations. For example, women students may have felt more comfortable speaking to a woman interviewer and found it easier to speak about personal matters. Second, there are a range of ideas drawn from feminist psychology. There are arguments that women (through their socialization) develop difficulties with self-esteem, blame themselves rather than outside events for their failures, are dogged by a persistent sense that they are imposters in settings filled with (other) bright, confident people, and associate achievement with danger and isolation (Sandford and Donovan 1985; Clance and O'Toole 1988; Stiver 1991). These arguments have been criticized for implying that outcomes for women are mainly consequences of their personalities and attitudes.

Third, also drawing on feminist psychology, are the perspectives from a standpoint sometimes labelled 'relational feminism', emphasizing women's focus on connected and caring relationships (Gilligan 1982; Belenky *et al.* 1986; Miller 1991). Such approaches tend to value and celebrate the ways women prefer to go about learning or arriving at moral judgements. These approaches have been criticized for essentialism and for paying insufficient attention to the social context that may have produced such preferences through women's experiences as subordinates (Hare-Mustin and Marecek 1990). Advocates of relational feminism have criticized the alienation offered by higher education due to its insistence on individualized and competitive achievement and hierarchical structures. Certain notions of feminist pedagogy take their lead from such arguments, aiming to construct courses that de-emphasize hierarchy and power, feature sharing and collaboration, and recognize experience as a base for knowledge (for critiques, see Kenway and Modra 1992; Manicom 1992). Perhaps some of the women interviewed for our study sense this disparity between their preferences and the structures they encounter. Even without subscribing to relational feminism, we can question why the university is structured to reward only certain virtues (those traditionally associated with what Thomas, 1990, calls 'middle-class masculinity') and what wider implications this situation may have.

Fourth, we can draw on the concept of discourses elaborated in poststructuralist writing. Here we could argue that men and women work within socially acceptable discourses, frameworks for viewing life and organizing language (Wetherell 1986; Gilbert and Taylor, 1991). The tales of self-doubts and panic before a performance are women's tales, recognized in the culture. Men have to be (or sound) more heroic.

Most of these writers emphasize that discourses are shifting and contradictory; for example, Walkerdine (1981) gives an example of how a woman teacher can be powerful as a teacher but disempowered as a woman. Our students show such contradictions, especially when those who are accomplished and confident in their other lives, for example as a teacher, or even as a research assistant on a project, find themselves uncertain and anxious when cast in the student role. The quotations given earlier also demonstrate that gender does not stand alone but mixes with other characteristics such as age or social-class background. The male supervisor and female student pairing is the expected one for the culture, reinforcing everyday differences in power based on gender. We also have examples of male supervisors and male students developing friendships based on shared leisure interests. There are fewer models available for female supervisors and students of either sex.

I am not yet in a position to choose among alternative interpretations. My point is different. Without a feminist perspective, I would be unlikely to have initiated this hunt for gender. Had I done so anyway, I would have brought certain sociological understandings to the analysis. For example, the asymmetry in power between male supervisors and female students would be expected to produce subordinate-like reactions from the students. Students who add to their accounts details of failures, panics and so forth may be showing role distance, using Goffman's (1961) concept. I am not rejecting these lines of thought, but rather am drawing on an enriched repertoire extended by feminist scholarship. It is in that sense I might make the claim that I am doing *feminist research*.

Conclusion

This chapter has told the story of a particular piece of research and the conditions that influenced its development. Given the numerous constraints on the free expression of feminist thinking, there is a good argument for the guardians of feminist research to be more charitable about what can be admitted through its gates. As feminist scholarship becomes increasingly institutionalized, there is a tendency for it to develop its own rituals and practices of exclusion. This tendency cannot be avoided simply by reference to sisterhood or women's caring proclivities. However, its more deleterious consequences can be recognized or at least discussed. For example, Stanley and Wise (1990) put forward the concept of 'generous reading', where a work is judged in its own terms. It contrasts with the conventional practice of setting up another's argument as grievously wrong in order to contrast the rightness of one's own position. My particular concern is that if research is shaped by the constraints and conditions of a particular academic setting, or indeed the laws and traditions of a particular nation, it may not meet the usual criteria of feminist research for that reason. Yet if the researcher brings a feminist framework to the analysis and the written or spoken product, this, too, could be feminist research. What I resist is the notion that a checklist of criteria must be built into the fabric of the research itself.

The research project on graduate students is a case in point. The project would meet few of the criteria listed earlier as typical features of feminist research. It was originally designed by a woman but carried out by a team of two women and one man. No critique of injustice to women or of a discipline's approach to women was incorporated into the research proposal; no centrality was given to gender divisions or women's experience. An intent to improve conditions for women was only present in the sense that we hoped to contribute to better supervisory practice for students and supervisors (of both sexes).

Nevertheless, the new phase of the analysis described above seems to me to be 'legitimate' feminist research. It is being conducted by women with some exposure to feminist ideas. I do not think that the sex of the investigators in this phase is as important as the exposure to ideas. What we are doing is building on the work of the earlier research team; we have data that reflect the assumptions, priorities and skills of the designers and implementers. We bring to these data frameworks influenced by our study of feminist scholarship, as I showed earlier in this chapter. I see no reason not to regard this effort as feminist research.

My account of the project on supervision is also intended to illustrate the way in which research is a social construction. I have described how the conceptions of the project followed the guidelines, which did not feature gender, and were developed at a time when I had begun to believe that the focus of my research would forever marginalize me in the reward structure of my institution.

In contrast, my current position was advertised for a sociologist who worked on gender issues in education. Although the overall representation of women among academics in Canada is similar to that in Britain (see Chapter 9), at my university, women are relatively well represented among faculty (about a third) and very strongly represented among students (around 70 per cent). A high proportion of students applying to my department want to pursue feminist studies, and there are a number of faculty offering such courses. I had little difficulty finding graduate assistants who were interested in the project and could draw on their own feminist and sociological background to improve the analysis of the data. The key point is that here I was hired as an associate professor and promoted to full professor two years later *because* of my record as a scholar of gender and education. In this environment, I no longer needed to weigh up so carefully the advantages and disadvantages of doing overt gender research.

The gendering of academic practice is a difficult terrain for women academics to write about, not only because of the danger of being thought to be 'obsessed' or showing pique or disappointment. To write about gender and academic life, they also need to see both the forest and the trees, the patriarchal structures and the everyday forms of maintenance and control. In an interesting ethnographic account of working as a waitress in a Chinese restaurant, Kay (1990) comments that it was much easier to classify phenomena related to ethnicity (e.g. insults) than to gender. Customers might be making sexist or sexual comments – or simply engaging in pleasantries. It was hard to tell. Because gender-influenced interaction is so routine, it is also ambiguous. It is just as difficult for a feminist academic to know to what extent the reception accorded to her work or the response to her teaching is related to her politics, her gender, or some other feature of her background, demeanour or ability, or whether it resides in the politics and practices of the institution, or even the culture and political economy of the society (Acker 1986; Gelb 1989; Arnot 1993).

There is a debate within ethnographic circles regarding the ethics of covert research, research done in situations where the individuals or community being studied are unaware of the researcher's purposes. What seems unethical – deception – is sometimes justified as contributing to a greater purpose, the ability to discover something important that otherwise could not be uncovered. I am not arguing that we should deceive our participants, and I recognize that there may be ethical questions attached to a decision to use research results for a purpose not originally proclaimed. On the other hand, a different slant in the analytical framework does not seem particularly deceptive. We need some way to make feminist research possible in more settings, and not insisting on rigid conformity to a feminist guideline, especially in the early stages of the research, might move us in that direction. Research that is not labelled feminist research can be done by feminists in situations where otherwise it could not be done at all.

Notes

1. Thanks to Edith Black, Kari Dehli, Roxana Ng, Si Transken and Kathleen Weiler for comments on the draft of this chapter.
2. I understand that there have been some improvements in the procedure in recent years, although it is still a competition for a restricted number of positions. Promotion procedures vary among universities.
3. My early publications from this research concerned the role of the head teacher (Acker, 1990b) and the response of the teachers to educational reform (Acker 1990c). Gradually, I became more and more intrigued with the effect of gender on women teachers' careers and the question of whether feminist ideas about women's culture or women's ways of working could be used to understand the close, collegial culture of this group of mostly women. Eventually, I made use of a feminist framework in this research, as well as for the project to be described in this chapter (Acker 1993; see also Chapter 7, this volume).
4. The support of the Economic and Social Research Council for this project is gratefully acknowledged. The work described was part of the Research into Training Programme supported by the Postgraduate Training Board, award number T007 40 100. The views expressed here are my own and do not necessarily reflect those of the ESRC. I would also like to thank the project co-director, Tim Hill, the research associate, Edith Black, and the graduate assistants who have worked with me on subsequent analyses of the data, Kate McKenna, Kelly McDowell and Si Transken.
5. It may help North American readers of this chapter to know that in Britain, graduate students who obtain their higher degree through a dissertation alone (the case for all doctoral students, and many master's students) are called 'research students'. Our study was concerned with students of this type. Students usually worked on their dissertations with one member of staff, deemed the supervisor, rather than with a thesis committee. For more detail, see Hill *et al.* (1994) and Acker *et al.* (1993).

PART 2

Women and Teaching

5 Women and Teaching: A Semi-detached Sociology of a Semi-profession

. . . no country should pride itself on its educational system if the teaching profession has become predominantly a world of women.

(Langeveld 1963: 404)

. . . there can be little doubt that in the past much of the sense of a second-rate profession attached to teaching has been the fact that it was predominantly female in membership.

(Morrish 1978: 234)

Is the teaching profession a 'world of women'? In 1990, 63 per cent of the 401,000 full-time teachers in maintained schools in England and Wales were women (School Teachers' Review Body 1993: 64). This figure conceals considerable variation by level: women constituted 81 per cent of primary school teachers, but only 48 per cent of secondary school teachers.[1]

Is school teaching female-dominated? While nearly all teachers and head teachers of nursery and infant schools are female, women become increasingly scarce as we move up the age range. In combined infant and junior schools, women constitute 78 per cent of teachers, but only 36 per cent of head teachers; in separate junior schools, they make up 70 per cent of teachers, but only 25 per cent of heads.[2] In the secondary sector, women hold 60 per cent of the Main Scale posts without incentive allowances, but only 34 per cent of the deputy headships and 20 per cent of the headships (Department of Education and Science 1992: 36). Interestingly, although only 12 per cent of maintained schools in England are single-sex, nearly one-third of the female secondary heads are in such schools, usually girls' schools, compared with 7.6 per cent of male secondary heads (Department for Education 1993c: 118). Most part-time teachers – 90 per cent of those in primary schools and 79 per cent of those in secondary schools – are female (Department for Education 1993c: 110). A consequence of differential representation in promotion posts is differential salaries. The average salary for men in 1990 was £16,780, for women £14,788. While a fifth of men earned £19,000 or more, the same was true for only 6 per cent of women (Department of Education and Science 1992: 40).[3]

If we consider the modal location of men and women teachers, we observe that men and women typically teach different subjects to different groups of children, hold responsibilities for different functions within schools, and generally have different chances for rewards within the system. Women are more likely to teach younger children, men older ones; women to teach girls, men boys; women to teach domestic subjects and humanities, men technological subjects and physical sciences; women to have pastoral responsibilities, men administrative and curricular ones. As Strober and Tyack (1980) put it, women teach and men manage. The divisions are not of caste-like rigidity, but the probabilities that the sexes will experience differential career lines and typical locations in school are striking enough to allow us to speak confidently of a sexual division of labour in teaching.

What have sociologists to tell us about this sexual division of labour in teaching? Such divisions appear to have been so taken for granted that the majority of books and articles on schools and teaching make hardly any reference to them, and many a school ethnographer has missed entirely the chance to tell us about the impact of gender on relationships among teachers, or between teachers and head teachers, or between teachers and pupils. When writers do consider women teachers, they frequently resort to commonsense and unsubstantiated assumptions about their deficiencies. Earlier works sketch a stereotype of the spinster teacher (Waller 1932/1965), later largely replaced by an image of a married women who shows a half-hearted interest in teaching while getting on with her 'family responsibilities' (National Union of Teachers 1980). This image is so powerful that it seems to have prevented sociologists of education asking a range of other questions about the nature of the sexual division of labour in teaching. Why are women in a subordinate position in the education system? Can we say anything about gender relations and power relations in schools? What do we learn if we try to make these divisions problematic, instead of part of the natural order?

This chapter gives an account of a journey through some of the sociological literature on teachers that I took in an attempt to answer the question of why a sexual division of labour occurs within teaching and appears to place women in a disadvantaged position. I concentrate on British and American studies of school teaching as a profession and as a career. Limitations of space mean leaving out interesting material on the role of the teacher, on teacher–pupil interaction and on teacher unionism, as well as confining attention to the primary and secondary phases. I examine not only the shortcomings of individual studies but also the deeper deficiencies of this literature, including the commonsense assumptions about women that (mis)inform much of it. The studies chosen for detailed review are frequently cited ones that should provide evidence for main themes that run through the literature. These studies all have in their favour the recognition of gender as in some way important; there are others, not reviewed here, that make no reference, or only very minimal reference, to gender. In the conclusion, I briefly consider some theoretical approaches to the analysis of sexual divisions and what promise they hold for improving the sociology of teaching.

Sociological work on women and teaching

Women teachers are most often specifically mentioned in discussions of commitment, careers and claims of the occupation to professional status. What seems to run through such discussions is a conception of women teachers as damaging, deficient, distracted and sometimes even dim. As the emphasis seems to change somewhat over the years, the literature can be considered in two parts, with the dividing line around 1970.

Semi-professions and sexist stereotypes

In the 1950s and 1960s, a number of commentators expressed concern over the disastrous consequences they supposed must follow from the predominance of women in teaching. Most educational psychologists, Lieberman reported in 1956, believe that young boys who lack suitable masculine role models among their teachers will not only become reading failures or behaviour problems, but might end up in the nearest pool hall in search of a gang leader to emulate (p. 245). For the profession itself, discontinuities in women's employment are 'devastating' (p. 249). Unlike many subsequent writers, Lieberman does discuss discrimination against women teachers. By noting that the existence of a huge reserve supply of female labour allows school boards to resist teacher demands for better pay and conditions (p. 253), he manages to go beyond the charge that women themselves are to blame for low status and salaries in teaching.

By the late 1960s, the subtleties of that distinction appeared largely lost, as is apparent in *The Semi-professions and Their Organization*, edited by Amitai Etzioni (1969). Semi-professions are school teaching, social work, nursing and librarianship. All are highly 'feminized'. The chapter in the collection that best represents the blame-the-woman approach is 'Women and bureaucracy in the semi-professions' by Richard Simpson and Ida Simpson. It is certainly a caricature and might almost be a parody. Simpson and Simpson see bureaucratic control (i.e. strong emphasis on hierarchical authority and rules and low worker autonomy) as a *consequence* of the presence of women:

> A woman's primary attachment is to the family role; women are therefore less intrinsically committed to work than men and less likely to maintain a high level of specialized knowledge. Because their work motives are more utilitarian and less intrinsically task-oriented than those of men, they may require more control. Women's stronger competing attachments to their family roles and . . . to their clients make them less likely than men to develop colleague reference group orientations. For these reasons, and because they often share the general cultural norm that women should defer to men, women are more willing than men to accept the bureaucratic

controls imposed upon them in semi-professional organizations, and less likely to seek a genuinely professional status.

(Simpson and Simpson 1969: 199–200)

Several pages follow on the harm women do to the professional hopes of these occupations. Psychological inventories of college students and workers show that women attracted to the semi-professions possess such damning characteristics as altruistic motivations, desires for pleasant social relationships with colleagues, and preferences to work with people rather than things. It is only by twisting the meaning of some of the research findings, and adding unsupported statements, that Simpson and Simpson come to their conclusions. For example, altruistic motivations towards work are dismissed by the argument that since women can satisfy their desire for service through family life without outside work, even strong humanitarian motives are insufficient to create vocational commitments. Statements like 'women seem less able than men to disagree impersonally, without emotional involvement' (p. 241) are thrown in without evidence. Women are accused of a lack of drive towards intellectual mastery on the basis of Coleman's (1961) research on adolescents, which found girls' marks in school concentrated in the 'B' category. Simpson and Simpson (1969: 219) also discuss career discontinuities and commitments: 'A woman's family situation makes it improbable that she will develop a strong professional commitment, or in the unlikely event that she had one to begin with, that she will be able to maintain it'.

In 1970, Timothy Leggatt imported some of these ideas into Britain. In his contribution to *Professions and Professionalization* (Jackson 1970), Leggatt dwells on the negative consequences for teaching of its high proportion of women, echoing many of the Simpsons' sentiments. He argues that the bureaucratic nature of the work context is compatible with women's traditional characteristics, which include submissiveness, acceptance of authority and lack of ambition. Women are unconcerned with collegial affiliations, he says, because their family activities are less compatible than men's with extra-familial group loyalties. High rates of 'turnover', plus the large size of the occupation, result in a loosely structured uncohesive occupation, reinforced by the 'tenuous loyalty of women members' (p. 165). Leggatt (1970) writes as if all women teachers are married (although he states only half are), and he gives very little evidence for most of his statements about women.

Teacher careers and double standards

From the mid-1970s, the accusatory tone in the works reviewed above lightens. Studies of this period are less preoccupied with 'profession' and more with 'career'. Many are explicitly or implicitly in the symbolic interactionist tradition, within which the study of 'work and occupations' is usually traced back to Everett Hughes and Chicago sociology.

Lortie was a student of Hughes and the influence is apparent in his major book on the sociology of teaching, *Schoolteacher*, published in 1975. He draws on survey and interview data, mostly from the 1960s, but goes considerably beyond simple reporting of figures to a sensitive analysis of teacher sentiments, meanings, rewards and interpretations. Lortie shows an awareness of sexual divisions in teaching at a number of points in his book, especially when he examines the interacting influences of sex, age and marital status on teacher satisfaction and involvement. Few women teachers, he reports, become heavily involved in teaching during their twenties, as they are 'hedging their bets' to cover contingencies related to a husband, to children or to a husband's job changes. Older married women teachers are split between home and work commitments but are 'serious about their work'; older single women are deeply invested in their work but not as satisfied as the married women, perhaps because they are more isolated from the adult world. Among men, secondary school teachers under age 40 who hope for promotion show very high involvement. My favourite finding is that the small number of male primary teachers in the sample had low commitment and low interest in their work. Nevertheless, they all hoped to be principals within 5 years (p. 95). Lortie does not discuss the influence of marital status on men. Unlike some of the other writers, he avoids the temptation to make simple equations between women and doomed professionalism, but he does observe that careers in teaching work out well for those with 'less than full commitment', from which they paradoxically gain a degree of autonomy (pp. 99–100).

In British studies of the 1970s, we also see a move away from sexism and towards a concern with a concept of career (see Chapter 7). In *The Socialization of Teachers*, Lacey (1977) starts promisingly by pointing to sex-differentiated opportunities in teaching. The career structure, he writes, favours men, and they dominate the higher posts. However, the remainder of the book, which explores ways in which teachers in training are socialized into orientations to teaching, fails even to question whether the process works differently for women and men.

The relative promotion chances of men and women vary by type of school, we learn from Hilsum and Start's (1974) *Promotion and Careers in Teaching*. Mostly their rather atheoretical report tells us that men do a lot better: they are promoted faster and further. Hilsum and Start are in little doubt that the reasons for the imbalances lie in women's lower aspirations. In answers to questions about aspirations, men consistently wanted headships more than women did: 54 versus 16 per cent for primary, 17 versus 4 per cent for secondary. The great majority of applications for vacant headships in 1972 came from men. Although 17 per cent of women primary teachers and 20 per cent of women secondary teachers believed 'being a man' aided promotion, the authors are not convinced. Despite lacking direct evidence, they blame sex differences in motivation, basing their conclusions on 'our general discussions with teachers, headteachers and LEAs and our own general acquaintance with the education scene' (p. 72).

Lyons interviewed 122 teachers in five comprehensive schools (Lyons 1980; Lyons and McCleary 1980). His theoretical framework is a symbolic interactionist one, and he is particularly concerned to develop the concept of 'career maps'. Lyons (1980) notes that more senior positions go to males, adding that females do not apply. He is one of the very few writers to note that promotions for women are concentrated in stereotypically female subject areas, and he also remarks that many young women interviewed expressed dissatisfaction with the career structure offered to them. Lyons looks at those woman teachers who have moved geographically following husbands and comments on how much effort it took them to obtain new jobs and how damaging to their promotion prospects these moves had been.

Lyons is more sensitive to problems arising from gender relations than many, but his book still reflects the obsession with the *married* woman teacher characteristic of such writing. The result is that women are discussed almost entirely in relation to their family roles. They are left out entirely in the main chapter on strategies, 'good' career maps, how to get to the top, sponsorship. The strategies of males in top positions are discussed there; women in senior positions are discussed separately in a context full of speculation about marriage and husbands. So again we have a double standard: we learn nothing about men's family commitments and we learn nothing about school-based barriers or supports to women's careers.

Underlying assumptions

Let us now go beyond charting the idiosyncratic inadequacies of representative studies and instead examine their underlying assumptions. I suggest that most conventional sociological writing on the influence of gender on teacher careers and on teaching as a profession suffers from the following shortcomings:

1. A 'deficit model' of women that leads to a blame-the-victim approach as well as conceptual confusion.
2. What appears to be a low regard for the intellectual capacities of teachers, perhaps especially women teachers.
3. A persistent tendency to see women exclusively in family role terms.
4. A poor sense of history coupled with an inability to anticipate social change.
5. An oversimplified view of causality.
6. A pervasive ideology of individual choice, deeply embedded in American writing about women's work and often uncritically applied in British literature.

Deficit models and conceptual confusions

Chapter 8 explores the idea of a 'deficit model' of women, analogous to the much-criticized deficit model of the working-class child in some educational literature. Components include a tendency to 'blame the victim' (and thus distract attention from structural obstacles) and to take male experience as the norm to which women are then (unfavourably) compared. These tendencies are apparent in the literature on teachers. Women teachers are frequently blamed for the low status of the profession and for their own low status within it. The male-as-norm assumption is also evident. As there are so many women in teaching, it seems this norm can only be sustained either by taking 'the norm' to be the established professions (to which teaching is then unfavourably compared) or senior posts in teaching (ambition for which is often called 'commitment'). Writers get tangled up trying to equate 'commitment' with what men do. 'Lack of commitment' turns out to mean interruptions for childrearing; 'commitment' to mean furthering one's own career, especially by moving out of classroom teaching. A study by Nias (1981a) suggests writers have only been investigating a narrow set of meanings for 'commitment'. To the primary teachers (of both sexes) interviewed, commitment usually meant a vocation for caring, or a concern with competence (doing the job well, working hard). Only 3 of nearly 100 teachers used commitment as career-continuance. This did not mean the teachers did not want 'careers': many did. Also, the National Union of Teachers' (1980) survey of women teachers reports that most respondents (82 per cent), married or otherwise, see themselves as 'consciously pursuing a career'; 77 per cent intended teaching until retirement.[4]

There are problems with other concepts that frequently appear in the literature. Most writers say teachers are 'isolated', but with little empirical evidence and various meanings (from one another? from the outside world?). Does this 'isolation' really prohibit collegiality or solidarity?[5] In a study of a primary school, McPherson (1972) comments on the solidarity teachers have with each other against the principal and parents, only broken by loyalty to the class they teach. The Simpsons (1969) dismissed women semi-professionals' concern with social relationships at work by assuming they talk about dress styles, not professional tasks. King (1978) found infant teachers discussing not only husbands, children and shopping in the staffroom, but also school affairs and incidents from the classroom.

All these concepts (commitment, isolation, collegiality, career-mindedness) need more refinement and differentiation: under what circumstances, in what schools, with what colleagues, with what pupils, teaching what subjects do we find commitment, collegiality, etc.? Simply distinguishing stereotypically between women and men is surely sociologically simplistic.

Not too bright?

Much of the literature on school teachers reflects a lack of respect, if not outright contempt, for their intellectual abilities. Traces of this orientation are evident in the literature reviewed here. Lortie (1975) and Leggatt (1970) both emphasize the lack of technical terminology in teachers' vocabularies. Lortie refers to an analysis of some of his interview tapes that showed teachers mostly used common English words rather than a professional argot. As David Hargreaves (1978) suggests in his critique of Sharp and Green's (1975) study, it may be that the interviewing context itself produces the particular type of response. Leggatt (1970) cites Philip Jackson's (1968) interviews with 50 outstanding primary school teachers (almost all women) as evidence for 'conceptual simplicity'. Jackson (1968: 144) writes that teachers show:

(1) an uncomplicated view of causality; (2) an intuitive, rather than rational approach to classroom events; (3) an opinionated, as opposed to an open-minded, stance when confronted with alternative teaching practices; and (4) a narrowness in the working definitions assigned to abstract terms.

If these are defects, many of the researchers on teachers show rather similar ones in their own work. Jackson (1968) does, in fact, conclude that the 'intuitive' approach is more suitable to the task than a highly rational one would be. He also raises the question of whether this intuition is merely due to women 'exercising their feminine birthright' (p. 146).

Women and marriage

Another defect in this literature is that women teachers are almost inevitably discussed in terms of their marital status. Four associated problems arise. First, the impression given in study after study is that all women teachers are married (ironically, in view of the history of marriage bars). Whenever reasons are advanced for lack of ambition and the like, marriage is always cited as one of these, even when not accompanied by any empirical evidence comparing single and married women.

Second, if all women teachers are married, apparently no men ever are. No published source to my knowledge discusses any conflicts arising from men's marriages. Interestingly, one unpublished study of a local National Union of Teachers Association found the men activists reluctant to participate further at a regional or national level because of their 'family commitments' (Walker 1981). Nor do researchers remark on the assistance men's families might provide towards fulfilling career ambitions. The literature on academic and certain other professional workers (and countless book prefaces) suggests that men are often enabled to immerse themselves fully in their careers because they have a 70-hour-a-week housewife backing them up (see Chapter 8). Is the same true for 'successful' male teachers?

Third, marriage and parenthood are never sufficiently distinguished from one another. Women are said to leave teaching 'on marriage', although they are more likely to leave upon becoming mothers (Ollerenshaw and Flude 1974). Child care may be the problem. Only a few writers mention the provision of child care or nurseries as relevant to teacher commitment or career continuity (Kelsall 1963; Purvis 1973; Ollerenshaw and Flude 1974).

Fourth, and most seriously, it appears that to discuss women teachers means *only* to discuss family–work conflicts. When other aspects of being a teacher are discussed, women, or sex differences generally, are rarely singled out. Lacey (1977) does not tell us anything about sex differences in socialization into teaching; Lyons (1980) does not tell us anything about differential access to sponsorship. Perhaps there was none, but how can we know? What we have here is the notion that beyond personality characteristics, the only remotely sociological factor that affects women teachers' careers is 'marriage'. The consequence is that there is no serious investigation of in-school or other factors that influence women's experiences and outcomes. Richardson's (1973) study of Nailsea School stands almost alone in the research literature in its sensitivity to double binds in which senior female staff find themselves. The way they were treated by male staff affected their ambitions as much as personality and family role characteristics did. Buchan's (1980) and Whitbread's (1980) autobiographical accounts refer to the negative pressures that male colleagues and superiors may bring to bear on women teachers.

Suspension in the present

It is easy, but incorrect, to assume that the sexual division of labour in teaching always has existed, and always will exist, in the form we see today. The relative proportions of men and women, of single women and married women, of female head teachers and male head teachers, have all varied over time in response to government policies, wars, population trends, social attitudes and economic circumstances. For example, the 'payment by results' system of the 1862 Revised Code led to reductions in education spending, teacher training and teacher status, and was followed by an exodus of men from the occupation (David 1980). The expansion of state schooling after 1870 relied on large numbers of untrained women 'supplementary teachers' and further 'feminized' the teacher workforce (David 1980; Purvis 1981). At other times, the balance has shifted towards men, for example after the Second World War, when two-thirds of those trained by the Emergency Training Scheme were men. Tropp (1957) remarks that the profession 'shed its mass of cheap untrained female labour' as the proportion of women in the 'old elementary' sector (primary plus secondary modern) dropped from 75 per cent in 1900 to 65 per cent in 1954.

Whether married women were allowed to teach also depended on demand and circumstance. In the first part of the twentieth century, many authorities operated bars against married women teachers, although they were not required by any government edict. Exceptions were made, for example, in remote rural areas, or sometimes when 'hardship' might result from dismissal upon marriage (Partington 1976). London ended its marriage bar in 1935 when the Labour Party came to power locally, and finally the 1944 Education Act ended the practice altogether (Partington 1976). During the world wars and in the severe teacher shortages of the 1950s and 1960s, married women were encouraged to teach.

Who heads schools has also been subject to change. The proportion of women head teachers in the primary sector was high in the 1920s but fell rapidly between the wars, with the closure of small village schools, amalgamations of infant with junior schools, fewer single-sex schools for 7- to 11-year-olds, and a campaign by the National Association of Schoolmasters to resist women being put in positions of authority over men teachers (Partington 1976). While women might still head small rural schools and infant schools, large mixed junior schools became the province of men. Similarly, where women have headed secondary schools, they have often been girls' schools, as noted earlier. The move towards co-education in state secondary schools reduced the proportion of head teachers who were women (Byrne 1978; Trown and Needham 1981).

It would be unfair to expect the studies of teaching as a profession and as a career to predict the future. But it is not unreasonable to expect that some sense of history might prevent them adopting a framework that regards women's status in teaching as *unchanging* and based solely on personal preferences. When studies (e.g. Simpson and Simpson 1969) use figures on women's labour market participation or surveys on college student values to back up their assertions, there is no suggestion these might reflect anything but eternal verities. Writers happily cite results of surveys of teachers done 10 or 20 years earlier without apparently recognizing that social change might have intervened.

Even if women teachers were much less career-oriented than men in the past, one cannot project such findings into an unchanging future. Women's labour market participation and attitudes about their roles have changed dramatically (Fonda and Moss 1976; Farley *et al.* 1977; David 1980). Changes in ideological, demographic and economic conditions, accompanied by shifts in government education policies, alter the context within which women teachers' commitments and career patterns are shaped. An example in the late 1970s would be the way in which a decline in opportunities for part-time teaching and re-entry, plus changes in maternity leave provision, resulted in more women making the 'choice' to take maternity leave and to continue teaching even if their personal preferences might have been otherwise (Trown and Needham 1980; Thurston 1981). It is to be hoped that future studies of career patterns of women teachers will build in a sensitivity to social change that was absent up to the early 1980s.

Causality

An oversimplified view of causality also characterizes much of the literature under review. For example, some writers assume that the predominance of women in teaching is the cause of the low status of the occupation. As Kelsall and Kelsall pointed out (1970: 118), if this is true it is a function of the status accorded to women in a given society, not simply of the presence of women. Another dubious argument is Simpson and Simpson's (1969) charge that women's personality characteristics *require* bureaucratic organizational control. In contrast, Kanter (1977) has argued convincingly that many so-called sex-difference findings about behaviour in organizations can be more satisfactorily explained by the differences in opportunities, numerical representation and access to power that often *coincide* with sex.

Hilsum and Start (1974) doubt that expectations of sex discrimination deter women from applying for head teacher posts. They may be right, but they also fail to note that there are a whole sequence of experiences and events that put someone in a position to apply for such posts. Women may have had less access than men to some of these experiences; they may less often be 'groomed for seniority and responsibility by their mainly male heads' (Byrne 1978: 227). It is too simple merely to assume that lack of ambition plus family responsibilities produce low commitment or lack of interest in promotion among married women teachers. The sequence of events and decisions may be more complex. Nias (1981b) reports that most of the 26 primary school teachers she interviewed who had left work to have children told her that their timing was precipitated by discontent with the particular school and its administration; they had children in order to leave work, so to speak, rather than the reverse. Moreover, the relatively strong numerical representation of women (including married women) in *certain* senior posts (infant school heads and deputies; secondary school 'senior mistresses') suggests modifications need to be made to any generalized thesis about women's reluctance to seek promotion. *Under what circumstances* do women seek promotion? And under what circumstances are women actively sought or encouraged to apply for promotion? Researchers should ask these questions rather than simply repeat commonsense views about women.

Choice and constraint

As should be clear by now, much of the literature under discussion displays what might be called an ideology of individual choice, and a corresponding neglect of constraint at any but a familial level. Aspirations and motivations have crowded out everything else. The roots of this approach may lie in what Bledstein (1976) calls the 'culture of professionalism', which he traces from its nineteenth-century origins and regards as a characteristic world view held by the American middle class. Diversity in standards of living is not seen as the result of class structures, but as the product of 'individual attainment at a fleeting moment in a career' (p. 21). Even the virtual confinement of nineteenth-century married middle-class women to the home was seen as a consequence of individual *choice*; such women merely chose to develop their special gifts and sensitivities in the professionalization of domesticity (p. 118).

Lortie (1975: 50) was perceptive enough to break free from this framework when he observed that choosing a career in teaching because of its compatibility with marriage and motherhood could be seen as a constraint as well as a choice. It is to be hoped that future researchers on women and teaching will clarify the subtle balance between choice and constraint, as they typically endeavour to do within sociology of education generally.

Conclusion

I have tried to make problematic some issues related to the sexual division of labour in teaching and the careers of women teachers. I have reviewed some key sociological studies on teacher careers and the teaching profession and criticized these studies on various grounds, perhaps the most serious of which is their insistence that women's aspirations and family role responsibilities are sufficient explanations for their subordinate position in teaching. In the late 1970s and early 1980s, a handful of textbooks on women and education and a few empirical studies brought sexual divisions in teaching to our attention and began to expand our knowledge of how these operate (e.g. Byrne 1978; Deem 1978; David 1980; Delamont 1980; Spender and Sarah 1980; Trown and Needham 1980; Acker *et al.* 1984). What can we do now, then, to ensure that future research avoids the pitfalls of the past?

If we begin by seeking guidance from the literature – feminist and otherwise – on gender relations, we speedily discover that it is a massive task, perhaps never fully to be accomplished, to review and synthesize the vast literature that attempts to answer the question of how women as a group have come to be subordinate to men as a group. One distinction that I have made (Acker 1984a) is between what we could call *fundamental* and *implementary* theories (using 'theory' loosely to include any attempt to impose an explanatory framework).[6]

Fundamental theories are those that try to explain *why* the different social positions of men and women exist. They seek to uncover a set of basic principles that makes sense of diverse observations comparing the sexes. They fall into two subgroups: the first includes those approaches that use a 'sex-difference' framework and see social arrangements, especially gender relationships, as rooted in and limited by human nature, specifically biology; the second contains theories that postulate some ultimate feature of the social structure as the limiting influence (at least for the immediate future) on human possibilities, especially on the life chances of women. This sub-group includes some of the functionalist theories (maintaining that the stability of society requires a sexual division of labour much like the present one) and those that look to capitalism or patriarchy to explain the oppression of women. Needless to say, theories that come under the heading 'fundamental' are not necessarily mutually compatible.

The other major group of theories, the implementary ones, are sometimes presented as 'why' theories, but I think they are better described as 'how' theories. Rather than seek first causes, they focus on how the subordination of women is perpetuated. Approaches that rely on processes such as socialization, sex discrimination or role conflict for explanations of sex inequality are examples of those we can assign to the implementary category, because they lack the 'fundamental' character of the theories that trace everything back to human nature or social structure. The 'how' theories are important in that they fill in the gaps: how it is that nature's demands or social requisites 'work' in the everyday world. They are more often situation-specific and culture-specific.

Most of the research on women teachers described in this chapter has remained at the implementary level, except when it has made reference to supposedly fundamental 'sex differences' of a bio-psychological sort. Most attempts to conceptualize women's position in teaching have been very limited. Even in their more sociological forms, they rely on an assumption that family responsibilities or marriage–career conflicts will produce attitudes and behaviours (low promotion orientation, willingness to submit to bureaucratic control) that have certain implications for the profession (lack of militancy, low status) and for individual women's careers (intermittent, uncommitted, 'flat'). Such approaches are extremely one-sided, placing the emphasis on the individual woman as 'actor' with little or no attempt to assess the structures within which action takes place. This emphasis is partly a side-effect of typical sociological techniques that are better suited to the analysis of individual attitudes than to capturing the subtleties of the school environment, let alone the impact of the wider society.

There has been considerable interest in recent years in the effects of teacher expectations on pupil behaviour. Why not also ask what effect the expectations of colleagues and head teachers have on the behaviour of (women) teachers? What kind of humour, what traditions, what beliefs about women teachers, married women, and women in general surround the woman teacher daily? In my years teaching experienced teachers on advanced courses, I have heard many stories about incompetent men given major responsibilities within primary schools; women teachers who continue to work after maternity leave believing they are under constant scrutiny from disapproving head teachers to prove no loss of competence; unsuccessful women applicants for senior posts told in confidence that a man was preferred in order to discipline the older children or satisfy village prejudices. I also hear complaints from men teachers about the lack of commitment and interest shown by some of the women in their schools. None of the stories has any but anecdotal weight; but where is the research that will show what gender relations are truly like in schools and how they influence women teachers' 'choices'? Such studies are likely to be on the 'implementary' level: they will not tell us 'why' sexual divisions occur, but they could do an immense service in telling us how they are perpetuated.

What about the fundamental theories, especially those that invoke capitalism or the patriarchal order? How do we draw upon these to understand the sexual division of labour and career chances of women teachers? A major theme to come out of feminist work at this level when applied to education is that the sexual division of labour among teachers contributes to the reproduction of the patriarchal and/or capitalist social order. It does this through providing models to students of male–female power relations and sex-differentiated responsibilities that reinforce the connection of 'femininity' with caring, serving, conforming and mothering (MacDonald 1980a). Some very interesting questions arise.

To take one example, why is it that teaching very young children is regarded as an occupation suitable only for women? Men who wish to teach such children run the risk of being branded 'sexually deviant' (Lee 1973). Once one stops assuming that the answer is rooted solely in natural proclivities such as women's love for children or their motherliness, a series of interesting possibilities emerges. At one level, answers may lie in tradition and the economic advantages to the state of a cheap mass female occupation (Lee 1973). The need for a mass teaching force that could be increased or decreased according to demographic change or political whim may have increased the preference for women teachers who would be 'dispensable'. Lortie (1975) tells us that schools in America were developed on an 'egg crate' model, so that rooms and teachers in them could be added on or taken away without disturbing the functioning of the school. There is also the possibility that once women had carved out this area of influence, they held on to it as one of the few arenas in which they could exert any power, even at the expense of further reinforcing stereotypes about women's sphere.

Another line of reasoning stresses more specifically the part schools play in social and cultural reproduction; some argue that the development of the 'male sex role' may depend on experiencing resistance against a 'feminine' environment in early school as well as at home (Lee 1973). There is no doubt that the image of women teachers as 'substitute mothers' is replete with contradictions.[7] Although the primary school teacher may appear motherly, it is a professional sort of motherliness, accompanied by the necessity to evaluate and assess impartially and to enforce what may be an authoritarian regime within the school (Parsons 1961; King 1978; Grumet 1981). Other contradictions, as David (1980) has shown, are located in the expectations that women teachers transmit a sex-differentiated curriculum to prepare girls for domesticity. In the past, such teachers were single (especially when marriage bars operated) and thus presumably had little direct experience of the life they were advocating; now they may be married, but are themselves choosing to work outside the home in preference to full-time domesticity.

Many interesting questions derive from fundamental theories about women and schooling. But how can we design research that confirms or disconfirms such theories? If we are simply looking for a 'good fit' between the phenomenon and the theory, some of the sociobiological theories seem to 'fit' just as well. Fundamental theories also have the disadvantage of leaving us terribly frustrated in any attempt to change things. It is certainly easier to imagine we can change socialization practices or role relationships in our schools and personal lives than to bring about the demise of capitalism or patriarchy.

While we cannot pursue, let alone resolve, all the methodological and epistemological questions that arise from an attempt to develop and apply fundamental and implementary theories, it should be clear that a *rapprochement* between certain feminist theories and the sociology of teaching could be promising and productive. Fundamental theories might lead us to investigate whether there is a correspondence between the sexual division of labour in teaching and the sexual division of labour in the family and the economy. Implementary approaches could result in empirical studies of schools, considering, for example, gender relationships among teachers, sexual harassment, sponsorship, the relationship of deskilling of teachers' work to gender, and the balance of resistance and accommodation in the lives of women teachers. I imagine there are other exciting possibilities, once we break away from the prison of the prevailing paradigm within which work has proceeded to date. The result should be a considerably enriched understanding of teachers and teaching.

Notes

1. I have updated the statistics found in the original version of this chapter, in order to help the reader to get an up-to-date picture of gender divisions in the teaching profession. Most of the discussion, however, is concerned with work on teachers in the 1960s, 1970s and early 1980s, reflecting the original publication date of 1983. Although there is contemporary feminist work on teachers that goes beyond the limitations described here (e.g. Biklen 1985, in press; Grumet 1988; Weiler 1988; Acker 1991, 1993; Sadker *et al.* 1991), it is still the case in 1994 that many studies of teachers and teaching fail to take gender into account more than superficially.
2. For the benefit of readers outside the UK, infant schools are for children aged 4 or 5 to 7 years, junior schools for children aged 7 – 11 years. In the most common case, infant and junior aged children are educated together in one school. All of these types of schools are considered part of the primary phase and can be referred to as primary schools. In a minority of districts, other breaks in schooling are found, e.g. between first and middle schools. The terms 'head teacher' and 'deputy head teacher' are equivalent to the American 'principal' and 'assistant principal'. UK statistics on teachers generally include administrators together with classroom teachers in the base used for calculations such as the percentage of women teachers, while comparable US statistics are often given for classroom teachers alone.
3. Divisions of class, sex and religion are deeply embedded in the history of teaching, and some writers argue that these divisions have facilitated state control and impeded the development of professionalism (see Parry and Parry 1974). The history of the campaign for equal pay for women teachers with men shows gender divisions were often accompanied by considerable hostility (Gosden 1972). Equal pay was not fully implemented until 1961. More details about gender divisions in teaching can be found in Chapter 7.
4. Various writers have suggested that the vertical model of 'career' needs supplementing or replacing by alternative conceptualizations more appropriate to women's lives (and probably to men's). See, for example, Biklen (1985), Lewin and Olesen (1981) and Chapter 7 in this volume.
5. See Acker (1991) for a more extended treatment of this issue.
6. Chapter 3 makes a different distinction specific to feminist theory. Although socialist-feminist and radical-feminist theories are often fundamental theories, and liberal-feminist ones often implementary theories, exceptions occur; also, non-feminist theories can be classified as fundamental or implementary.
7. I explore this point further in Acker (1993).

6 Teachers, Gender and Resistance

Many studies in the gender and education literature imply that teachers play an important part in the thwarting of girls' potential. This impact can happen in a variety of ways. Sometimes there is direct action, such as treating the sexes differently or holding differential expectations for them. Sometimes the input is more indirect, part of the school's 'gender regime' (Kessler *et al.* 1985) or 'gender code' (MacDonald 1980b), whereby messages about models of masculinity and femininity are contained in everyday school practices such as pupil grouping and timetabling, and in the sexual division of labour among teachers. A more neglected category involves teachers failing to take action where such action (which may include intentionally different treatment of the sexes) might reduce bias or improve opportunities. I shall review literature from all three categories, but the third is the main concern of this chapter. Doing nothing is a form of action itself, with consequences (Bachrach and Baratz 1962). It is not necessarily a conscious decision, and teachers are hardly the sole culprits. But it is important to try to understand why, despite popular perceptions to the contrary, gender issues have made so little headway in schools.

Research on gender and education

Identifying the problem

What is 'the problem' about gender? The debate is not straightforwardly about educational achievement. There is no pattern whereby girls consistently do worse than boys, and in some ways they tend to do better. In the later years of secondary schooling, the pathways through the system begin to diverge. On entry to secondary school, girls are, as Byrne (1978: 116) put it:

> . . . in theory, starting out on the same fast motorway or slower country road to their destination, as their brothers. But whereas we teach boys the intricacy of the Spaghetti junctions of curricular routes . . . we leave our girls on single tracks or at best, dual carriageways, with very few side

turnings, junctions, or crossroads. The traditional arts/science split dies hard.

Girls' apparent avoidance of physical science and technical craft subjects is practically the only gender issue to receive national attention (Acker 1986). There is, however, a wide range of other issues found in the feminist literature such as sexual harassment, career blocks against women teachers, unequal teacher treatment of boys and girls, and the weaving of gender differentiation into the very fabric of school life.

Attempts to account for social class differences in educational achievements have variously blamed the family ('working-class values'), the teachers ('teacher expectations'), the educational policy-makers and the requirements of capitalism. Hypotheses about the relative achievements of girls and boys draw upon similar models. There has also been a parallel change over time in the choice of targets for blame (Yates 1986). Pre-1980s studies of the 'sex-roles' genre, especially in the United States but in Britain too, conceptualized the problems as involving achievement, aspirations or ambition, the sources of which were located either in childhood socialization, leading to aversions to public accomplishment and male-dominated occupations, or in role conflict dilemmas for married women. The inadequacies of this approach (blaming the victim, taking the male life pattern as the norm, and ignoring structural in favour of attitudinal constraints) gradually became apparent, as they did in social class and educability research. Sociological and feminist attention eventually shifted away from the individual and family socialization, towards the school and the educational policy-making process within the parameters of capitalism and patriarchy.

Inequality in the classroom

Apart from historical studies, most of the empirical work on gender and education concentrates on processes within classrooms and schools, especially teacher–pupil interaction. Since the mid-1970s, such research has tended to suggest that boys get more teacher time than girls do. Using a computer technique called meta-analysis to review and combine data from more than 80 studies on the topic (many of them from the United States), Kelly (1986) reported the general trends as follows. Boys got more teacher interaction. Girls on average participated in 44 per cent of classroom interactions, although they were as likely as boys to volunteer to answer teacher questions. Male teachers gave less attention to girls than did female teachers. Girls got less criticism but also less instruction; boys received more academic and more behavioural criticism. Girls' share of instruction was smallest among the oldest age groups and in mathematics, but generally subject differences were minor. Equity training for teachers reduced bias.

Despite the impression of consistency conveyed by this summary, the teacher–pupil interaction studies are not all unanimous in their conclusions. Contradictions remain unresolved. Before the mid-1970s, researchers (e.g.

Sexton 1969) firmly saw boys as the sufferers, noting particularly their greater tendency to have difficulty learning to read. Douglas (1964: 73–4) reported teachers' preferences for girls in no uncertain terms:

> The teachers tend to see the boys as less hard-working, less able to concentrate and less willing to submit to discipline than the girls. These judgements are made mostly by women, and might have been different if they had been made by men . . . These differences in the way in which the teachers see the boys and girls . . . suggest a lack of sympathy and understanding of the boys.

But by 1982, Spender could assert confidently (and less rhetorical researchers would agree with her):

> In many classrooms, as teachers persistently spend more time with the boys, accord more value to male experience, treat the boys more as named individuals and identities, the pattern of making females marginal is relentlessly reinforced. (p. 69)

It may well be that the introduction of feminist perspectives has transformed researchers' abilities to see what 'really' happens to girls in classrooms. There may also be a concomitant historical change, for example towards less formal, less ritualized schooling (King 1982), which may have had unintended effects on sex-differentiated experiences.

A recent trend in classroom interaction studies is to ask under what conditions teacher behaviour of the sort described is produced. To what extent are teacher characteristics or ideologies responsible (a point to which I return later)? The role of prior understandings and strategies pupils bring with them into the classroom is increasingly stressed (Measor 1983; French and French 1984; Kelly 1985), as is the impact of the subject being studied and the type of instructional activity, for example formal versus practical sessions (Randall 1987). Others suggest that to consider gender without reference to class or race produces an incomplete picture: 'gender variables may operate quite differently in the multiracial classroom from an all-white classroom' (Wright 1987: 184).[1]

Gender regimes

A second popular approach to understanding gender differentiation involves scrutinizing the school as a whole for the dominant motifs and models of masculinity and femininity that pervade it. Kessler *et al.* (1985: 42) use 'gender regime' to describe 'the pattern of practices that constructs various kinds of masculinity and femininity among staff and students, orders them in terms of prestige and power, and constructs a sexual division of labor within the institution'. Arnot's 'gender code' (MacDonald 1980b; Arnot 1982) is similar. Codes have 'varying degrees of boundary strength and insulation between categories of masculine and feminine' (Arnot 1982: 84). Students are actively involved in inferring the underlying rules, learning to 'recognise and make sense of a wide range and variety of contradictory and miscellaneous inputs' (ibid.)

Although relatively little empirical research has made explicit use of these guiding concepts, many studies could fit fairly easily under the rubric. They demonstrate that gender is a major organizing principle, applied to uniforms, curricular subjects, administrative practices, classroom activities and even the use of space within and around the school. Even single-sex schools highlight gender classification by their very existence (MacDonald 1980b: 23). What is the most striking is the unselfconscious way in which mixed schools have used sex as a convenient administrative divider to organize registers, seat allocation, queuing, even coat-hanging and story-telling (Shaw 1976; King 1978; Delamont, 1980). The secondary school option choice system (Ball 1981; Grafton *et al.* 1987), the stereotypes in textbooks, stories and examination materials (Buswell 1981; Spender 1982), and the division of labour among the teaching staff (Marland 1983; see also Chapter 5, this volume) have all been singled out as providing a lightly hidden curriculum of gender differentiation.

Analysis of gender regimes, gender codes or hidden curricula does not result so readily in blaming the teacher as the classroom interaction studies do, for the school processes appear hegemonic enough to carry along teachers unwittingly in their wake. Teacher action seems rooted in tradition and common sense rather than malice. Yet there is a legitimate question here of how, when and why teachers do challenge the hegemony or, conversely, why they often do not. These questions lead us to focus on the *teacher* herself or himself, rather than the pupil or the nature of the interaction between them.

Teacher resistance?

In some sociology of education literature, refusal by pupil groups to acquiesce to school authority is called 'resistance' (Anyon 1983). Resistance, while appearing specifically directed at the immediate agents of social control (that is, the teachers), tends to be analysed as a symptomatic response by youth to control and authority more generally, especially as used in the service of capitalism and the production of a docile workforce. We meet the term again in another relevant but different context: the study of innovation in educational institutions. There is a substantial literature on the latter topic (for reviews, see Fullan 1982; see Ball 1987). One phenomenon addressed in this literature is the rarity of planned changes with long-lasting impact. Among other reasons for unsuccessful innovation are said to be teacher responses such as defensiveness or conservatism (Mulford 1982: 184). As Ball (1987: 31) points out, there is a tendency to see change as progress and to ascribe teacher resistance to individual irrationality. So 'resistance', depending on one's theoretical preference, is either the last stand of the brave underdog or the last gasp of the doomed dinosaur. Does either model help us to understand teachers' responses to gender issues?

First, *do* teachers 'resist' anti-sexist initiatives? Feminist teachers think so: Joyce's (1987: 69) interviews led her to conclude that there is 'massive resistance and refusal even to consider the arguments'. Using larger samples, survey researchers have asked teachers about their attitudes to equality for the sexes.

The results suggest teachers are reluctant to accept equal opportunity initiatives such as Girls into Science and Technology (GIST), a project intended to increase the proportions of girls opting for physical science in secondary school (Whyte 1986). The GIST researchers found science and craft teachers, who were mostly men, believing there are natural sex differences and that sex equality is not an educational problem. They worried that positive action for girls would mean unacceptable discrimination against boys (Whyte 1986). Other surveys of secondary teachers (Pratt *et al.* 1984; Kelly *et al.* 1985; Pratt 1985) find that there is support for equal opportunities in principle, but that teachers are disinclined to believe schools actually favour boys and are wary about interfering in the processes whereby girls make traditional career choices.

There is less information available on primary teachers.[2] In an innovative ethnography of a primary teacher training course, Skelton (1985) reports that gender was (on the face of it) a 'non-issue'. In the words of one of the tutors: 'It's interesting that you've said that because I've never thought about it' (p. 65). The general response of students to direct queries was to suggest that 'gender' was a secondary school problem, connected with option choice or adolescent sexuality. Patrick Orr (1985: 21) draws on his experience with HMI to summarize for both phases: 'There are still large numbers of schools where there is very little understanding of the issues involved . . . little genuine interest in positive action to promote equal opportunities'.

Set against all this gloom might be reports of anti-sexist projects initiated by individual teachers and groups of teachers, as contained, for example, in Adams and Arnot (1986) or Taylor (1985). Clearly they exist and in some local authorities are given support by special advisers. But, 'most authorities provide relatively little practical support for reducing sex differentiation in schools; the issue is seen as one of a large number of causes arguing for priority treatment in the allocation of resources' (Orr 1985: 16). It seems an uphill struggle.

Why is gender not on the agenda?

We see that feminist literature makes a strong case that girls and boys are treated unequally. Teachers are committed to advancing the interests of all the individual children in their charge. Yet gender equality initiatives, while not unknown, are scarce and apparently failing to transform teachers' attitudes and actions. How can this happen? There are a few studies that I shall draw on to help solve this puzzle (notably Cunnison 1985; Whyte 1986; Ball 1987; Riddell 1988), but to a large extent what follows is speculative and remains to be explored empirically. I argue that explanations for teachers' 'resistance' to equality initiatives may be sought in four categories:

1. The characteristics of the initiative and its introduction.
2. The type of people teachers are.
3. The ideologies teachers hold.
4. The conditions in which teachers work.

The nature of the initiative

Innovations concerned with gender face some of the same difficulties as any other educational innovation. Conditions that make successful implementation of any innovation likely are often absent. Channels for dissemination from one school to another are not well developed, so that ideas emanating from one teacher or school may never find their way to others with similar needs. Academic writings are rarely read by teachers other than those on in-service courses and there is a strong tradition that 'experience counts, theory doesn't' (Hargreaves 1984). David McNamara's (1976) classic article about his return after working as an educational researcher to a term of primary school teaching explains why this happens: 'I lost all desire to keep up to date with the literature . . . the world of the academic journals seemed completely irrelevant to classroom life'. Educational research deals in abstractions, but 'as a teacher I had to act in particular and concrete situations and, moreover, be committed to and believe in what I was doing' (p. 155).

In other respects, 'gender' may be a more difficult arena for innovation than others. Some of the more accessible writing such as Spender (1982) or Mahony (1985) is forcefully feminist, when there is considerable evidence teachers are wary of feminism (Whyte 1986; Ball 1987: 75–6). Ethnographic studies suggest that teachers sympathetic to feminism are not only few in number but junior in age and status (Cunnison 1985; Riddell 1988). This is not to argue that radical-feminist ideas should be disguised in equal opportunities clothing, for even the very mild feminism of the GIST project was looked upon with suspicion (along with social science and qualitative research) (Whyte 1986), but to point to the possibility that social acceptance of feminism has not progressed sufficiently in Britain to allow schools to move smoothly in that direction.

Some local education authorities have issued policies on gender. How many have done so, and with what effects, is 'anybody's guess' (Joyce 1987: 83). In certain cases, LEAs introducing anti-sexist guidelines have run into accusations of insensitivity (Wells 1985) or left-wing political bias (Joyce 1987). The LEAs have also attracted feminist criticism, usually on the grounds of their anti-sexist initiatives being insufficiently resourced or indifferently enforced. The equal opportunities policies of LEAs have also faced difficulty in tackling the full range of educational 'disadvantage', which encompasses (at least) class, sex, race, disability and sexual orientation. To date, multiculturalism and anti-racism have attracted far more public debate and have penetrated LEA and school-level policy making to a greater extent than gender issues or anti-sexism (Davies 1987). The relationship between anti-racism and anti-sexism is complex and contradictory (Williams 1987), presenting further problems for practitioners.

Apart from the policies of a few LEAS, there is no concerted outside pressure for teachers to adopt innovations concerned with gender (Acker 1986; Davies 1987), at a time when central government is compelling schools to change in a number of other ways. The introduction of a National Curriculum was justified in part by an argument that it would prevent pupils from dropping subjects too soon. This concern could be seen as a response to anxieties about girls and science, but such a procedure will only go a little way to meet the feminist critique without concomitant changes in the way in which science is packaged and taught (Kelly 1985).[3] Gender equality initiatives appear to have penetrated the consciousness (and consciences) of educators more deeply in some other countries, including the United States and Australia, where there have been greater central government support, relatively lavish funding and stronger legislation than in Britain (Klein 1985; Yates 1986). These initiatives have not been unmitigatedly successful and have produced some backlash. But it is interesting to consider Hatton's (1987) point that when there are no negative sanctions for failing to be innovative, and when an innovation would make significant extra demands on time and energy, teachers (seen as workers) would be irrational if they did pursue it.

One additional point is important to the success or otherwise of initiatives specifically on gender. Much of the educational literature is implicitly or explicitly critical of teacher practice (McNamara 1976). The gender literature is no exception here, and indeed goes further than some other critiques. The evaluators of the GIST project pointed out that many of the teachers did not appreciate that the intervention was intended to change their own attitudes as well as those of pupils. Those who did catch on were likely to react negatively, for it 'was criticism of the most fundamental kind, of teachers' professional competence' (Hustler and Cuff 1986: 182). Taylor (1985: 105–106) points out that 'the best way of ensuring that anti-sexist initiatives fail is to foist them on teachers . . . without preparation or time to reach an understanding of the issues, and then be helpless in the face of things going wrong'. Teachers are not simply being asked to adopt new textbooks or adapt the curriculum but to alter fundamental aspects of their practice, tantamount in some cases to admitting years of malpractice. We cannot expect such conversions to come easily.

Teacher characteristics

Any initiative will be filtered, so to speak, through the characteristics, ideologies and working conditions of the teachers who have to accept or reject it. There is a stereotype that teachers are fundamentally conservative souls who instinctively reject progress (Lightfoot 1983). Generalizations about teacher personality have always been suspect in such a large profession. Might there, however, be common characteristics of teachers that result in particular difficulties in accepting anti-sexist initiatives? In an American study, Grant and Sleeter (1985) argue that the social characteristics of most teachers – white, from relatively comfortable backgrounds – make it hard for them to empathize with children from distinctly different origins. Extrapolation of this argument might explain opposition or indifference to gender equality from male teachers, but it is clearly not only men who 'resist'. If teachers' characteristics have an impact, it is likely to be a complex one. Delamont, for example, hypothesizes that there is an interaction between sex and social class origin. The lower-middle-class origins of many teachers, especially men, give them a view of gender tending towards the conventional stereotypes of their own childhoods.

Middle-class women who go into teaching tend to be those who aim for limited career targets rather than challenging occupational barriers (Delamont 1980: 73–7).

There may be differences in teachers' attitudes to gender equality according to subject taught (Pratt 1985). On the other hand, much of this variation may be due to other factors like sex, age and type of qualifications, which tend to be systematically associated with subject taught (Kelly *et al.* 1985). Age is one characteristic that is frequently mentioned. Most studies suggest younger teachers are more reform-minded about gender (Cunnison 1985; Kelly *et al.* 1985; Ball 1987; Riddell 1988). There are various reasons why this might be so, including greater exposure of young teachers to the women's movement and feminist ideas, and older teachers more likely to be in management positions, with a greater stake in the *status quo* (Riddell 1988). It may also be that the conditions of teaching progressively drain teachers of energy and enthusiasm as they carry on over many years (Feiman-Nemser and Floden 1986).

To the extent teachers have been exposed to similar experiences and ideologies during their training, they may share common perspectives about gender. It is only very recently that teacher education has explicitly tackled questions of racism and sexism, perhaps explaining younger teachers' more favourable views on reform. But simply introducing gender issues into initial teacher training does not guarantee the production of committed anti-sexist teachers. Students on the secondary Postgraduate Certificate in Education course Hanson studied took equality issues more seriously when they were included in 'methods' rather than 'professional studies' components, when they were raised in planned fashion by tutors rather than incidentally, and when they were sensitively presented (Skelton and Hanson 1989).

An interesting line of work is beginning to locate teachers' attitudes and actions in their own biographies and life situations. Little attention has as yet been paid to attitudes about gender, although several recent studies consider women teachers' own career attitudes and patterns in biographical context (Evetts 1986; Spencer 1986; Grant 1987; see also Chapter 7, this volume). Evans (1982) found women primary school teachers he interviewed displaying 'ambiguity of self': that is, caught in a contradiction between personal identification with traditional gender roles and a competing identity as career women deserving equality with male colleagues. Clarricoates (1980a) points out the down-to-earth difficulties of going home exhausted and doing the housework. She suggests that when women teachers are already doing two jobs, their lack of enthusiasm for taking on additional responsibilities of promotion (and by extension, innovation) is understandable. There is scope for further research to link the characteristics of past and present lives of both sexes to their beliefs and actions *vis-à-vis* gender.

Teacher ideology

Beliefs about education and about gender may be particularly important as a source of resistance to anti-sexist initiatives. Fullan argues that for implementation of an innovation to occur, changes to materials, teaching approaches and beliefs are necessary. Materials are the simplest to alter, beliefs the most difficult, as they may be 'buried at the level of unconscious assumptions' (Fullan 1982: 247). Beliefs about education can be elaborated into an ideology, 'the network of beliefs, values and assumptions about children, learning, teaching, knowledge and the curriculum' (Alexander 1984: 14). As with the search for teacher personality, the idea of discovering a quintessential teacher ideology may possibly be chimerical, but the search itself yields important insights.

Ideologies specifically about sex and gender have been referred to earlier in this chapter. As we have seen, teachers appear to be in favour of gender equality in its most general terms but sceptical about feminism and often unmotivated to take practical steps to alter school practices. What perhaps needs more analysis is teacher ideologies that are not specifically about gender but that may set limits to what changes and challenges teachers are likely to accept. Three possibly relevant sets of beliefs are: (1) ideologies about child-centred learning; (2) ideologies about the determining role of factors outside school on educational achievements; (3) ideologies about political neutrality of the school.

Child-centred learning

Primary teachers' 'child-centred' ideologies have come in for criticism on various grounds, among them discrepancies between beliefs and behaviour and their potential for masking curricular and pedagogical weaknesses (Alexander 1984). Although typically associated with the primary level, child-centred rhetoric is also heard at the secondary stage, one of Riddell's (1988) teachers, for example, insisting 'I teach characters, not sexes'.

It is possible to make connections between such an ideology and perspectives on educational change (Alexander 1984: 180). Carrington and Short (1987) argue that an explanation for primary teachers' slow response to certain ideas about anti-racist teaching might be found in their ideological stance. They suggest that teachers' belief that children develop along a sequential path leads them to conclude that political education is too abstract for young pupils' comprehension. Similarly, teachers' belief in young children's innocence results in attempts to protect pupils from facing harsh realities like racism. To take these ideas any further, one would need empirical study to demonstrate that the teachers holding the particular educational ideologies most strongly are the same ones who are reluctant to implement anti-racist strategies.

Skelton (1985) and Skelton and Hanson (1989) give us some empirical evidence to make the case for a link between primary teachers' child-centred ideology and their failure to challenge gender inequality. Students on the primary teacher education course Skelton studied believed and were encouraged to believe that attention to children's individual differences, needs and development was paramount. They took this one step further (implicitly), so that individualization effectively eliminated categorization. If children were truly treated as individuals, it would be impossible to discriminate against a social group. In the process, this stance ruled out positive action as well as negative discrimination. The course itself was marked by numerous examples of taken-for-granted gender differentiation and bias in school observations, curriculum materials, films and lectures. (Ironically, the films on race and special educational needs dealt almost entirely with boys.) The trainee teachers (and tutors) appeared to absorb these instances uncritically.

It should also be noted, however, that child-centred ideologies have in other contexts been considered particularly compatible with feminist pedagogy (Joyce 1987; Middleton 1989). Both approaches stress values such as respect for the individual's perceptions and experiences, cooperation and self-esteem. There is a contradiction here that remains to be resolved.

Environmental determinism

A little dose of sociology, such as one gets (or used to get; see Chapter 1) in initial teacher training, is sometimes said to do more harm than good, and has been blamed for teachers' eagerness to locate working-class underachievement in family values and language usage rather than school processes. A similar point can be made about gender and schooling. The teachers in Riddell's (1988) study were wont to ascribe responsibility for girls' stereotyped subject option choices or narrow vocational horizons either to biological sex differences in ability or to childhood socialization, with some reference to parental, peer and employee expectations. The inference was that there was little the school could do. 'By the time they're at primary school it's too late', said the director of sixth-form studies. Only a minority of those Riddell interviewed (all under age 45 and not in 'the hierarchy') believed the attitudes and practices of the school were at all implicated.[4]

Neutrality

Pratt (1985) and Riddell (1988) found some teachers holding an ideology of 'neutrality', a belief that it would be morally or ethically wrong to intervene to alter differential preferences shown by the sexes. To do so, they thought, would be a form of indoctrination or political bias and not an educational activity. Riddell's teachers believed strongly that the job of the school was to provide a value-free environment in which pupils could exercise freedom of choice (over subject options, in this case). There were, as she notes, contradictions between this claim and a number of administrative practices in the school that clearly limited free choice.

The GIST teachers, even when they supported the project, were hesitant about tackling sex inequality directly, as if the location of the problem in the hidden curriculum required the solution to remain there as well. For example, when women scientists were brought in to talk to the pupils and serve as role models, the teachers introducing them frequently avoided any direct reference to their being female (Whyte 1986).

The ideology of 'neutrality' needs some further comment. It appears reactionary where racism or sexism is concerned, and Carrington and Short (1987: 11) condemn it soundly, arguing that teacher training will have to 'show teachers that political and racial attitudes can be taught as well as caught and, moreover, such an undertaking may begin in the infant school'. But the injunction not to take advantage of the teacher's access to impressionable minds was hardly invented by resistant teachers: it has been espoused by many from Weber (1946) to Warnock (1985). The two faces of resistance draw close here as teachers' views about proper educational practice might also insulate them from the blandishments of all the would-be quick change artists of the curriculum. When it is the secretary of state who calls the tune, teachers may have to sing it, but they do not necessarily have to give it full voice.[5]

Alexander (1984) develops a concept of intellectual (as opposed to executive) autonomy for teachers. This does not simply mean 'freedom from interference' (or reflex resistance to new ideas), but implies a rational, questioning scepticism, whereby choices are made in view of their thought-through consequences. There are tendencies in educational organizations that work against such an ideal, he points out. But a consequence of his argument for mine is that we shall get further by according teachers' views (however misguided in our opinions) some respect. They are not simply irrational, without foundation. Ideology cannot be the whole answer, since we need to know its sources and reasons for its persistence. Daily work experience may reinforce ideologies, if not create them, and it is to this topic I now turn.

Conditions of work

To discuss 'conditions of work' fully, it would be necessary to review a large and unwieldy body of sociological work on teachers and teaching. Here I pick out those aspects most likely to assist or undermine attempts at innovation, especially anti-sexist innovation. Those concerned about tendencies towards stasis in schools tend to argue that the 'modal conditions' (Weinshank *et al.* 1983) of teaching are unlike, even prohibitive of, those required for effective implementation of innovation. I shall discuss: (1) the teacher's classroom focus; (2) isolation and time for consultation with colleagues; (3) micropolitics in the school; and (4) the ever-expanding teacher's role.

Teachers and classrooms

Most often cited in the literature is the teacher's adhesion to a classroom base and the singular features of classrooms. Classroom complexity demands full teacher attention. Managing so many children in a small space puts a premium on routine and predictability (Feiman-Nemser and Floden 1986). Most innovations represent some threat to that precarious classroom order. Doyle and Ponder (1977) explain that as a consequence, teachers' main reaction to a proposed change will be a judgement of its potential as 'practical' or otherwise for classroom use. They suggest that to be 'practical', a proposal must be (a) *instrumental* (explain what is to be done rather than appeal to principle alone), (b) *congruent* (fit in reasonably well with the way the teacher normally works and the type of pupils she teaches) and (c) *cost-effective* (expected to produce a return worth the effort and sacrifice involved).

Instrumentality seems particularly relevant to anti-sexist initiatives, as most of the literature on gender and education tends toward exposé and exhortation rather than specifying alternative practices with any precision. Both Hargreaves (1984) and Hatton (1987) emphasize the inadequacy of consciousness-raising or 'cultural interruption' when structures (conditions of work) remain unchanged.

Teachers and colleagues

Often mentioned in tandem with teachers' classroom focus is the supposed isolation of the teacher (e.g. Lortie 1975) and consequent dearth of collegial consultation. Most innovations require some kind of cooperation between colleagues, according to Doyle and Ponder (1977: 3), while the teacher culture is thought to emphasize autonomy in its usual sense (Pollard 1985), and the geography of the school sometimes imposes it. 'Professionals (teachers) wish to be left alone. At best they wish to be critics' (Mulford 1982: 195). My view is that although 'isolation' from colleagues is the lot of some teachers most of the time and most teachers some of the time, it is not an inevitable and unalterable feature of schools. What is missing is probably not contact *per se*, but sufficient specific time set aside for planning and consultation. Many commentators agree that this time is necessary for successful implementation (Fullan 1982; Weinshank *et al.* 1983; Hargreaves 1984; Hatton 1987) and it is clearly a rarity. Time given voluntarily represents a 'cost' and teachers are only likely to accept this cost either under compulsion or when it is seen by them as a means to a desirable end. Either the ideology has to be there already or the conditions changed to allow it to develop.[6]

Teachers and micropolitics

Schools are much more than a collection of class teachers, and an increasingly popular approach is to see them as organizations in which individuals and groups compete and manipulate events, using whatever power resources they possess to try to maximize their own interests and satisfactions (Hoyle 1986; Ball 1987; Sparkes 1987). This dimension of organizational life is called 'micropolitics'. The metaphors are those of conflict and exchange (Hoyle 1986). Ball (1987: 31) argues that change in schools or resistance to it cannot be fully understood without taking into account the micropolitical dimension. One potential interest group he singles out is women teachers (are men teachers *qua* men an interest group, we might wonder in passing?).

If women teachers are such a group, we might expect them to take an initiating role towards anti-sexism. But while some do, many do not, and the micropolitical perspective suggests the roots of their inaction may lie in their structurally relatively powerless position in the (mixed-sex secondary) school rather than in simply 'being women'. Several ethnographic studies of mixed secondary schools give support to this interpretation (Cunnison 1985; Ball 1987; Riddell 1988).[7] Cunnison found a small group of women teachers keen on career advance for themselves, but showing relatively little interest in changing the situation for their girl pupils. She describes the women's difficult, contradictory and largely powerless position in the school. A 'macho culture' (especially regarding discipline) flourished in the school, which marginalized the women teachers who could or would not wield that sort of authority. Ridicule also acted as social control. Women who held senior posts were without exception the butt of jokes (see also Woods 1979; Delamont 1980) and young women teachers encountered sexual banter focused on their dress and appearance (Cunnison 1989).

In her study of two rural comprehensive schools, Riddell (1988) also sees women teachers as relatively powerless when it comes to improving their own situation. Very few women held positions of responsibility in either school. All the male teachers interviewed, and some of the women, believed women's free choice to have children was equivalent to renouncing interest in a career. Those women who did get 'to the top' in teaching were criticized as 'too wrapped up in it, too emotional and much too intense' (cf. Waller 1932/1965: 409, on 'sex starvation' of spinsters) and their heterosexuality questioned. A few women teachers protested against this stereotyping, but many accepted an inevitable opposition between 'children' and 'career' and rejected allegations of discrimination. Women's lack of power seemed natural to them. The divisions among the women, Riddell argues, left those who thought of protesting too isolated to carry it through.

Riddell (1988) and Ball (1987) report almost identical instances where women teachers in a mixed secondary school, concerned about an evident lack of promotion opportunities, held a meeting on their own to discuss the issue. In Greenhill (Riddell), 'the Headmaster was so furious . . . that he absolutely forbade anything like that ever to take place again . . . So it sort of filtered out then, petered out'. At Casterbridge (Ball), 30 women teachers signed a letter to the head protesting, mildly it appears, the fact that the head, three deputies and six tutors were all men. 'The response from the head was that the right people were given the jobs' (p. 74). And that was the end of it.

In both cases, the seeds of resistance were planted but failed to grow, and the implication is that women rendered powerless to help themselves will resolve the cognitive dissonance between their ambitions and their opportunities by coming to terms with the limits placed on their careers (see also Chapter 7, this volume). In the process, they cannot pose any effective challenge to the gender reproductive processes their students undergo, and the gender regime continues.

Teachers' expanding role

A final, and important, feature of school life that discourages innovation is the teacher's role itself: infinitely expanding, some argue, and weighed down by attempts to meet high standards with declining resources and by traditions of endless accountability to diverse significant others (see Pollard 1985; Nias 1986; Broadfoot and Osborn 1987). The conscientious teacher works harder and harder just to keep going. In 1987, following long and bitter industrial action, the secretary of state scrapped the Burnham Committee, which previously carried out negotiations over teachers' salaries and conditions, and himself specified contracts in much detail. A National Curriculum and testing at certain ages loomed. American writers argue that federal, state and local mandates have intensified and deskilled teachers' work (Apple 1986). Weinshank *et al.* (1983) show how different schemes introduced into schools conflict with each other, cut across other goals the teachers may have, and ultimately leave them unable and unwilling to be creative and innovative on their own account. The long lists of areas British teachers are already expected to understand and implement given by Stewart (1986) and Pollard (1985: 113) do not even include gender inequality. If Britain moves further in the direction described by Apple and Weinshank *et al.*, teachers will simply be too tired for optional innovations.[8]

Conclusion

The starting point for this chapter was the gap between gender-based inequalities in schools, amply demonstrated by feminist research and increasingly accepted within mainstream sociology of education, and anti-sexist initiatives in schools, conspicuous more by their absence than their success. It could be said that teachers 'resist' such initiatives, in most cases simply by not recognizing or accepting that there is an educational issue involved. The remainder of the chapter drew upon the literature on implementation of educational innovations, on teachers' work, and on gender and education to suggest four areas that influence teachers' reactions. These are the nature of the proposed innovation and the characteristics, ideologies and working conditions of teachers. It is unlikely these are all equal and independent influences. Further research might produce a more exact model of the innovation process as it affects initiatives concerned with gender. There are indications that gender might not be just like every other area of innovation. The reforms called for by the feminist literature are fundamental and possibly threatening; teachers' own gendered histories, roles outside school and positions within the school shape their beliefs about what reform is possible or desirable. 'Resistance' appears double-edged, preventing progress but also protecting against illegitimate pressures and impossible demands.

In a situation where neither government dictates, conventional teacher ideologies nor conditions of work promote and support anti-sexist innovation, feminist futures seem grim. Not everything, of course, can be accomplished through education, as sociologists well recognize, and feminism probably needs to make a greater social impact in Britain before it can permeate the schools. On the other hand, women teachers appear more career-conscious than in the past, and gender issues are increasingly raised in teacher education courses. One gap (indeed, chasm) badly needing filling is the one between feminist and sociological scholarship on gender on the one hand and teachers' everyday school experience on the other.[9] The 'cost' of implementing anti-sexist innovations will decrease when it becomes clearer what they are and how one goes about putting them into practice.

Notes

1. A recent study from the United States with a similar finding is Grant (1992).
2. Since the National Curriculum was introduced, researchers have paid greater attention to primary teachers' responses to innovation, specifically the new curriculum and assessment arrangements. See, for example, Acker (1990c), Brehony (1990) and Broadfoot and Abbott (1991).
3. For an assessment of the National Curriculum's chances of encouraging girls to study science, see Miles and Middleton (1990).
4. Riddell's study is now available in book form Riddell (1992).
5. See Bowe and Ball (1992) for further consideration of this point in the context of the educational policy developments of the late 1980s and early 1990s.
6. Hargreaves (1994) explores relevant issues about teachers' work conditions, including the use of time.
7. There are also recent studies that consider the consequences gay or lesbian teachers face when trying to counter homophobia among students while protecting their own position (Anon. 1989; Squirrell 1989; Khayatt 1992).
8. The original version of this chapter (published in 1988) was written before the Educational Reform Act (ERA) of 1988 was implemented. The ERA introduced a raft of changes in the curriculum, the assessment requirements, the management and the financing of schools. These were reforms that were not optional, although teachers still had some latitude in their pedagogical responses. Gender equity was not among the priorities of the Conservative Government, and as Hey (1993: 330) puts it: 'EO [equal opportunities] in most schools is going out of fashion as fast as yesterday's news'. It could be said that my 'teachers will be too tired' prediction has come to pass (see also Arnot 1992, 1993).
9. Kenway and Modra (1992) note a gap between studies of gender and schooling, and writing on women's studies. Each body of literature theorizes feminist pedagogy rather differently, without much reference to each other, perhaps a function of the different audiences they address.

7 Creating Careers: Women Teachers at Work

'Career' as a concept seems to fascinate certain sociologists, myself included. We grope for a way of understanding its shades of meaning. Distinctions are made, for example, between objective and subjective careers (Hughes 1958; Evetts 1990), or personal and structural career contingencies (Carlson and Schmuck, 1981).

In one sense, a career clearly is an individual construction. Individuals have work histories, perspectives on the past and desired future, the capacity to make choices. Yet at the same time there is inevitably a structural dimension. Structures are social arrangements largely outside our control, such as the size of steps on the pay scales, the number of teaching vacancies in a locale, the probability women will be appointed to senior posts, even the configurations of national political and economic systems.

I begin this chapter by elaborating on 'individual' and 'structural' approaches to understanding teachers' careers and raising the question of what lies between. Then I turn to the stories of teachers in two primary schools in England, to support my contention that we need to extend (or deconstruct) our conventional notions of teacher careers, especially for women.[1] The study also attempts to bridge the gap between scholarship on gender and teachers' everyday experiences that was remarked upon in Chapter 6.

Conceptualizing careers

The individual level

The individual level is easy to relate to. We all make decisions, take actions, hold perspectives and so forth. Some of the sociological and educational literature on teachers' careers has conjured up an image of teacher as *rational career planner* (e.g. Hilsum and Start 1974). Or, more precisely, some teachers, usually male, are seen as rational career planners, busily plotting career maps and climbing career ladders. Chapter 5 described the commonsense sexism often found in such accounts. Feminist reaction against the androcentrism of these approaches produced a *female rational career planner* (e.g. National Union of Teachers 1980). She, too, tried to climb a ladder but found it had missing rungs and fewer hands reaching down to haul her up the steps.

Then, in the 1980s, British studies of teacher careers tuned into a different theoretical tradition and created the *interactionist teacher* (Woods 1983; Ball and Goodson 1985; Pollard 1985; Sikes *et al.* 1985; Nias 1989). These individuals interpreted and negotiated their careers in the process of everyday interactions, constructing and reconstructing the 'teacher self'. How gender might shape this self was, oddly, not often asked.

Meanwhile, in the United States, feminist scholarship was discovering *the woman as teacher*, in Casey and Apple's (1989) phrase. In this approach, the researcher retreats and lets the woman speak for herself. This approach has affinities with one that collects *teacher narratives*. These narratives are sets of stories about a teacher's past that are thought to help comprehend the present (her/his classroom practice) and create purpose for the future (Connelly and Clandinin 1988).

What the most recent studies and commentaries have in common is the foregrounding of the 'teacher's voice' (Goodson 1991). Critics note that this voice may masquerade as androgynous (Grumet 1990), while women teachers' voices are silenced (Pagano 1990). Also typically silenced are voices of those different from the majority on grounds such as sexual preference or ethnicity (but see McKellar 1989; Squirrell 1989; Khayatt 1990).

There are, then, a number of competing perspectives that give pride of place to individual interpretations, experiences and narratives. Other scholars, however, prefer an approach at the other end of the analytical spectrum, one that highlights social and economic constraints.

Wider structures

It seems indisputable that wider social influences shape and limit teachers' careers, although the extent is difficult to assess. Historical studies demonstrate this shaping particularly clearly. Differential opportunities for men and women teachers and restrictions on married women teachers' employment have a long history (Littlewood 1989; Oram 1989; C. Reynolds 1990; Prentice and Theobald 1991).

Demographic fluctuations are particularly important in determining labour market conditions for teachers. Evetts (1990) describes how teachers in England in the 1960s were implored to return to the classroom to teach the influx of young pupils and offered incentives to do so. In contrast, a 'career break' was so widely regarded as disastrous in the 1980s that many women struggled on with the aid of maternity leave rather than risk the destruction of their careers (Grant 1989).

Some writers see long-term economic and social change altering the nature of white-collar work in the direction of reducing skill and autonomy. Teachers are among those said to be deskilled or proletarianized, as their autonomy is reduced and the pace of their work intensified (Apple 1986; Ozga and Lawn

1988). Certain accounts, especially those from the United States, create an image of a teacher-worker heavily controlled by curriculum packages, state mandates and external testing (Apple 1986; Smith 1991). The issue is highly topical in Britain, too (Acker 1990c), as 1988 saw the introduction of a sweeping package of 'reforms' that reduced the considerable classroom and curricular autonomy British teachers traditionally enjoyed, by measures such as the introduction of a National Curriculum and testing. Furthermore, the legislation changed the balance of power in the governance of education, reducing that of local education authorities and increasing it for central government, for school governing bodies[2] and to some extent for parents.

One might ask whether changing social attitudes towards women and the rise of feminism are not also reshaping the parameters within which teachers operate. In Britain, as elsewhere, there has been a sharp rise in the proportions of married women, and women with children, in the labour market (often part-time), and there has also been a steady increase in the likelihood of young women staying on longer at school, gaining examination qualifications, and going on to undergraduate degrees (see Chapter 10). Certain professions have opened doors to women that were closed 20 years ago. Women now have more alternatives than in the past to teaching as a career. However, the teaching force itself seems only marginally influenced by feminist ideologies, perhaps reflecting the lack of support central government has given to feminist initiatives (Joyce 1987; Gelb 1989; see also Chapter 6, this volume).

Teacher career structures

Such historical, demographic, economic and political structures are part of the context in which teaching careers must be constructed. We can see their operation around us only dimly. What we perceive more clearly is the structure of the teaching career itself: its sequences of positions, rules for moving between them, duties expected, etc. Here, incidentally, there is considerable cross-cultural variation (Dove 1986; Davies 1990).

A few details about teaching in England and Wales will put the rest of this chapter into context.[3] Teachers' pay is negotiated (or prescribed) nationally. During the late 1980s and early 1990s, while my research was being conducted, teachers were paid on a main professional scale or grade, also called the standard scale. They moved up the scale with annual increments. Some teachers received, in addition, one of a series of 'incentive allowances'. Although school governors were responsible for the allocation of these allowances, head teachers usually had considerable influence. The allowances available for distribution depended on the size of the school. In theory, allowances could be given for teaching excellence, shortage subjects, or difficult-to-fill posts, as well as for extra responsibilities, but the latter criterion was by far the most common (School Teachers' Review Body 1993: 17).

Primary schools usually had only A and B allowances – the smaller ones – and the proportion of primary teachers receiving any allowance was smaller

Table 1   Representation of women teachers and women heads by type of school in England and Wales, 1990

Type of school	Numbers of teachers in each type of school	Percentage of teachers who are women	Numbers of heads in each type of school	Percentage of heads who are women
Nursery	1,614	98.5	598	99.3
Infant	23,892	98.1	2,992	97.2
First	18,350	90.1	2,461	72.1
Junior with infant	92,206	78.3	11,663	36.1
First and middle	4,564	80.5	379	37.7
Junior without infants	28,274	69.9	2,908	25.0
Middle deemed primary	6,855	68.4	593	23.1
Unattached and visiting	2,983	75.1	238	50.8
All nursery and primary	178,738	80.6	21,832	48.6
All secondary	203,934	47.8	5,020	19.7
All teachers[a]	385,177	63.1	26,971	43.2

[a] This category includes 2,505 teachers categorized as divided service (primary and secondary) and miscellaneous who are not included in the separate primary and secondary figures above.
Source: Calculated from Department of Education and Science (1992: 36).

than that of secondary teachers, about 32 and 60 per cent, respectively in 1989 (Interim Advisory Committee 1990). These features of the system represent a hidden disadvantage for women teachers, who were 81 per cent of primary and 48 per cent of secondary teachers in 1990 (School Teachers' Review Body 1993: 64).[4]

Secondary schools offer a more complicated career structure, with layers of middle management. Informally, there are two career pathways in secondary schools – academic (including heads of subject departments) and pastoral (welfare or counselling roles, such as head of year). Women are more often in the pastoral roles, thought to be more difficult to use as stepping-stones to headships (Cunnison 1989).

Table 1 shows that in England and Wales during 1990, 48.6 per cent of primary head teachers and 19.7 per cent of secondary head teachers were women. These figures may look high, especially by North American standards,[5] but it is important to note, first, that they still mean significant under-representation of women at senior levels compared with their presence in the occupation, and second, that they come about in part because of the many schools for younger primary pupils counted in the figures. These 'infant schools', which include children from ages 4 or 5 to age 7, are almost entirely

Table 2   Percentage distribution of each sex across the grades in England and Wales, 1990

	Nursery and primary		Secondary	
	Men	Women	Men	Women
Heads	32.4	7.4	3.8	1.0
Deputy heads	19.0	8.5	6.4	3.6
Main scale with incentive allowance				
E	0.1	0.0	6.2	2.1
D	0.5	0.2	19.3	8.2
C	1.3	1.1	7.7	6.2
B	14.0	13.3	23.6	23.9
A	8.6	16.1	8.1	13.5
Main scale without incentive allowance[a]	24.1	53.4	24.9	41.5
Total %	100.0	100.0	100.0	100.0
Total number	34,619	144,119	106,467	97,467

[a] Includes a small number listed as paid on 'any other scale', e.g. those for unqualified teachers.
Source: Calculated from Department of Education and Science (1992: 36).

staffed and headed by women, as Table 1 shows. Women are less likely to head combined (5–11 years) primary schools or the junior schools, which contain older primary pupils only (7–11 years).

Table 2 gives some idea of what the probability is for each sex to move into senior positions or be rewarded with allowances. It shows women concentrated in the lower categories. Over half of women teachers in primary schools are on the standard scale without an incentive allowance, compared with just under a quarter of the men. In secondary schools, 41.5 per cent of the women, but only 24.9 per cent of the men, have no incentive allowance. Note, too, that just over half of all the men in primary schools occupy headships or deputy headships. Also, the figures in Tables 1 and 2 are for full-time teachers only. Part-time teachers are usually female and rarely hold an allowance (Department of Education and Science 1991).

Careers in the workplace: Two English primary schools

I have discussed approaches that emphasize on the one hand individual actions, and on the other the wider structures in which teachers must operate. I have also described the teaching career structure itself. What remains to be considered is how the individual perceptions and decisions about careers are formed in the context of the structures. There have been surprisingly few attempts to find such middle ground, reflecting both the usual difficulty of reconciling agency and structure and the fervour with which some of these positions are held and defended. Evetts (1989) constructs one such bridge in developing the concept of an internal labour market for teachers. She argues that characteristics significant for promotion, and the extent to which sponsorship mechanisms and occupational community networks can support women's career opportunities, vary over time and are linked to economic, political and demographic contexts.

Deborah Britzman (1991:11) develops an approach to teacher narratives that highlights their placement in 'a context characterized by an unequal distribution of power that acts to construct people's lives . . . [structuring] their investments, interpretations, and practices'. Like Britzman, Norquay (1990) draws upon a version of post-structuralism to stress the influence of historical and social structures on the formation of subjectivity. Both point out that the creation of an apparently unified self through narrative or life-history methods runs the risk of de-emphasizing the contradictory realities and social constraints under which identity is negotiated.

I believe that teachers arrive at perceptions about careers through their daily experiences in families, communities and workplaces, experiences that reflect gender divisions in society. In Chapter 5, I noted the need for more studies of the everyday lives of teachers, especially if we are to understand gender relations in schools. Workplace experience is a largely missing level of analysis in the literature on teacher careers. My own study involves observations in two primary schools over several years, using an ethnographic approach that allows description of the everyday lives of teachers in and to some extent out of school. The overall intent of the study was to depict the reality of teachers' work and workplace cultures in the primary school (see Acker 1990b, 1990c, 1991).

Details of the study

My main school I call 'Hillview'. I began observations there in April 1987. Hillview is an inner-city school, with a mixed social class and ethnic intake. It has about 200 children, aged 4–11 years, in seven classes. In 1987–89, the teaching staff consisted of a female head teacher, a male deputy head teacher, five full-time and three part-time teachers. All but one of the teachers were female and white. There were two general assistants, one working mostly as school secretary.

A year later, in April 1988, I began observations in a second, contrasting, school. 'Rosemont' is larger, in a middle-class area, with about 360 children in 12 classes. It caters exclusively to juniors (aged 7–11 years). Of the 13 teachers in 1988–89, 4 were men. The head teacher was male and the deputy head female. There were two general assistants as well as a secretary. All of them were white.

The most intensive period of fieldwork took place in the 1987–88 and 1988–89 school years, adding up to about 880 hours in Hillview and 200 hours in Rosemont. These estimates do not include telephone conversations, social occasions or interviews outside school. I spent time with teachers in class-rooms, in the staffroom, and in other sites within and around the school, as well as participating in school activities such as concerts, fairs, trips and parents' meetings. I took field notes during observations. I also taped semi-structured interviews with all the teachers at Hillview, some on several occasions, and about three-quarters of those at Rosemont. I continued occasional visits and regular staff meeting attendance at Hillview until December 1990, when I moved to Canada.

Among other themes emerging from the data was 'lives and careers'. My analysis suggests that career plans are provisional and changeable, especially but not exclusively for the women. Most teachers in my study believed that men in primary schools have a career advantage, but it is taken more as a fact of life than a call to feminist protest. The career structure for women is actually more complicated than the outline I gave earlier, for there is a shadowy world of part-time posts and temporary contracts, most of which are held by women. People often look back and feel that they have made mistakes in their career decisions, but most of those 'mistakes' seemed sensible at the time. Careers are influenced by family stage and the work needs of teachers' spouses, as well as by unexpected life events. They are also strongly shaped by the school experience itself. I now turn to the results of my study, in three sections: career plans, women's place in teaching, and lives outside school.

Career plans

Expectations

Teachers planned careers, but the plans were provisional. Several responded to my questions about intentions 10 years hence with humour: 'sunning myself on a lovely beach somewhere', 'haven't got a clue', 'running a charter yacht business in the Caribbean'. Some wanted incentive allowances or deputy head-ships or to change schools. The two deputies and a few others hoped for headships. Dennis Bryan, the deputy head at Hillview, expected to head two or three schools in the next 10 years, then do something else, perhaps becoming an adviser: 'I'd hate to think I'd still be a teacher in 20 years' time, when I'm 50', he said.

Reservations and alterations

Even conventionally ambitious teachers tended to express reservations about the negative consequences promotion might bring. Alison Holly, the deputy head at Rosemont, hoped to become head of a middle-sized primary school. But she added:

> Don't get the idea I'm so dedicated I would want to go on to the last day. I enjoy the job; I find a lot of frustrations about the job; it's very stressful at times; and I think for that reason, I genuinely think I ought to retire early.

Others had altered their ambitions according to circumstances such as child-birth or lack of perceived encouragement for their aspirations. Some reacted to the 1988 Education Reform Act and its intensification of their workload with thoughts about leaving teaching entirely.

Accidents

Another major source of hesitation was what I came to think of as simply 'life's unpredictability' or 'accidents'. During 1987–90 at Hillview, to my knowledge, among the teachers and general assistants two children were born (with two maternity leaves), there was one ectopic pregnancy and three miscarriages, one husband's death and another's heart attack, a marital separation, and several deaths of parents and grandparents. As well as these serious life events, there was a stream of 'everyday' illnesses, injuries, car breakdowns, house moves, problems with children, and so forth. Three long-serving teachers left the school for promotions elsewhere. Part-time or fixed-contract staff moved on more frequently. Teachers went on courses or sabbaticals.

While there were generally sufficient core staff to provide stability, there were times when this stability could easily have been threatened by absences and leaves. Sometimes many of these events coincided, causing unanticipated consequences. Such fluctuations could provide valuable experience for individual teachers, however. For example, when Liz Clarke, Hillview's head teacher, had a term's secondment, Dennis Bryan acted as head teacher for a term, and Helen Davies as deputy. Later, Dennis's foreign exchange allowed Debbie Stevens to become acting deputy head. Kristen King, who started out as a part-time teacher, moved into full-time teaching and during the unsettled time described above was able to emerge as a strong teacher and a 'rising star', 'manning' the office in a few cases when all the senior staff were away.[6]

Re-entry

Teachers' past careers also carried themes of accident and unpredictability. This was especially true for the older teachers. Several had moved around the country or abroad with their husbands, or had been in and out of teaching but with a basic commitment to the occupation, much like Biklen's (1985) puzzling interviewees who described their discontinuous careers in terms of 'always working'.

Re-entry after starting a family provided complex stories. Marjorie Howard explained in a lengthy interview how she had started out in secondary teaching, later moved into junior school teaching, stopped when her children were born, then came back first into supply teaching, then part-time teaching and eventually a full timetable. During her whole career, she had never had an interview – it was always a telephone call, a chance meeting in the village, someone who knew someone:

> Anna was born in December 1969. I never actually expected to go back to teaching, I don't know why, it just never occurred to me then. I had this idyllic thing that I would be like my mother, stay home and bring up my children, spend all my time with them. That's what people did, and that's what I thought I would be doing . . . Then after a couple of years,

there was a knock on my back door one day. I was playing in the kitchen with the girls and it was the headmistress of St Hubert's, Sister Teresa, at the door and she said could I come up quickly: Mrs Brown, a teacher of the second year infant class had bent over the bath rinsing out her tights and couldn't get up, she'd slipped a disc or something. 'I'm desperate, she can't come in, she's in Valleyton, and she's bent double . . .', and I said, 'Well, look, I've got to bring the girls, because I've got the children here, I can't just leave them . . .'. So I gathered up the girls, and I just managed . . .

She did a fortnight's supply work then, after which she would be telephoned for 'odd bits of supply', and later, when a teacher left suddenly, she taught a junior school class for the year at St Hubert's. Then there were falling rolls and a lot of publicity about teachers being unemployed and numbers dropping in the schools. Marjorie concluded that she wouldn't work again:

Then the 'phone rang, and it was Mrs Temple who was the head of Hillview. [This statement is followed by a lengthy explanation of how Mrs Temple knew someone who knew Marjorie.] 'You don't know me, but I know you; you were at Lilymead. Can you come and do three days a week for me?' I said, 'Nope, I can't drive to Wesley, I only ever work in Bayview'. 'Of course you can work in Wesley'. She wouldn't take no for an answer, she just would not.

Marjorie explained how her husband showed her how to drive to Wesley, and how she insisted on doing only 2 days, later 3 days, a week. A few years later, Mrs Clarke replaced Mrs Temple as head teacher and talked Marjorie into 'going into the infants'. She also asked Marjorie to do it full-time. Marjorie resisted and then agreed to a compromise, that she would do 4 days but plan the fifth; however, Mrs Clarke soon convinced her to teach all 5 days.

Job changes

Job changes sometimes arose through 'accidents' such as school closures or reorganizations, or even a chance remark. Alison's career illustrates some common themes. At the time of my research, she had been teaching for 18 years, was single, and was deputy head at Rosemont. She enjoyed her first school, but its rural location created travel problems. When the school was reorganized, after 2 years, she took the opportunity to leave and applied to schools nearer home. She stayed in her second school about 10 years, where she became a scale 3 (later equivalent to incentive 'B') responsible for 'PE and girls' games, country dancing, senior member of staff, general dogsbody, country dancing club and display at summer fête'. When someone left, Alison shifted away from this pot-pourri of responsibilities and took on mathematics and computers. After a few years she began to feel unhappy. She explained:

I just found it difficult to keep my head above water at doing the jobs I was expected to do, and I wasn't totally happy at the way I was allowed to handle it, and then it was almost a series of events which caused me to move on and further myself again . . . Other people started to say, 'Look,

Alison, you're not so happy, you've spent long enough here, why don't you go for deputy headships', and I began to think, yes, why am I not moving on? So I started applying for deputy headships, but I didn't get shortlisted, you don't if you're down in Moresborough and not known in Wesley. I felt very depressed, couldn't see if I was going anywhere, was fed up with Moresborough, decided to physically move out, recognized things weren't right for me.

Then, 'suddenly it all went click'. Her subsequent move she described as 'a fluke, really'. Her deputy head told her about a mathematics advisory post, and by coincidence she was at an event that night that the local education authority senior adviser for mathematics also attended. She explained she'd been ill and hadn't seen the advertisement in time to make the deadline; was it, she asked, worth applying? 'He looked about to say "No", but changed it to "Yes", if I got it in right away', she said. The advisory job lasted several years and gave her the experience to secure a deputy headship, as well as renewed enthusiasm for her work.

Alison's story, like Marjorie's, illustrates how career plans and job moves are shaped by chance occurrences and interpersonal contacts, rather than simply being outcomes of either individual decisions or structural forces. An additional factor, which operates across structural, individual and 'middle' levels, is gender. The next section takes up this theme.

Women's place in teaching

Disadvantage

Teachers were asked in interviews if they thought there were any particular advantages in being male or female teachers in primary schools. Most stated that men had a career advantage. Several had concluded that the crux of the problem was the scarcity of men and the surfeit of women. Every school wanted some men, so men got preferential treatment in hiring and promotion.

Teachers thought that appointing committees, especially the parents and school governors on them, were working from stereotyped ideas such as women inevitably leaving to have children or not having the strength or strictness to keep the school in order. Some teachers had been to look at schools or attended job interviews where 'it was quite clear they wanted a man'. They, or their friends, were asked questions such as how they would manage when their own children were ill.

In their interviews with me, a few teachers broadened the definition of disadvantage. George Middleton at Rosemont thought a man might be at a disadvantage if 'for promotion reasons' he ended up isolated in a staffroom composed of older women teachers. Alison Holly pointed out that a woman in a mixed-sex staffroom finds it difficult to protest about sexist banter without being labelled aggressive and becoming disliked (see also Cunnison 1989). Both Alison and Helen Davies at Hillview believed that women had to work harder than men for equivalent rewards.

Marginality

Women who had children were thought to experience further disadvantages. Either they carried on, with only a short break for maternity leave, or they were faced with returning to a lower-status, often marginal, position. Grant's (1989: 44) review of studies of women teachers' careers identified the 'career break' as particularly deleterious to women's chances of career advancement in a system where 'promotion is tied to age-related norms'. Alison, who herself had not had a career break, offered her observations on the fate of women who dropped out to look after children:

> They come back into teaching having been deputy heads, having even been heads, scale postholders, and they have to go back to the beginning and they're often derided. And feared, because they used to be something high up, and in fact they often don't get jobs for a long time and have to go through supply and fixed-term contracts, and it's hell for them.

Nias (1989) discusses the sources of satisfaction and dissatisfaction for the primary teachers she interviewed. Those who were temporary, supply or part-time were particularly likely to express 'disappointment, resentment or frustration' (p.127). Chessum's (1989) interviewees voiced similar sentiments, one terming herself a 'part-time nobody'.

Certainly, such teachers provide flexibility for the *schools*. For the teachers there could also be advantages. Marjorie said, looking back, 'It suited me beautifully, doing part-time, with two children and a home to run'. Yet frustration and insecurity were evident, too. Helen Davies explained how difficult supply teaching is when you don't know where the staffroom, the lavatory and the office are. The children are hard to control and you have nowhere to keep your resources and records. Fixed-term contract teachers were by definition only temporary. Part-time teachers were subject to sudden changes in routine.

Delegation of (what were often inadequate) budgets to individual schools, one of the features of the 1988 legislation, was beginning to threaten all the 'marginal' teachers. It is important to realize these teachers are nearly always *women*. The problem is not only a lack of job security. These teachers, like the others, had high standards. It was not unusual to hear a remark that a part-time teacher was trying to do a full job in half the time. It is not surprising if they feel, as Nias (1989) suggests, that there is a discrepancy between their desired self-images as teachers who should work hard and make a difference, and the reality of limited relationships and smaller accomplishments imposed by their position.

Fatalism or feminism?

Interview questions and staffroom conversations suggested that teachers believe that men have an advantage in promotions, and the statistics presented earlier also point towards this conclusion. Moreover, it is mostly women who inhabit the world of temporary and part-time positions. What was the response to such evident inequity? Although I have quoted from interviews that showed an awareness of sex discrimination, the topic came up only rarely in staffroom discussions and any anger was fairly muted. The stance was more fatalistic than feminist. 'Discrimination' and very occasionally 'sexism' were part of the explanatory framework, but never 'patriarchy' or 'oppression'. People did not self-identify as feminists in any informal conversations recorded in my field notes.

There were even a few examples in my research where teachers (tacitly) supported the sexual *status quo*. No-one, except perhaps Helen Davies, who was trying hard to secure a deputy headship herself at the time, seemed to object to the understanding that the new deputy at Hillview should be male, as the rest of the staff were female. The appointment of a new head teacher at Rosemont brought out certain contradictions. One woman and three men were being interviewed for the post. The teachers, who in other contexts favoured equal opportunities, by and large reacted very negatively, almost on sight, to 'The Woman', as she was termed, objecting to her demeanour: 'We've all crossed her off our lists', Rosemary Walker said.

It was unlikely that the teachers would adopt an overtly feminist perspective to explain their own career patterns, for several reasons. One is probably the marginality of feminism in Britain, which means teachers may lack access to ideas that would give them an alternative framework for their experiences (Middleton 1989). Another reason is the reality of their competing domestic commitments. In interviews, several teachers said that women were less likely than men to seek promotion because of their dual role:

Question: Why do you think there are relatively few women primary heads?

Helen Davies: Well, either because they've opted for their families and think that they shouldn't have a career, either they think or they've been told that it doesn't go hand in hand, and the pressures of life are so much that you can only do one or the other.

Debbie Stevens: I don't know; it's probably the same sort of reasons that most of the cabinet ministers are men and most of the everything else . . . it's the same thing, isn't it. I think a lot of women probably take time out to have families, people like Sheila, who were very ambitious before they had children, and have taken the time out and now feel that they've jumped back so many years.

Rosalind Phillips: Often they are trying to do two things, aren't they, they are trying to hold down family responsibilities and do their work on a par with their male colleagues.

It was difficult to feel discriminated against, as Cogger (1985) also found in a study of Welsh teachers, when the *choice* to have a family is believed to be the cause of career blockage.

Moreover, as Table 1 showed earlier, there *are* significant numbers of women in primary headships, even if they are under-represented. People tended to look at their schools and their own experience (the 'middle ground') for guides, not to national statistics or feminist literature.

Question: Do you think there's any particular advantage or disadvantage in being a woman in primary teaching?

Rosemary Walker: I used to think it was easier for a male to get a promotion but I don't think that's so now. I'd have said it was fair, at the moment, it's become that way . . . I was expecting a man to be appointed here for science, because I thought, well, we're losing a man, but in fact he's been replaced by a female, and Alison replaced a male, so my experience is that it's fair at the moment.

'Mistakes'

This tendency to look at one's own experience rather than analyse structural constraints led teachers, especially women, to highlight 'mistakes' they had made in the past. 'Staying too long' in a school was a typical 'mistake'. Alison felt she had done this, as we saw, as did Helen, who had great difficulty securing a deputy headship elsewhere because she had spent her whole career, 19 years, at Hillview. During that time, she had worked under five different head teachers and seen many other changes at the school. She had become strong and influential, becoming the head's deputy in all but name: 'Helen is the school', Liz Clarke told me. But her repeated efforts to move into a deputy headship were thwarted by the convention that one's experience had to be gained in more than one school.

Rosemary Walker provides another example. She was highly frustrated at not getting an incentive allowance or a major curriculum responsibility at Rosemont, although she worked extremely hard. She organized all the educational visits for the school. She attended many in-service courses. She was active and visible in extra-curricular activities with the children. Her teaching was relatively traditional in style but very creative. One half-term her room became a ship, for example, in both decor and linked educational activities. A parent said to me that she was the best teacher her child ever had.

But when the incentive allowances were made available by someone leaving or an extra allocation to the school, they were often used to attract new, well-qualified staff, rather than rewarding more of the teachers already there. Although Rosemary recognized certain decisions taken by the head teacher had not been helpful to her, she also looked back with regret at some of her own actions. She had moved schools and counties several times, shifted from secondary to primary teaching, taught abroad and had periods doing work outside teaching. She told me:

> I would like to have done things in a different way. I haven't exactly tried to plan it; I should have started a long time ago. I left it too late. No, I'd like to go back to college again, I'd do far more courses at a younger age . . . be a head.

Rosemary's story illustrates the tension between individual and structural explanations, as well as the importance of workplace experiences for teachers' careers. We all want to be active shapers of our destiny, and this requires acceptance of our wrong as well as our right decisions. What is difficult to hold onto is that strength and sense of possibility without engaging in self-blame for conditions beyond our control.

Lives outside school

School goes home

School follows teachers everywhere. Nearly all the teachers said that they thought about school while at home, although only rarely did they think about home at school. If things were going wrong or they were in crisis situations, they might be 'in tears at home', or 'doing action replays in my head'. Even in normal circumstances, as Hillview's Debbie Stevens put it, 'It's always there'.

The double shift

The men tended to be family-oriented and spoke of playing with and looking after their children. But it was the women who worked a double shift, juggling domestic work and teaching commitments with the finely honed skills of circus performers. Most of the women teachers were in relatively traditional domestic roles. Several were adept at domestic arts such as sewing and baking, and their efforts enriched the school productions and staff get-togethers.

Women teachers generally felt they had support from their husbands. Marjorie explained that when there were concerts or school events, 'all our relatives come'. 'Fred will build anything I need for school. Mike the same for Helen', she added. A husband's support might be practical, financial, or moral, but it was less often domestic. Like many people, Debbie's husband didn't comprehend the difficulty of the teacher's job:

> I do think Jack underestimates how tiring teaching is. The zoo visits that we went on, I'd gone on two like you had, and I came home one night and it was about half past seven, eight o'clock, and Jack pulled up and I was just absolutely worn out. I mean I was lying on the settee and Jack said, 'What's there to eat', or something, and I said, 'I just can't move. I'm going to lie here and I'm going to go to bed in a minute'. And he said, 'But you've only been to the zoo for a couple of days'. I mean it's that sort of not understanding the real tiredness that you can get. I mean I'm sure he thinks it's an exaggeration when I see him and say, 'Oh, I just can't move to go up to bed, I'm that tired'.

Faced with demands from all directions, teachers devised strategies for being economical with their time. Many mentioned that they came in early in the morning, worked through much of their lunchtime and sometimes after school too. Some preferred this routine in order to keep some separation between work and home. Most, however, said they took school work home, some every night, and the additional demands of recent legislation were clearly increasing the pressure.[7] Others cut down on leisure activities or confined them to holidays. Several told me that they were not now active in pursuits (e.g. choir singing) they had enjoyed in the past. All of the four men interviewed referred to sports or hobbies that took them away from their families at weekends. Two mentioned some consequent feelings of guilt. Only women mentioned caring for relatives other than children or doing housework.

Question: What do you tend to do in your non-teaching time?

Helen Davies: At home? The washing, and the ironing, and the cleaning, and the cooking . . . [laughs]

The triple shift

Women teachers with young children had to be even more skilful at juggling, for they had a triple shift, namely, work, home and child-care responsibilities.[8] At Hillview, two teachers had live-in nannies; others worked part-time and made complicated arrangements with child-minders, relatives, play groups, nurseries, and eventually, when the children were old enough, schools. Teacher-mothers had to have plenty of stamina.

For some teachers, having young children did not appear to have sapped energies and ambitions so much as encouraging a kind of flexible, even fatalistic, outlook. In a staffroom conversation, Rosalind Phillips told Debbie Stevens and myself that she had held a management position in a secondary school before her children were born. 'I'll never get there again', she commented, 'my age is against me'. But she doesn't mind, she said: she's religious, and she believes things will work out. Debbie agreed, saying that when she had Katy and her husband moved jobs to Wesley, she thought she'd never be working again – but here she was.[9]

Conclusion

Teachers' perceptions and interpretations are clearly a major component of any approach to career – the 'subjective career' as it has been called. These interpretations sometimes seemed wrong to me – for example, Rosemary's assessment of no discrimination against women clearly clashed with the accounts presented by other teachers – but the important point is that such assessments have *consequences*. Irony pervades the lives of teachers. They have to believe that they have some power to shape their own destinies; otherwise, schools would grind to a halt under the weight of demoralized teachers. They cannot afford a full-blown feminist analysis, with its risk of inducing discontent and anger, in the context of a society where feminism is regarded as on the fanatical fringe. They have to live with patent inequities of preferment for men in promotions and, in many cases, domestic arrangements that give them double or triple shifts. At the same time, their ideologies induce constant, committed, dedicated hard work. As Nias (1989: 197) says, 'Primary teaching is an occupation which requires the ability to live with, and handle constructively, a multitude of dilemmas, tensions, contradictions, uncertainties, and paradoxes'.

It could be argued that women primary school teachers are contributing to the reproduction of gender inequality by their acceptance, unwilling as it may be, of the inequalities in their own lives. My teachers weren't overtly fighting the *status quo* like those studied by Weiler (1988) or Middleton (1989). A forcible feminism would have been counterproductive in the circumstances, as Alison's remark about the price to be exacted from someone who protests about sexist comments in the staffroom testifies. A 'strategic fatalism' (Cogger 1985: 64) seemed much better adapted to the realities of their lives. They remake definitions of careers and commitments to suit their preferences and their possibilities, strategizing for security and maximum flexibility within the particular 'patriarchal bargain' (Kandiyoti 1988) offered by their circumstances.

In the process of perceiving and interpreting, the teachers are guided by their immediate experiences in the workplace culture of the school. Much has been made in the literature of the isolation experienced by teachers in the classroom. These generalizations do not seem to apply as well to Britain as to North America (Acker 1991), although there is considerable variation from school to school. Nias *et al.* (1989) were able to identify what they called 'collaborative cultures', and the term could apply to my research schools, too. Basically, a collaborative culture is one where teachers work closely together, in a mutually caring community.

The culture not only provided sustenance, but also a framework for creation and sharing of views and experiences (Metz 1989; Acker 1990c). When someone went to look at another school, or for an interview, the other teachers got detailed feedback. The teachers could see by looking around them how careers would be affected by time out for child-rearing or what advantages men had. Debbie, in working out at what ages she might expect promotions, said she was just going by what she saw other people doing. Gillian Evans at Rosemont said she had not been promotion-minded but now began to feel 'irritated', observing others less competent than herself rising in the system. On the other hand, her observations of what extra work was expected from the deputy head also confirmed her suspicions that as a single parent she would be unable to put in that amount of time.

So we have individuals making tentative plans and judgements, in the context not only of their family situations and wider social constraints, but guided by experiences and observations in the school. The plans could never be firm, as life presented too many upsets and unexpected chances. It is an oversimplified view of reality to regard teachers' careers as the unproblematic product of either individual choices or societal constraints. Currently popular post-structuralist approaches teach us to be suspicious of arguments that give any concept, career included, an essential core. My empirical data support such a view by illustrating how careers are provisional, kaleidoscopic constructions, made up of everyday events and interchanges, part of 'the search for meaning in a world of contradictory information' (Lather 1991: 146). But it is not sufficient to see the search solely as an individual enterprise. Meaning is negotiated in the culture of the workplace and is constrained by the patriarchal and other bargains available in the society at large.

Notes

1. I am grateful to the head teachers and teachers at 'Hillview' and 'Rosemont', without whose cooperation and support this study could not have been conducted. Thanks are also due to university colleagues who shared with me their knowledge about primary school education, especially Tim Hill and Marilyn Osborn.

2. Schools have governing bodies, made up of appointees of the local education authority (who reflect the political composition of local government) and representatives of parents and teachers. If a school is affiliated with a church, as many are, the church ('voluntary body') also appoints governors. Schools not so affiliated will make up numbers by bringing in individuals from the community, such as local businessmen. The head teacher may either be a governor or attend *ex officio*. Hillview, one of the schools in this study, with about 200 children, had 11 governors. During the 1980s and early 1990s, school governors were given increased responsibilities by the Conservative Government, including staffing, finance, overseeing the implementation of the National Curriculum, publishing information for parents about the school, and developing a policy on sex education (Statham and Mackinnon 1989).

3. The statistics in this chapter have been updated from the original article, published in 1992.

4. The proportions of teachers receiving incentive allowances grew during the time the system operated, although the gap between primary and secondary school teachers remained. In 1992, 43 per cent of primary school teachers and 69 per cent of secondary school teachers held allowances (School Teachers' Review Body 1993: 65). In 1993, it was announced that the system would be replaced by an alternative that abolished incentive allowances and instead gave points for a number of possible achievements and responsibilities on a common scale. Some points are mandatory, and some discretionary, their award to be determined by the school governors.

5. In the United States, women held 28.8 per cent of elementary school and 11.6 per cent of secondary school principalships in 1988 (Sadker *et al.* 1991). In Canada, Rees (1990), using data collected from 12 provinces and territories, reported women's percentage of principalships ranging from 15 to 38 per cent for elementary schools and 0 to 12 per cent for secondary schools. The provinces used different dates and reporting conventions, making comparisons and summary figures difficult.

6. Mrs Clarke, the head teacher of Hillview, made great efforts to give teachers experiences that would help their career development. I have analysed her role elsewhere (Acker 1990a, 1994). Kristen King became deputy head of another primary school in 1993.

7. It is interesting to contrast this picture with the writings about female teachers showing inadequate commitment to their work that I discussed in Chapter 5.

8. My students at OISE pointed out to me that teachers like themselves, enrolled in part-time higher degree courses in the evenings, had a 'quadruple shift'.

9. This conversation took place in spring 1987. Subsequently, Rosalind Phillips completed an MEd, moved into a full-time job in another school, and in July 1991 was appointed deputy head at a third primary school. In 1992, Dennis Bryan moved to a headship in another school and Debbie Stevens became deputy head at Hillview.

PART 3

Women Academics

8 Women, the Other Academics

Under the impetus of the women's movement, numerous American books and articles have pondered the plight of the woman professional (e.g. Theodore 1971; Rossi and Calderwood 1973; Abramson 1975). What of her British counterpart? Some will consider her part of a privileged elite, in a labour market where most women work physically harder, under more supervision, for less money. Yet in comparison with male colleagues, she emerges with second-class status. Whether envied or pitied, the woman professional worker occupies a position potentially of interest to sociologists.[1]

If there is anywhere that women professionals should be successful, it is in the universities. We think of teaching as a women's forte and universities as meritocratic institutions. Yet there is ample evidence that career patterns of women university teachers differ from those of men. Women are a minority (12 per cent in the late 1970s) among full-time teachers and researchers in UK universities and better represented in lower than higher ranks (Department of Education and Science 1979).[2] A 1969 survey of British academics reported that women university teachers were less well paid than men, that they were less likely to hold doctorates (except in social and applied sciences), that they published less (except in social sciences), and that they were concentrated in humanities and nearly absent in applied sciences. Women, especially older ones, were also less likely than men to be married or have children (Williams *et al.* 1974).

Most published works on British women academics focus on discrimination in pay and promotion. My purpose here differs. I shall instead consider three of the more subtle problems that any working woman but especially the woman professional faces, in varying form and degree according to the nature of her work and her family circumstances. None is so dramatic as overt discrimination; rather, they are embedded in everyday life. The first of these problems involves conflicting demands of family and career; the second, relative powerlessness of minorities; the third, male domination of knowledge and practice. I shall examine each, focusing on university teaching as an occupation where all three are encountered. Little research has been done on the everyday experiences of women academics, so this account is necessarily speculative. I draw upon British and American studies on professional and executive women, as well as personal experience as a woman academic in a British university.

Greedy institutions

The first problem is coordinating, over time, the demands of two 'greedy institutions' (Coser 1974): the work setting and the family. This dilemma arises whenever the job is a career; that is, it requires continuous commitment, spilling over into otherwise leisure time. 'Greedy institutions' is Lewis Coser's (1974) term for those organizations and groups that demand total, undivided loyalty, such as the church for priests, Utopian communities for members, the family for (some?) housewives. They differ from 'total institutions' in that they do not necessarily impose physical boundaries. Despite the eight major books listed as 'also by the author', Coser (1974) fails to mention the greediness of universities as workplaces, but the concept is easily extended.

Meeting demands of home and work is problematic for both women and men trying to have egalitarian partnerships. Many professional women no longer think in terms of a choice between family and career but expect themselves to cope with both. Sociologists, rather dismissively, used to call the problems that arose 'role conflict'. A more adequate conceptualization suggests that the difficulty lies in the timing of family and career cycles (Fogarty *et al.* 1971; Hochschild 1975). Even if a woman postpones having children until her higher education is complete, the arrival of young children will still coincide with the age and career stage when she is expected to make an impact on the field. Youth and performance are especially associated in the sciences, less so in the humanities, but equally linked for all fields in the sense that when good jobs are scarce and competition is fierce, performance is more convincing than potential. Young children are time-, energy- and emotion-consuming. Nor is housework a trivial task. Rowbotham (1973) points to the process whereby setting one's own standards for housework ('autonomy') results in compulsive attempts to increase self-worth by repeatedly upgrading performance targets. Most of the housewives in Oakley's (1974: 92) study put in between 70 and 89 hours a week on housework; the one with a full-time job cut back to 48 hours.

Like housework, academic work is never really 'done'. Making an impact on the field involves, for all but the most talented, considerable time and effort. In one survey, British academics claimed to work a 50-hour week (Committee of Vice-Chancellors and Principals 1972), and there are indications that American academics, haunted by pressures to publish or perish, put in more hours still. To a large extent, academic success rests on research and publishing 'productivity', measured against age. Productivity is most enhanced when someone else does all the support work (laundry, dinners), avoids making competing demands, and types, edits and looks up references, as so many book prefaces remind us. Here is an example from Holmstrom's interview study of traditional and two-career professional families:

> In one traditional couple, for example, the wife followed the husband as he moved from job to job. She did all the housekeeping tasks herself. She also managed the family's money and did the yard work. She was responsible for buying the car and having it serviced; she did all the driving . . . while he frequently worked all weekend . . . She said her husband was used to quite a bit of service and used to having her adjust to his hours. She said she had done everything she could to make things easy for him so he would have all the time available for his work.
>
> (Holmstrom 1973: 82)

Of course productivity, even merit, is no guarantee of success, but a (say) 60-hour man with a 70-hour housewife to back him up is off to a running start compared with everyone else. Single persons are disadvantaged, persons with family responsibilities even more so, if the 'two-person career' (Papanek 1973) sets the norm.

Even if publishing does not suffer from competition with family needs, something else might. An American study of faculty in high-quality universities found married women in lower ranks than other academics, even after controlling for publishing productivity (Freeman 1977). Discrimination is one obvious explanation, but one might also suggest that such women, while keeping up with family, teaching and research, have less time and energy left for committee work and image-enhancing departmental activities.

There are a number of possible responses to overload. Some may regard it as a challenge and redouble their scholarly efforts, while for others feelings of inadequacy result in a lowering of aspirations. Some come to question the worth of a reward system that penalizes anyone who lacks traditional wifely services and support. However, in a tight job market, when subtle distinctions must be made among numerous qualified candidates, there is little chance that institutions of higher education will reject productivity as a key criterion for hiring and promotion.

Negotiating from weakness

The second problem is the management of colleague relations while occupying minority or token status in a work setting. This dilemma is most obvious for women in clearly male-dominated occupations. Yet even the 'women's professions' are so often administered by men that successful women in these fields will at times be a minority among men.

In attempting to develop a theory that speaks to the importance of relative numbers − 'the dramas of the many and the few in the organization' − Kanter (1977: 208–209) distinguishes between uniform, skewed, tilted and balanced groups. All people in *uniform* groups are of the same social category. In *skewed* groups, 'dominants' and 'tokens' appear, in ratios from 99:1 to about 85:15.

The few, the tokens (who may be solos, if only one is present), 'are often treated as representatives of their category, as symbols rather than individuals'. In *tilted* groups, dominants become 'majorities' and tokens 'minorities'. Minorities are more powerful than tokens, as they can form coalitions, influence group culture, and be seen as individuals as well as representatives of a social type. Finally, when the ratios range from about 60:40 to 50:50, the group is *balanced*. Using Kanter's terminology, women university teachers, comprising 12 per cent of the profession, are typically 'tokens' in skewed, male-dominated colleague groups. The extent to which this is the case will vary by subject field.

Being the only woman, or one of a small minority of women in a university department, makes one paradoxically both invisible and extra-visible. Invisibility may be a consequence of a tendency for dominants to express solidarity in reaction against the presence of an outsider (Kanter 1977). At one extreme, women may be overtly excluded from the informal networks (Epstein 1970; Fogarty *et al.* 1971); on a more subtle level, they may be challenged to show a sense of humour by accepting jokes at the expense of their sex (Kanter 1977). In the university, invisibility is what one feels in a large committee meeting with many men and few women, perhaps a secretary and oneself. This is hardly the most comfortable position for speaking out to advance the cause of women. It takes a certain aggressive style even to enter the discussion. It is necessary to begin speaking at precisely the moment a previous speaker finishes and before another begins, while a number of others are trying to accomplish the same feat. A tentative, polite, soft-spoken person finds herself making a critical point after the moment has passed, if not while coffee is being served.

People expect a woman academic to show just the right degree of emotion, an impossible task if colleagues are likely to condemn both wishy-washy speakers and emotional women. Studies of conversations between women and men suggest that men complete women's sentences, interrupt without negative sanctions, and give minimal response to topics initiated by women (West and Zimmerman 1977). Smith (1975) gives several examples of ways in which women's contributions to meetings are restricted, including the practice of pausing while a woman speaks, then responding to the previous speaker or topic as if she had not spoken. A woman encountering this pause-and-continue pattern might begin to wonder if she is in fact invisible. The language of the meeting – talk of 'chaps' and 'fellows' and the ubiquitous 'he' – is unlikely to give much reassurance.

At the same time, tokens face the limelight simply because they are different. Women executives in Kanter's (1977) study were subject to gossip and scrutiny of what they wore, with whom they spoke, how they spent their leisure time. Moreover, the actions of tokens took on a symbolic significance, as their behaviour was taken to be representative of their social category, a sign of what one could expect from a woman in an executive position (Kanter 1977: 212–16).

One way to become uncomfortably visible in a university department is to become the department feminist, protesting about practices that show some degree of sexism. Examples of such practices might be the listing of male students with initials (J.A. Smith) but female students with full name plus marital status (Mrs Jane Smith),[3] or course outlines that ignore relevant gender-related issues. While a timely remark may be highly effective, it is difficult to gauge its likely impact in advance. Too much protest may result in responses to the person rather than the remark ('we were waiting for you to say something'). Hochschild (1975a) reports such reaction from university colleagues to her feminism and relates how clippings on all subjects vaguely related to women appeared on her desk, unread by the senders. The gestures were friendly, but they showed that her colleagues had not been forced to think about feminism, only about her as department feminist.

What consequences follow from this combination of visibility and invisibility? 'The token does not have to work hard to have her presence noted, but she does have to work hard to have her achievements noted' (Kanter 1977: 216). In Hennig and Jardim's (1979) study of women executives, one kind of 'hard work' for the women was trying to dress and behave so as to hit exactly the right (near-impossible) balance between 'feminine' attributes (seen as inappropriate to job requirements) and 'masculine' ones (unacceptable in women). Another kind of hard work was the attempt to demonstrate exceptional superiority at assigned tasks. But instead of receiving commensurate rewards for outstanding achievements, women executives got stuck at middle management levels. Their intense dedication meant either that they failed to note advancement opportunities or that they became so identified with the particular responsibility that no-one thought of them as candidates for promotion. A team of British researchers who studied women in selected professional and business occupations made almost exactly the same point, as well as suggesting that creativity may dissolve under such conscientiousness (Fogarty *et al.* 1971: 414–15). Hennig and Jardim (1979) also noted a strongly sex-differentiated perception of 'career', with women speaking of a career as a focus for the demonstration of competence and dedication, while men visualized it as a series of planned steps to a goal. If these findings, taken together, can be generalized to the university situation, they suggest that what is often thought of as a reluctance to seek promotion or positions of influence may not be due to personality traits or even family responsibilities but to the dynamics and dilemmas of token status, as filtered through both self-perceptions and opportunity structures.

At least there is the consolation for tokens that 'marginal men' are thought to possess special sociological insight. But another consequence of being different is less desirable. In his study of references written for university job applicants, Lionel Lewis (1975: 141) concluded:

> There are relatively clear standards among academics regarding what is acceptable or socially normal behaviour, and those who in one way or another are not prototypical are less welcome as colleagues than those who conform.

In other words, conventions of social acceptance tend to keep tokens in their (token) place.

Consciousness of women

Problem number three is understanding and confronting biases that reflect male dominance in our stock of accepted professional knowledge and practice. The sociology of knowledge suggests that what is known is a product of the historical and socio-economic position of the knower. Those who rule have the 'ruling ideas', preserving their hegemony through the ability to convince subordinates of the validity of these ideas. In a feminist version of this thesis, men impose their conceptualizations of the world on women, whose own experience is regarded as a less valid, less convincing, less scientific basis for understanding. 'Men . . . govern, administer, and manage the community', while 'women have been largely excluded from the work of producing the forms of thought and the images and symbols in which thought is expressed and ordered' (Smith 1975: 354). A problem for the woman professional, particularly the woman academic, is to identify gaps and distortions of knowledge in her field, while searching for alternative conceptualizations that confirm rather than deny the experiences and consciousness of women.

What is this experience of women that is ignored or excluded? A theme in some feminist writings is the concept of a 'women's culture': a way of looking at the world rooted in experiences women share by virtue of being women. Such experiences may be physiologically unique to women (menstruation, childbirth) or consistently assigned to women by the wider society (domestic labour, child-rearing). In studies of marriages and of organizations, some sociologists have argued that men and women in effect inhabit different worlds (Bernard 1972; Kanter 1975). Anthropologists search for the structural duality underlying the two worlds: usually a version of nature (women) versus culture (men), or domestic versus public domains (Ortner 1974; Rosaldo 1974). Bernard (1973) suggests that men live in a cash-nexus world, characterized by bonds of exchange, and women in a status one, characterized by bonds of love and duty. Berit Ås (1975) points to values such as cleanliness and conservation as typical of female culture. Smith (1974) sees women's immersion in children, cleaning, cooking and general maintenance as providing a realm of experience outside the comprehension of most males.[4]

If there is a women's culture, largely invisible to those who conventionally produce knowledge, then what we think we know about the world must be highly partial. At the simplest level, feminists over the past decade have exposed enormous gaps in prevailing knowledge about women. Such gaps stem in part from the tendency to conduct research on men only. In sociology, this has been characteristic of research on a great range of topics that come to mind: inequality, workers' lives, streetcorner groups, deviance, anti-school subcultures. Generalizations derived from research on men are suspect; not to generalize ignores half the population. These gaps are narrowing. In my particular interest area, women and education, special journal editions have appeared, conferences have been held, and texts have been published in the past few years. Yet, as of 1980, 'mainstream' sociology of education remains untransformed (see Chapter 2). Courses have been established and research initiated on women and education, or more generally on sexual divisions and society, but down the corridor somewhere, as optional extras. There is still some way to go before women's studies courses are incorporated throughout the curriculum.

Perhaps more important than the gaps in our knowledge about women are the distortions. I propose that sociology and psychology (including some feminist analyses) have created or at least reinforced what might be called a deficit model of women, analogous to the much-criticized deficit model of the working-class child.

Two related phenomena together constitute a deficit model. First, there is *blaming the victim*. In the 1960s, a popular approach in sociology and psychology of education was what Byrne *et al.* (1975) call the 'class-culture paradigm'. Trying to find explanations for the relatively poor school performance of working-class children (in Britain) or black children (in the USA), researchers shifted away from arguments based on genetics towards those based on deficient motivational dynamics of disadvantaged families. By the last few years of the decade, this paradigm, too, was being seriously questioned. In the United States, Valentine (1968: 18) attacked 'doctrines that point to presumed defects in the mentality or behaviour of disadvantaged classes then go on to explain their social position and deprivation as resulting from these internal deficiencies'. And in England, Bernstein (1972: 107) criticized compensatory education, 'because it distracts attention from the school itself and focuses upon deficiencies within the community, family and child'.

Much the same can be said of a considerable amount of academic writing, not to mention popular commentary, on women. As de Beauvoir (1949/1972: 616) said: 'Her wings are clipped, and it is found deplorable that she cannot fly'. For example, women's career aspirations, a popular topic in vocational psychology and 'sex roles' literature, have consistently been reduced to questions of value systems and personality constellations (for critiques, see Ferber and Huber 1975; Levine and Crumrine 1975). Even sophisticated sociological analyses of women and work still tend to blame the victim. Thus Kelsall *et al.* (1972), asking why all but a handful of women in their sample either taught or kept house six years after university graduation, put the major share of the blame for 'second-rate careers' on the ideological stance of the women themselves. While Fogarty and co-workers' (1971) chapter 10 could be read to suggest that employers hold remarkably stereotyped views of women's capabilities, the authors nevertheless chose to see 'women's lack of availability' (due to their life-cycles) as the 'most serious obstacle to women's promotion into top jobs' (p. 423). Another example can be found in Chapter 5 of this volume, which critiques the practice of blaming women teachers for the low status of the teaching profession.

The second facet of the deficit model of women is the *male-as-norm bias*, or in more general terms, the practice of making invidious comparisons between advantaged and disadvantaged groups so that the superiority of the advantaged group's characteristics is never questioned. The problem is seen only as explaining why the subordinate group fails to resemble the dominant group in

some way. Bernstein (1972: 108), writing about comparisons between middle-
and working-class children, says:

> We take one group of children, whom we know beforehand possess
> attributes favourable to school achievement; and a second group of chil-
> dren, whom we know beforehand lack these attributes. Then we evaluate
> one group in terms of what it *lacks* when compared with another. In this
> way research, unwittingly, underscores the notion of *deficit* and confirms
> the *status quo*.

The important point here is that social research itself, for all its pretensions, is in
large measure conducted within the 'natural attitude' (Schutz and Luckmann
1974), especially in determining what is problematic for study. We ask why
girls lack the science orientation of boys or why women fail to apply for
promotion like men, without questioning why science alienates girls or how
career structures exclude women. Nor does it occur to us to ask why boys
avoid the arts or infant school teaching, or why some men sacrifice health for
career advancement.

What consequences for women academics follow from the hidden nature of
'women's culture' and the gaps and distortions in our knowledge of women?
One problem may be coping with a sense of alienation. Smith (1974) believes
that women academics, particularly sociologists, will be caught in the contradictions of 'bifurcated consciousness', alienated through the lack of fit between
the theoretical world and the experiential one. A second problem is how to
break set. To the extent to which our thinking is culturally channelled, neither
women nor men will find it easy to move away from prevailing deficit models
and to realize that what is often taken for granted as an answer may in fact be
part of the problem.

Feminist questions

What links all three problems discussed above is the 'Otherness' of women
academics. De Beauvoir (1949/1972) argues that men have taken themselves
to represent humanity, casting women into the position of being 'the Other'.
Women are marginal to the academic enterprise, because full tribute to greedy
institutions is only feasible for persons without competing claims from other
greedy institutions; because token status results in invisibility, powerlessness
and lack of opportunity; because dominant groups deny the contributions and
distort the characteristics of subordinates.

The barriers to equality encountered by women academics have their roots
deep inside the structure of higher education, itself influenced by norms and
values of the wider society. It will not be easy to change this situation. British
women academics are so scattered around, in token positions, that their vul-
nerability is high and their political potential low. And in a contracting market,
lavish reform campaigns seem unrealistic, and individuals cannot risk their own
job chances to become martyrs. Must we then give in to the 'exaggeratedly

pessimistic view' to which Mackie (1977) argues feminist sociologists are subject?

If nothing else, women academics can ask feminist questions. Perhaps this is the area where they can ultimately have the most impact, being in the knowledge business, so to speak. Asking feminist questions opens up the possibility of radical alterations in prevailing paradigms. Examples can be given in various fields of study where such a process has begun. Literary critics have seriously challenged conventional wisdom on women writers. Anthropologists have criticized common explanations for the universality of female subordination, called attention to sexist biases in ethnographic accounts, and written illuminatingly on women in cross-cultured perspective. Health specialists have undermined (male) medical claims to expertise on childbirth and women's illnesses. Sociologists have sought the source of women's oppression in the workings of capitalism and patriarchy. Social workers, educators and the general public have been challenged to expose 'sophisticated myths' (Sharpe 1976).

All intellectuals, feminists included, have their own ways of seeing and not seeing. Some choose not to see the struggles of academic women as particularly problematic. In defending her decision to exclude discussion of academic women from her book on women and education, Eileen Byrne (1978: 17) argues that such women are 'best qualified to fight for their own equality'. In effect, she is saying that if women academics cannot fight their own battles, who can. However, we cannot expect women academics automatically to have superior insights and strategies. This chapter has been an attempt to help equip academic women for the 'fight' by revealing the conditions and cultures that threaten to constrain our careers and our creativity.

Notes

1. Before its 1980 publication in the *British Journal of Sociology of Education*, this chapter started out as a talk given to the British Sociological Association Education Study Group in 1979. Geoff Millerson, Caroline St. John Brooks, Michael Berry, Miriam David, Philip Gammage and Sara Meadows all gave helpful comments on the draft version.
2. Chapter 9 contains more recent statistics on the representation of women in academic life.
3. This example may seem rather quaint, but at the time I wrote the original version of this chapter, the university department in which I worked followed this practice of initials for male students and title with first name for female students on class lists.
4. Relational feminism, stimulated by work such as Gilligan's (1982) identification of an 'ethic of care' said to be more pronounced among women than men, emphasizes differences between the sexes and women's preferences for caring, connected, cooperative ways of thinking, teaching, learning, etc. Although such accounts successfully put women's worlds or cultures at the centre of analysis, they often sound deterministic and essentialist. They have also been criticized for failing to appreciate the many differences among women, or the similarities between women and men found in some cultures but not others (Collins 1990). Sociological writings about women's worlds generally see them as socially produced rather than responses to essential qualities of women.

9 Contradictions in Terms: Women Academics in British Universities

This chapter[1] asks two deceptively simple questions: How can we best conceptualize the situation of women academics in British universities? How can we
change it? Having spent my working life as a woman academic and sociologist
of education and gender, I have strong personal and intellectual interests in
these questions. For nineteen years I taught in a British university. My move to
Canada was in part a search for a more nourishing environment for women, for
feminists and for women's studies scholars.

There is, of course, the view that there is no real problem. Otherwise, the
'problem' can be variously located: in sex-typed socialization; family–career
conflicts; under-investment in women's education; sex discrimination and
career structures; the workings of capitalism and patriarchy. I shall discuss these
perspectives in the context of feminist theory – that is, ways of understanding
gender relations and the structural subordination of women – as theory helps to
group the 'explanations' and to extend our thinking. I shall use the familiar
divisions of liberal, socialist and radical feminism that were discussed in Chapter
3, recognizing that they are much-criticized for making artificial distinctions
which divide the women's movement (Delmar 1986); for failing to include the
full range of women's experiences, especially the experience of black women
(Carby 1982); for being country-specific (ten Dam and Volman 1991); and for
making overstated claims to be essential truths (Fraser and Nicholson 1990).
For me, these theoretical approaches are still very useful, both in describing the
dominant discourse about women academics (which, if feminist at all, is liberal-
feminist) and in pointing to ways in which our conceptualizations, arguments
and strategies might be extended by drawing upon socialist-feminist and
radical-feminist perspectives.[2]

In recent years, feminist writers have furiously debated how differences
among women can be accorded the respect and analytical importance they
deserve without destroying the integrity of the concept of 'woman' upon
which much of feminism as a political practice rests (Hirsch and Keller 1990).
Yet ways in which 'differences' among women academics are typically

construed can be rather limited. For example, differences may refer to levels of success in achieving publications or promotions (Davis and Astin 1990). Feminist work can become more sensitive to diversity when it crosses national borders, for women's position within higher education responds to particular social, cultural and economic forces (Moore 1987; see also Chapter 4, this volume). Feminism itself takes different forms in different countries (Gelb 1989; Eisenstein 1991).

I begin my discussion by summarizing some of the statistics on academics that demonstrate the differential positions typically occupied by women and men in the hierarchical structures of British universities.[3] The statistics confirm that a problem, indeed, exists. In the main body of the chapter, I examine the three major forms of feminist theory in terms of their contribution to an adequate conceptualization of the situation of women academics. I also look at some 'missing links', areas where scholarship is underdeveloped yet required for further progress on this topic. I argue that while the typical rhetoric about women's place in the university derives from liberal feminism, other theoretical approaches are necessary if we are to grasp why resistance to change is so entrenched. Designation of some theoretical approaches as providing better explanatory frameworks than others does not, however, preclude the use of political strategies derived from less satisfactory frameworks.

Documenting the differences

Among academics in Britain, women are not only a minority but are found disproportionately in lower ranks and in less secure posts. In 1991–92, women made up about 22 per cent of all full-time academics in universities (Universities Funding Council 1993). The figures can be broken into two subsets, as shown in Table 3: those faculty who teach and are expected to do research as part of their normal work (termed 'traditional academics' in Table 3) and those who do 'research only'. Women are much more likely than men to be in the second category, so much so that the 22 per cent figure becomes misleading: women constitute 32 per cent of the research-only group but

Table 3 Distribution of academic staff across ranks by sex in Great Britain, 1991–92

	Traditional academics		*Research-only*	
	Men	*Women*	*Men*	*Women*
Professor	17.4	4.4	0.9	0.3
Reader/Senior Lecturer	31.0	17.1	3.4	1.9
Lecturer	51.0	73.9	69.1	59.6
Other	0.6	4.6	26.6	38.2
Total %	100.0	100.0	100.0	100.0
Total number	25,579	5,234	12,385	5,923

Source: Universities Funding Council (1993).

only 16 per cent of those following traditional university careers. Even this figure of 16 per cent obscures subject variations. Women constitute 32 per cent of the 'traditional academics' in language, literature and area studies and 29 per cent of those in education. At the other extreme, they form 7 per cent of academics in biology, mathematics and physical science and an even smaller 4 per cent of those in engineering and technology (Universities Funding Council 1993: 82).

Most of the people in the research-only group are on contracts, which generally means that their salaries come from bodies outside the universities, such as research councils. Their job security only extends for the duration of their contract, which might be as short as 6 months. For some, a succession of contracts constitutes a career. Contract researchers are often excluded from other academic employee benefits such as maternity leave and are not always well integrated into departmental life. The contract research sector, which now contains over a third of full-time academics, is the growth area in British universities, up from around 5000 in 1972 to 14,000 in the late 1980s (Rees 1989; Universities Funding Council 1993).

Do women in the traditional career lines fare any better? As I explained in Chapter 4, the lectureship is the so-called career grade in British universities. The next level includes readerships and senior lectureships, different from one another on promotion criteria but equivalent on salary scale. Only a small proportion of British academics achieve the rank of professor. There are rarely more than one or two in a department and apart from a small number of 'personal chairs', more can be hired only when a position is vacant. The system does not favour women. Among men, 17 per cent are professors and 31 per cent readers or senior lecturers; among women, 4 per cent are professors and 17 per cent readers or senior lecturers.

Figures such as those shown in Table 3 tell us what proportion of each sex reaches a given academic rank. They give us an indication of career chances for each sex. Our other option is to show the relative proportions of each rank that are held by women and men. The two options give us different information. If women are severely under-represented in the academic population as a whole, then even if most were to rise to the top level, they would remain a small proportion of that grade.

Table 4   Representation of women and men in each rank in Great Britain, 1991–92

	Professor	Reader/ Senior lecturer	Lecturer	Other
Men	95.4	90.5	78.4	41.8
Women	4.6	9.5	21.6	58.2
Total %	100.0	100.0	100.0	100.0
Total number	5,035	9,443	17,924	411

Source: Universities Funding Council (1993).
Note: 'Research-only' staff are not included.

Table 4 shows the figures arranged accordingly. It gives us an idea of what the outside world sees. Nearly all professors in Britain are men; men also hold the vast majority of other senior positions. The impact of the imbalance on British academic life is extreme, especially when combined with tendencies towards hierarchy and elitism still found within many of the universities. Professors in British universities are the people who head departments, represent the university to the government, serve on working parties, act as external examiners, make hiring and promotion decisions. In many universities, the numbers of women professors can literally be counted on the fingers of one hand, while the men number in the hundreds. When I left my British university post, in December 1990, only two women there were professors. The number has since increased to six.

Explanations and strategies

What needs to be explained is why we find women academics so relatively disadvantaged and men so firmly in control – why we have a man-centred university (Rich 1979) with some women in it. The literature on academic women in Britain is rather sparse, probably reflecting a tendency to consider them members of an elite rather than a disadvantaged group worthy of feminist concern (Acker 1984b). Interested readers tend to rely on articles in *The Higher* (formerly the *Times Higher Education Supplement*) and the very useful *AUT Women*, a newsletter supplement published by the Association of University Teachers.

To answer the question posed here, we have to go beyond works specifically on women academics and extrapolate from feminist theory. The next sections review the three main strands of feminist theory in terms of their potential for explaining the unequal position of women academics in British universities.

Liberal feminism

Most accounts of women in higher education draw at least loosely on liberal-feminist perspectives. The aim of liberal feminism is to alter women's status and opportunities within the existing economic and political frameworks. It concentrates on removing barriers that prevent girls and women from attaining their full potential. Key concepts include equal opportunities, sex stereotyping, socialization, role conflict and sex discrimination (see Chapter 3).

In Britain, the liberal-feminist discourse of 'equal opportunities' is the most widely acceptable analysis (Acker 1986; Weiner 1986), despite a number of limitations. With respect to higher education, there are several strands. Liberal feminists consider the impact of socialization, conflicting roles, inadequate social investment in women's education, and sex discrimination. Strategies that follow from these arguments tend to depend on individuals changing their practices, in response to better information or appeals to fairness. The extent to which observed patterns are rooted in structures resistant to change is de-emphasized.

Socialization

A common explanation for women's 'failure' to achieve high status places responsibility on parents, schools and other socialization agencies which have encouraged
women from early childhood to develop a constellation of characteristics not easily
compatible with achievement, especially in certain traditionally male fields.
Women are said to display lack of confidence, low aspirations and ambition,
concern with people and nurturing, need for approval, desires for dependency,
motives to avoid success. Feminist researchers have moved away from simplistic
versions of such conceptualizations, recognizing their potential, as noted in Chapter 8, for 'blaming the victim' and taking the 'male as norm'.

Conflicting roles

A similar argument adduces that women put family first ('domestic responsibilities') and thus are unable to compete effectively. In this view, they are held
back by overload and time problems; by guilt; by the demands of a husband's
career; by anticipation of the demands of a husband's career; and by their
consequent inability to plan a career for themselves that is compatible with the
age norms of high-status occupations. It is necessary to look carefully at these
arguments. Many studies report that women academics are less likely than male
colleagues to be married or have children, although the gap may be culturally
and historically variable (Sutherland 1985). Researchers in various countries
have tried to calculate the effects of marriage or parenthood on publishing
productivity, with contradictory results (Lie 1990).

The many variables interacting here – age, experience, subject, ages of
children, rank and others – make it difficult to come to any firm conclusions.
Accounts which invoke family–career role conflict as an explanation too often
simply blame the victim for not achieving a successful resolution of competing
commitments or suggest that women are powerless in the face of social expectations. These are inadequate conceptualizations. Yet marriage and parenthood
are facts of women's (and men's) lives.

A more convincing approach considers the role of marriage and parenthood
in conjunction with institutional factors that make these statuses more or less
compatible with academic life. For example, a report from Cambridge University (Spurling 1990) finds that women academics experience strains caused by
conflicts between family and work. These strains are analysed, however, in an
institutional context specific to Cambridge University and King's College, a
formerly all-male constituent college within it. The university offers no part-
time posts and no assistance with child care, holds meetings in the late after-
noon or evening, and operates age restrictions affecting access to jobs or funding for those whose careers have been interrupted.

Investment in 'womanpower'

Another view of the problem is that society fails to invest sufficiently in
'womanpower'. This approach can be pursued with or without feminist input.

In the 1950s and 1960s a frequently encountered argument was that individuals benefit from investment in education and so does the country. With women there was too much 'wastage' (movement out of the labour force; failure to practise after training; failure to train up to capacity). Authors writing about graduate women claimed 'the country needs them' (Arregger 1966). These arguments are often elitist, as it is 'talented' or 'able' women who are needed, not the others (except perhaps to look after the children of the talented?).

Discrimination

Can we explain the position of women in higher education in terms of sex discrimination? This is a common argument, made both by feminists and others concerned with equality and justice. Legally speaking, sex discrimination consists of less favourable treatment of a member of one sex than would be accorded to a person of the other sex whose relevant circumstances are the same or not materially different. There is parallel legislation for race relations. Built into the UK legislation is greater concern for the fate of individuals than for the welfare of groups. In most cases, discrimination has to be established by means of comparisons between individuals rather than by demonstrating statistical patterns. Discrimination may be *direct* (unequal treatment because of one's sex) or *indirect* (unequal treatment using some other criterion that puts one sex at a disadvantage and is not otherwise justified).

Figures collated by the Association of University Teachers (AUT) demonstrate women's poor chances for promotion (Aziz 1990). For example, in 1986, 536 people were promoted from lecturer to senior lecturer or reader, only 53 of whom were women. From 1984 to 1986, the figures hardly varied; 'the proportion of women promoted is consistently smaller than the proportion of women in the pool of lecturers from which the promotions are made' (Aziz 1990: 36).

However, these figures are not proof of discrimination, according to the law, which requires direct comparisons between named individuals. In a recent example, four women lecturers from what was then Newcastle Polytechnic took their case under the Sex Discrimination Act to an industrial tribunal, with support from the Equal Opportunities Commission (Buswell vs. Newcastle City Council 1989). They claimed they had been directly discriminated against for promotion. A principal lectureship (a senior position) had been advertised within the department, and four women and two men applied. One of the men was appointed. The women felt he was junior to them in seniority and experience, and less qualified than some of them in other respects. Various witnesses appeared for each side before a tribunal made up of two men and one woman. The women *lost.*

The official report shows, first, the enormous difficulty of proving discrimination in cases where 'academic judgements' are involved (see also Evans 1993). It is clear the tribunal was unable to understand in depth the politics of academic institutions; 'this was a foreign world' the chairman admitted (Buswell vs. Newcastle City Council 1989: 10). Second, it shows how a tribunal is itself likely to rely on stereotypes about the sexes. The tribunal was impressed by the coolness and rationality of the polytechnic management; it declared itself unimpressed by the 'obsessive, emotional involvement' of the women (ibid.: p. 12).

Turning to indirect discrimination, several interesting legal cases have concerned part-time work in universities. The figures in Tables 3 and 4 were for full-time academics only. Part-time workers are more likely to be female. In one successful case involving a woman scientific researcher at the University of Dundee, a tribunal ruled that making part-time workers as a group redundant would affect women more adversely than men, thus constituting indirect discrimination. Also successful in establishing indirect discrimination have been several cases challenging age requirements, using the argument that women are more likely than men to be older when they reach certain points of their occupational careers, especially if they have taken time out from work to look after children.

Indirect discrimination may take more subtle forms. Simply working in a mostly male environment imposes pressures on women, as I noted in Chapter 8. The career structure is designed on a 'male norm' – career breaks or part-time work do damage to promotion chances. Time out from full-time work may be even more damaging in areas where knowledge is proceeding rapidly and where there is little provision for catching up (Jackson 1989). Women may also be at a disadvantage in the informal socializing that aids promotion chances.

Strategies

What strategies follow from the liberal-feminist perspectives reviewed above? If the problem lies in women's attitudes or personalities, as formed through socialization, the solution appears to be for the individual simply to make the best of a bad situation. One can just try harder. I have a post-it note pad from the United States which sums it up as the 'career women's checklist for success: look like a lady, act like a man, work like a dog'. Women are to 'dress for success', learn career planning strategies from mentors and develop assertiveness through training.

This path is full of pitfalls, for double standards make such strategies difficult. Women academics who are highly successful at publishing or obtaining research funding, or who try to be 'one of the boys', risk disapproval for breaking norms for feminine women. Meanwhile, feminist women criticize them for their lack of concern about other women's progress. Those who do take a feminist stance are regarded as eccentric if not actually strident and uncongenial. Whatever one does seems only to reinforce the male-as-norm definitions.

For family–career conflicts, a helpful partner, clever manoeuvring, luck and money might provide a nanny or other solution. But again, these are *individual* solutions, and not open to all. One woman finds a way, but the same problem is there for the next.

The womanpower and discrimination arguments shift the analysis some-what, still staying within the liberal framework, but examining structures rather than individuals. We become more sociological, understanding women's ac-tions within the frameworks that constrain them. But there are still difficulties. The demand for womanpower is bound to fluctuate over time and some groups are not perceived as being in shortage. For example, there has not yet been a call for women to come into university teaching comparable to those made occasionally for school teaching, although a 'womanpower' argument appeared in a project which recruited highly qualified women returners to university fellowships in science and engineering (Jackson 1988). There have also been rumours that contract researchers in universities are becoming more difficult to recruit, perhaps because of their poor remuneration and prospects. The university academic population in Britain is ageing, a result of expansion in the 1960s and early 1970s followed by contraction since the 1980s. At some point, mass retirements from the 'bulge' will require replacement. But recent government policies have squeezed the universities and starved them of funds, hardly auspicious circumstances for extending equal opportunities to women or minorities. Arts and humanities, and certain social sciences, have experi-enced particularly severe cutbacks. It is difficult to defend a 'womanpower' argument that supplies talent only to fields designated by the government of the day as in the national interest.

If discrimination is seen to be the problem, use may be made of the law, the Equal Opportunities Commission and union procedures. Steady pressure can be put on colleagues. The situation can be brought to the notice of the wider public. Generally, strategies rely on persuasion, rational argument, the assump-tion of goodwill and distaste for injustice. Using the law and publicizing successful outcomes, as the Equal Opportunities Commission does, may raise the level of consciousness, but there is little evidence of fundamental change. The number of successful cases is small and there are few effective sanctions to stop the same discriminatory treatment occurring again elsewhere.

Extending the analysis: Socialist and radical feminisms

The approaches discussed thus far give us an idea how social arrangements operate to the detriment of women but not why they have developed this way. We can deepen our understanding of women in higher education if we go beyond the various varieties of liberal-feminist thought outlined above. Both socialist-feminist and radical-feminist theories are concerned with underlying causes.

Socialist feminism

The long-term political aim here is to end oppression under capitalism, but most scholars analyse the processes involved in sustaining women's unequal position in institutions such as the economy and the family. Those concerned with education try to discover how education contributes to the reproduction of gender divisions within capitalism (Arnot and Weiner 1987a).

Socialist feminists note that women and men occupy different typical spheres in the labour market as well as in the home; details of such divisions change but the broad outlines are perpetuated over time, or 'reproduced'. Questions arise. Why is it that women are concentrated in certain manual occupations with little job security and few fringe benefits? Or in lower white-collar (secretarial) work? Or in the caring professions? Why is it that within professional occupations, women are found in lower grades and lower status specialities? If education is about increasing social mobility, why does the same amount of education bring a lower rate of return for women and minorities than for white men?

The internal labour markets in institutions of higher education contain gender and other social divisions. Universities now even have their own 'academic proletariat' (Aziz 1990): temporary contract research staff, disproportionately female, who act as a kind of reserve labour force. The abolition of academic tenure in universities (for all who join, move or are promoted) through the Education Reform Act 1988 would seem to suggest 'traditional' academics are vulnerable, too.

Higher education can be seen to reinforce divisions in other ways. It is a scarce prize that legitimates an elite, dividing those with credentials from the remainder. Figures for 1990–91 indicate that 14 per cent of boys and 13 per cent of girls leaving school enter a degree course (Department for Education 1993b). The overall participation rates are somewhat higher because some students go first to further education or tertiary colleges to get the requisite qualifications for entry to higher education, but nevertheless higher education is still only available to a small minority.

This minority is disproportionately white and middle class. The latter monopoly is scarcely news, as British sociology of education has a long history of interest in 'political arithmetic', charting the probabilities of children from different social class backgrounds achieving educational outcomes such as examination passes or access to higher education (Gray 1981). Gray (1981: 82) comments that the universities are still 'comparatively inaccessible to the working class'. Over a decade later, Blackburn and Jarman (1993: 203) state that 'class inequalities in higher education have remained fairly constant'. Reid (1989: 320) shows that in 1988, 68 per cent of the candidates accepted to universities came from the top two categories of the six-part Registrar General's social class scale (based on father's occupation). These categories contain only 27 per cent of the population at large.

Official figures on ethnic minority participation in higher education have only been collected since 1990. In an analysis of these statistics, Modood (1993b) concludes that 'there is no simple black–white divide' but differences among institutions, sectors, subjects and ethnic groups. In the new universities (the former polytechnics), most ethnic minorities are over-represented, given their proportions in the national population of 18- to 21-year-olds, but are concentrated in certain regions and institutions. (Ethnic minority categories appearing in the tables include Bangladeshi, Indian, Pakistani, Chinese, Black

African and Black Caribbean.) Minorities are less likely to be in the 'old' universities, and African-Caribbeans and Bangladeshis are significantly under-represented. Success rates for applications are lower for ethnic minorities, especially those of African-Caribbean origin, said by the Universities Central Council on Admissions to result from factors such as disproportionate applications to popular subjects with high rejection rates like medicine and law (Modood 1993a,1993b). It remains the case that only about 1 per cent of home university students and 4 per cent in the former polytechnics are classified as Black African or Black Caribbean (Utley 1991; Modood 1993a, 1993b).

One difficulty with such statistics is that they rarely record more than one social division at a time. 'Women' as a category are approaching parity among undergraduates (Universities Funding Council 1993). But what are the inter-connections of class, sex and 'race' (as well as other attributes such as age and disability) in determining access to university? We also lack figures on the class background and ethnic composition of the academic profession (and other workers in higher education); we have no easy way of assessing the combined effects of class, sex, 'race' and other characteristics such as sexual orientation (Kitzinger 1990) on subject specialties, promotion prospects, or any other aspect of being an academic.

Radical feminism

In radical feminism, the operation of patriarchy is the fundamental reason for observed social patterns. Although there are different definitions of patriarchy, most depict a system whereby men as a group (not necessarily every individual man) are dominant. Figures shown earlier amply support the argument that men dominate universities numerically. Radical feminists want to eliminate patriarchal structures and put girls and women at the centre of concern. In higher education, male dominance is expressed through curriculum, pedagogy and the sexual politics of everyday life.

Feminists have produced extensive critiques of scholarship in many fields. A classic of this genre is Dale Spender's (1981) collection, *Men's Studies Modified*. Jeri Wine (1989) identifies stages feminist criticism goes through, starting with correcting the record and finally attempting to construct woman-centred alter-natives. Writers like Stanley and Wise (1983) try to develop a specifically feminist research methodology (see Chapter 4, this volume).

Feminist scholarship is exciting, 'producing a critical and analytical literature of an intellectual liveliness and practical relevance unmatched in any other field of social science' (Connell 1985: 260). Nevertheless, there are numerous examples of im-portant ways in which feminist work is outside the mainstream. For example, Sara Delamont (1989) shows that the Winfield Report on submission rates for social science higher degree theses ignored all the research on *women* graduate students. Specializing in feminist scholarship may harm one's promotion chances (Gumport 1990; *The Higher*, 29 November 1991; see also Chapter 4, this volume).

How much scope is there for finding a feminist way to organize pedagogy, curriculum and management? Women's studies are gaining ground quietly in

Britain (Brookman 1991), but the field is subdued in comparison with develop-ments in the United States, where a different organization of higher education permits new courses and programmes to flourish provided they attract students. Attempts to create new ways of working within the relatively rigid world of British higher education can be painful, as high expectations held by the students clash with university conventions. Women who do become heads of department or professors find themselves allowed in as individuals to a culture which is shaped by men. They are always highly visible (Chapter 8). Simply being a woman academic in a male-dominated institution brings forms of 'sexual politics' – dilemmas of power, visibility, relationships – into everyday life (David 1989).

The power men hold over women can, at an extreme, become sexual harassment. Harassment means unwanted sexual attentions or advances, which may be looks, gestures, pictures, physical advances, threats, etc. In the United States, many institutions have developed policies on harassment and there have been widely publicized court cases. Consciousness was further raised by the issue surfacing during the confirmation hearing of Supreme Court Justice Clarence Thomas. American surveys suggest widespread sexual harassment in higher education institutions (Simeone 1987), but little is known about its incidence in British universities.

Strategies

The goals of socialist and radical feminism are not realizable in the immediate future; one cannot devise strategies for ending capitalism and patriarchy in the same way one might introduce an equal opportunities policy or encourage women to apply for promotion. Consistent with socialist-feminist analysis would be efforts to develop further a class-gender-race analysis of the univer-sity's social role; to encourage alliances of university workers, especially women, across occupational segments and social divisions; to raise conscious-ness of oppression among these groups; to increase awareness of, and commit-ment to, gender issues in the more left-leaning political parties and trade unions; to increase access to universities for groups traditionally deprived of it.

Radical-feminist strategies focus on putting women at the centre of concern: developing woman-centred knowledge, making institutions safe for women, finding space for women within (or outside) the academy. Putting women first may mean encouraging women-only courses and groups. The difficulty is that the territory is still controlled by men, as the figures show. Women's studies courses in Britain – as, indeed, is any input on 'gender' to any course – are frequently marginal, poorly resourced and dependent on the energies of a few committed individuals doing the work 'on top' of their responsibilities in traditional departments.

Missing links, alternative models

It seems to me that there are at least three underdeveloped areas within British feminist work on women in higher education. These are socialist-feminist writing on the topic, consideration of 'race', and imaginative projections towards a woman-centred university.

First, in the literature on universities, there are few examples of a socialist-feminist (or even a socialist) perspective. Earlier I referred to questions of access and the lack of simultaneous consideration of class, sex and 'race' divisions among the student body, academics and other staff. Other questions could be raised concerning the extent to which the university operates in tandem with the interests of industry and in support of capitalist development (Esland and Cathcart 1981; Buchbinder and Newson 1990). Under the Conservatives, central government has intervened extensively in British higher education in recent years, for example by modifying the curriculum in initial teacher education, abolishing academic tenure, taking polytechnics out of local government control and later giving them university status, differentially distributing funds so as to increase institutions' accountability and dependence on market forces.

What implications have these developments had for women? How do the subject divisions and hierarchies of the university contribute to the reproduction of gendered divisions of labour in society at large? How do particular forms of knowledge become enshrined in academic discourses? Do they then become differentially accessible to different groups? Do their curricula transmit messages that aid in the cultural reproduction of beliefs about gender? We need more scholarship and research from a socialist-feminist perspective on higher education; that there is so little, especially when British socialist-feminist work is so strong in other areas, is itself a 'problem'.

Second, there is a near silence about 'race' and ethnicity in terms of their impact on British academic women. This is perhaps surprising in view of the incisive critiques of ethnocentrism that have been levelled against some British feminist work (e.g. by Carby 1982; Murphy and Livingstone 1985) and the reconceptualizations that followed. Although there is a body of literature on experiences of black and Asian schoolgirls in Britain (e.g. Amos and Parmar 1981; Fuller 1983; Brah and Minhas 1985; Mirza 1992), there were only a few studies of black women students in higher education before the 1990s (Tomlinson 1983; Bryan *et al.* 1985). Recent studies of students are more likely to focus on race as well as gender (e.g. Edwards 1993), and there is an increasing literature on black women students in teacher education (Siraj-Blatchford 1990; Blair and Maylor 1993; Crozier and Menter 1993).

As noted earlier, there is an almost total absence of information about the ethnic composition of the academic profession, and little evidence of serious effort to increase the representation of minority ethnic groups, despite institutional claims to be equal opportunities employers (Williams *et al.* 1989). Similarly, there are very few studies of academics from ethnic minorities. One exception is McKellar (1989), who gives an account of her own experiences as a teacher-educator. McKellar (1989: 69) cites a study that found only 27 black teacher-educators in England, Scotland and Wales, only 8 of whom were in universities. Powney and Weiner (1991) conducted a small study of women and minority managers in higher and other educational institutions, identifying strategies being used to accomplish greater equity (see also Burton and Weiner 1993).

With the exception of Leicester (1993), who argues that anti-racist continuing education can set a norm for changes in all aspects of university practice and policy, we lack commentaries that explore the consequences for the curriculum, role modelling or other aspects of university life of the dominance of white academics. Although Leicester makes some reference to gender and to certain feminist approaches, she does not really integrate race and gender in her analysis. Recognizing and combating racism in the university is the priority, she believes, containing the potential to transform provision for other disadvantaged groups such as women.

In North America, where representation is somewhat better, one regularly finds discussion of ethnic diversity among academic women (e.g. Pearson *et al*. 1989; Welch 1992). A recent Canadian volume (Bannerji *et al*. 1991) provides a model of a collection written by women working in universities as students and academics that engages seriously with class, gender, race and sexuality issues in academic life and their impact on the construction of knowledge and the shaping of subjectivities. The authors 'recognize that this is a racist, classist and heterosexist society and that the university is structured to perpetuate those relations' (Bannerji *et al*. 1991: 8). In their individual chapters they examine their own 'different – and sometimes contradictory – locations in these relations' (ibid.).

Third, a leap of the imagination might allow us to go beyond the structures and inequities of universities as we know them. In reviewing research on women graduate students for Chapter 4, I noted that a typical concern of the 1970s and early 1980s – the extent to which women were taken seriously and sponsored by male faculty members – had in the more recent North American literature nearly disappeared. The themes of feminist pedagogy and radical revision of the curriculum, which I have linked to radical feminist scholarship, had developed further into an exploration of women's preferred ways of learning and working, thought to involve valuing community over competition, attachment and caring over justice and objectivity (Desjardins 1989). Gray (1989), for example, speculates what education would look like if 'the culture of separated desks' gave way. In a 'woman-centered university' (Rich 1979), the figures on women's under-representation in the upper reaches of the hierarchy that I gave earlier would no longer provide the linchpin of an argument; they would be beside the point, as the hierarchy itself would dissolve. Meanwhile, we can at least think creatively and innovate wherever possible.

Moving towards equity, slowly

The feminist theories discussed in this chapter advance reasons for the structural subordination of women. Those considered under the liberal-feminist umbrella tend to answer the question of *how* women become disadvantaged – for example, through processes of socialization and discrimination. The socialist-feminist and radical-feminist approaches aim for a deeper, more fundamental understanding, addressing the question of *why* such disadvantage occurs (Acker 1984a). As it is impossible to ascertain 'why' with any certainty, we are left with competing but untestable hypotheses. Moreover, behind every 'how' question, a 'why' is lurking, untestable as it may be; for example, if we believe socialization to be the cause of women's subordination, we still must question why socialization operates in this particular fashion.

While feminist theory gives broad reasons for inequalities of gender, focused studies in specific countries and educational systems are necessary to fill in the detail. Britain appears to lag behind other, similar, countries in its commitment to improving the status of women in general and women academics in particular (Johnson 1990). Reasons might be sought in its particular historical and political traditions. Gelb (1989) argues that in comparison with the United States and Sweden, British feminist groups are more radical, ideological and decentralized. Like other grassroots groups, they lack input into the policy-making process. Britain has no active and effective liberal-feminist network of committees and pressure groups pushing for implementation of feminist priorities. There has been no extensive feminist infiltration into bureaucracies such as that described in Eisenstein's (1991) account of 'femocrats' in Australia. Feminism in Britain remains outside the dominant discourse. The years of Conservative government have enshrined this principle; a few women, like Mrs Thatcher, could 'make it', but only by their own efforts, not by virtue of socially progressive policies.

Canada provides an interesting contrast. In neither Britain nor Canada is there a network of privately financed universities, as found in the United States. Women make up 18.8 per cent of Canadian academics, a figure similar to the British one (Statistics Canada 1992). There is also a tendency for women to be disproportionately located in contractually limited appointments and part-time positions (Drakich *et al.* 1991). But once in the 'tenure track', women's chances of advancing to middle levels are greater than those of their counterparts in Britain. A third of women and 35 per cent of men hold the middle rank of associate professor. The difference comes at the full professor rank, which is held by 13 per cent of the women and 40 per cent of the men (Statistics Canada 1992).

In Canada, there are policies at both federal and provincial levels which have as their aim the reduction of gender (and other) inequality (Breslauer and Gordon 1990; Canadian Association of University Teachers 1991). The Federal Contractors Program requires employees of more than 100 people who wish to receive federal contracts for $200,000 or more to put into place plans to increase equity for women, visible minorities, aboriginal people and the disabled. Many universities have joined this programme. Some provinces have introduced additional equity measures. Canadian universities also benefit from a higher level of feminist activism than British ones, reflecting the greater prominence of the women's movement generally, and there is evidence that such efforts have been influential (Drakich *et al.* 1991).

Education in Canada is a provincial responsibility. In contrast, central government is particularly influential in the British case; local and county levels of government have no control over universities. Although the central government in Britain has pursued a number of aggressive higher education policies in recent years, none is concerned with gender equality.

The use of a competitive promotion procedure in British universities, together with minimal commitment from the government to redressing gender inequities, may produce the contrast with the Canadian situation. Unlike the American practice of allowing individuals to compete against a standard to attain higher ranks, judged by one's peers, the typical British university makes its candidates for internal promotion (senior lectureships and readerships) compete against one another for a restricted number of promotions, usually judged by senior personnel (professors and deans) (see Chapter 4, this volume). Thus, Toren's (1993: 450) description of the norm (if not the actuality) in Israel and America that 'everyone [in academe] is expected and expects to climb the whole ladder and reach the peak' simply does not apply.

Given that even the more open structures in other countries still result in systematic slower progress through the ranks for women (Toren 1993), reforming the British system seems even more remote. Moreover, demographic trends and educational policies that expanded and then contracted the system have led to an ageing academic profession with large numbers at the top of the 'lecturer scale' (reached at about age 40) competing for promotion. Because promotions to middle levels are typically internal ones, the system discourages geographical mobility (why start over again in a lectureship somewhere else?), and it is open to micropolitical influences as heads of department struggle to get 'their' candidate promoted.

The individuals making these judgements, as we have seen, are almost all men. Few will be familiar with research on gender, thus placing women doing research and scholarship in that area at a possible disadvantage (*The Higher*, 29 November 1991). The disadvantage is deepened by the suspicion that greets feminist work in some quarters (Gumport 1990). Because women are concentrated in relatively few subject fields, they will also be competing against one another if promotions are 'shared out' among departments. It is also likely that when promotions are restricted, and many candidates are of equal merit, that male preference will operate, however unconsciously (Evans 1993).

A further, ironic, consequence of the small numbers of women in the system is that opportunities for organizing to improve matters are thereby limited. Women academics are too scattered to provide a critical mass, nor do they hold many positions of influence. Johnson (1990) makes this clear using the example of music, a subject with a majority female undergraduate enrolment. As of 1988, two-thirds of university music departments had no women academic staff. There were no readers or professors. Wales had no women lecturers. One of the limitations of women's studies is that it will make few inroads where there are few women already present.

Finally, the economic situation has been perilous for some time in Britain. Universities have been experiencing cuts and retrenchment since the early 1980s (P. Reynolds 1990). It would not seem the best of times to push for feminist reform. But there are always contradictions and points for intervention. For example, the increasing impact of market forces means that students' preferences should be a factor in shaping provision. Women have been steadily increasing their share of student places (see Chapter 10, this volume). During the 1990s, mature women are expected to be in demand to make up some of the shortfall left by an unusually small cohort of individuals of traditional university-going age. The massive rise in temporary teaching and research staff has unsettled old certainties about the meaning of the university as a workplace and undermines the image of the academic as an autonomous professional. The very business of education carries contradictions in its simultaneous reproductive and liberating potential. The institution is reproducing the divisions of the labour market, while at the same time providing the means for challenge and critique.

So feminists need not give up just yet. As I have suggested, liberal-feminist analysis is inadequate to explain the persistence of deep gender divisions in academic life. Socialist and radical feminisms go further to explain why the barriers to women are so strong. Yet when considering strategies, we confront something of a paradox. Either strategies are long-term (working towards the end of capitalist or patriarchal oppression) or provocative and likely to arouse opposition or even ridicule (challenging the disciplines with women's studies; constructing feminist methodology). Liberal-feminist strategies, on the other hand, tend either to put too much responsibility on the individual to make changes, often in herself, or to rely on arts of persuasion and assumptions of goodwill. Nevertheless, it may be that even those with radical or socialist sympathies need to pursue liberal strategies in the short run, given that the liberal ones – as in the Canadian case – may be as, or more, constructive than the others. The difference is that for liberal feminism they are an end, for other feminisms a means to an end. Liberal strategies have not failed in Britain, they have not sufficiently been tried.

The strategies will need to be adapted to their context: institutions complacent towards certain issues but in flux and crisis. Working through academic unions may provide a relatively 'respectable' base. Feminist academics need to use their skills as scholars to look at their own institutions. For example, the pioneering work of Thomas (1990) and Greed (1991) draws our attention to ways that institutional, disciplinary and departmental cultures in higher education transmit a hidden curriculum of gender and thereby create or reinforce gendered subjectivities – a phenomenon that demands further study. In examining her own situation, Evans (1993) makes a distinction between institutional and intellectual power within the university. With little of the former, feminist academics have developed the latter, to the point where challenges to the institutional power structure, even if mounted by individuals, increasingly carry the support of a collective understanding. She shows how a liberal-feminist strategy can rest on a more sophisticated feminist analysis.

Feminists are not as happy about our theories as we once were. The postmodern critique has forced us to deal with the puzzle that in arguing 'women's' case, we downplay disparities of class, race and other divisions which fragment the category 'women'. The theories I have worked with here are not convincing as total truth (did we ever think they were?), yet played off against each other they give us different angles of vision on an elusive 'problem'. As Linda Alcoff (1988) argues, we cannot afford to abandon our politics because our theories lack perfection. We need to recognize the historical and cultural specificity of our case, and within it actively take up the position and the identity which feels most compelling as a political point of departure (Alcoff 1988; Nicholson 1990). Feminist theories help us to understand how serious the situation is, and why change is so frustratingly slow. Accepting this, we can work at deepening the cracks, crevices and contradictions of the patriarchal university.

Notes

1. I would like to thank Madeleine Arnot, Kari Dehli, Maureen Dyer and Kathleen Weiler for their comments on drafts of this chapter or similar conference papers that preceded it; Carol Buswell for providing transcripts and other materials from her tribunal proceedings; Andrea Spurling for encouraging me to collect my thoughts together on women in higher education; Linda Fitzsimmons for updating me on Association of University Teachers activities concerning women; Helen Breslauer and Dorothy Smith for pointing me towards materials on Canadian women academics. Over the years, I have had many relevant discussions with friends and colleagues at the University of Bristol who shared their experiences as women academics, among them Sally Barnes, Liz Bird, Patricia Broadfoot, Miriam David, Eileen Gillibrand, Clara Greed, Ursula King, Ruth Levitas, Ann Low-Beer, Kate Lyons, Sara Meadows, Vieda Skultans and Jackie West.
2. Chapter 3 contains an extensive treatment of the these three types of feminism and their implications for educational research on gender and for feminist reform of education. The discussion here is more specific to the situation of women academics in higher education.
3. I have concentrated on the traditional universities rather than the former polytechnics, given limitations of space and my own experience in the university sector. However, women's representation in the former polytechnics is similar to the pattern in traditional universities, i.e. they are a minority overall and are scarce in top positions (Department of Education and Science 1987). Similarly, I have considered women academic staff rather than other university workers, many of whom are women in support positions, such as secretarial or library staff. Little is written about women in universities who are neither students nor academics.

10 Conclusion: Continuity and Change

The chapters in this book have explored aspects of gender issues in education. The introductory chapter considered the development of the sociology of education and the sociology of women's education. Each of the three main sections of the book shows the development of my thinking over the 1980s and early 1990s, with respect, first, to issues of feminist scholarship and research; second, to the sociology of the teaching profession; and third, to the study of women academics in universities. The chapter to follow concentrates on social and educational changes that occurred during the period of my writing. Do women still experience educational inequality? Are we approaching a period of greater social justice? What directions should we be taking in our research?

Women, education and social justice

The concept of educational inequality seems to have gone through its own post-structuralist revision before it was fashionable, taking on shifting and contradictory meanings. In the 1960s, 1970s and into the 1980s, inequality in British educational studies almost always meant social–class inequality. In contrast, work in the United States frequently blurred class and race to create a notion of educational or cultural disadvantage. British studies of the 1970s and early 1980s, such as those of Wedge and Prosser (1973), Rutter and Madge (1976) and Mortimore and Blackstone (1982), firmly equated disadvantage with social–class handicap. But by the mid-1980s, chapters on race, gender and special needs began to appear in books on inequality (Purvis and Hales 1983; Hartnett and Naish 1986; Rogers 1986). 'Equal opportunities' became a phrase used in local education authorities, often to refer to race and gender inequalities alone.

Problems in the conceptualization of 'inequality of educational opportunity' had been apparent for some time (e.g. Coleman 1968), but critiques escalated, from diverse commentators (Murphy 1981; Yates 1986). David (1993) shows that in the political sphere, cross-party support for expansion of provision and greater access to education was met by a backlash of right-wing views, starting around the late 1960s. By the mid-1970s, some of those arguments had found their way into government policy, which was turning to an emphasis on the needs of industry and the economy rather than on equity issues. In subsequent years, the shift to the right became far more pronounced in Britain, as it did elsewhere. Replacing social justice on the agenda were goals such as upholding standards, regulating the curriculum, increasing parental choice, reducing the influence of local government and increasing school effectiveness (see Flude and Hammer 1990; David 1993). With such an agenda, attention to the rights of minority ethnic groups, the working class or women came to be seen as pleading for special interest groups, rather than responding to the needs of most of the population.

Nevertheless, almost paradoxically, educational trends in the past several decades do show significant improvements in educational opportunities. Selective secondary education was largely replaced by comprehensive schooling; young people were leaving school better qualified; higher education was becoming more accessible; and as a result of such trends, the adult population gradually increased its educational qualifications. Educational outcomes were changing markedly for women, as the next section shows.

Routes and destinations in education[1]

Over the years, school-leavers have become less and less likely to leave without some paper qualifications (based on public examinations). In the mid-1970s, around a fifth of school-leavers (21 per cent of boys, 19 per cent of girls) fell into this category, but by 1989–90, only 9.9 per cent of boys and 6.7 per cent of girls had no leaving qualifications at all (Central Statistical Office 1993: 42). If we look for a middle level of accomplishment, we can trace the percentages of boys and girls with at least one O-level or one to four General Certificate of Secondary Education (GCSE) examination passes at Grades A–C. In 1970–71, 43 per cent of boys and 44 per cent of girls leaving school reached this standard; and then the percentages went up steadily, reaching 61 and 70 per cent, respectively, in 1989–90 (Central Statistical Office 1993: 42). Looking at a slightly higher level of achievement, we see that 34.1 per cent of boys and 42.7 per cent of girls aged 16 in England achieved five or more A–C grades in GCSE examinations in 1991–92 (Department for Education 1993a: 1).

Clearly not only are achievements increasing, but girls do 'better' by most of these calculations, especially in recent years. A similar trend can be seen for A-levels, the examinations required for university entrance. Figures for England and Wales showed only 8 per cent of boys and 5 per cent of girls with two or more A-levels in 1960–61 (Central Statistical Office 1970: 130). (Figures are for examinations taken in schools rather than further education establishments.) Later statistics, for the UK, show gradual increases in the percentages with two or more A-levels, with boys slightly ahead: 15 per cent of boys and 13 per cent of girls in 1970–71; 15 and 13 per cent, respectively, in 1980–81; 15 and 14 per cent, respectively, in 1985–86. In the late 1980s, we see a sharp rise for both sexes but a greater one for girls: 20 per cent of boys and 22 per cent of girls achieved two or more A-levels in 1989–90 (Central Statistical Office 1993: 42).

Boys have also traditionally been more likely to move from school to university education, with girls more often going into teacher training and other forms of further and higher education. In 1960–61, only 5.3 per cent of boys and 2.4 per cent of girls went directly to university; the vast majority, 88 per cent of boys and 84 per cent of girls, went into employment (Central Statistical Office 1970: 130). The numbers entering employment (or seeking work) have dropped steadily to under 60 per cent for both sexes (including those for whom destinations are not known) in 1990–91, while entry to a degree course upon leaving school is 14 per cent for boys and 13 per cent for girls. Girls are still more likely than boys to enter teacher training, although the percentages are very small for both sexes, and are also more likely to enter other forms of further and higher education (35 per cent of girls, 27 per cent of boys: Department for Education 1993b: 13).

Some of the most dramatic increases in female participation can be seen in higher education over the past 20 years (Blackburn and Jarman 1993: 207). In Britain at the end of the 1960s, women constituted less than 30 per cent of full-time undergraduates and just over a fifth of full-time postgraduates – a figure that includes those in graduate teacher education courses (Central Statistical Office 1970: 133). These figures climbed to 40 and 35 per cent, respectively, for 'UK domiciled' (or 'home') students in 1980–81 (Central Statistical Office 1992; figures for the UK); then continued to rise to 46 and 42 per cent, respectively, in 1991–92 (Universities Funding Council 1993; figures for Great Britain). Participation is slightly higher if undergraduate and graduate levels and different venues for higher education (universities, polytechnics and colleges) are combined. In Great Britain in 1991–92, women made up 48 per cent of full-time home students, and 38 per cent of those from overseas (Department for Education 1993d).

Fulton (1993) analyses patterns of university access in more detail, paying attention to interactions of full-time and part-time enrolment, age and gender. He notes that 'whereas in 1981 57 per cent of all full-time first degree entrants were male, by 1991 women outnumbered men in the oldest age group and had almost reached parity in the under-21s' (p. iii). Among part-timers, it is women from the older age groups that have 'poured into higher education'. He concludes that: 'The 1990s have truly been the decade of the woman student' (p. iii).

When I was teaching sociology of education in Britain, I sometimes summed up the trends in female participation in the education system as 'the higher the fewer'. We see that by the early 1990s, it is a great deal more difficult to sustain that claim within the formal education system, although it is still applicable for those who work in it as teachers or lecturers. Chapters 7 and 9 contain recent statistics on women's status within teaching in schools and universities. For example, in 1990, women constituted 80.6 per cent of nursery and primary school teachers, but only 48.6 per cent of nursery and primary head teachers; 47.8 per cent of secondary school teachers, but only 19.7 per cent of secondary head teachers. In 1991–92, 22 per cent of university academics were women (16 per cent of those in mainstream positions). At professorial level, women are barely visible (4.6 per cent of mainstream professorships), although this is an increase on their 2.7 per cent representation in 1980 (Acker 1984b).

Another common observation in my courses pertained to the different subjects studied by the sexes, at every level of education. These trends have been somewhat moderated over time, although they are still noticeable. In the 1960s, student entries for O-level examinations were sharply differentiated between arts (for girls) and sciences (for boys) (Central Statistical Office 1970). By 1991–92, patterns for GCSE, the successor to O-levels, were less differentiated, with 78 per cent of boys and 82 per cent of girls aged 16 in England entering for a combination that included English, mathematics and science. Differences could be seen in the percentages attempting GCSEs in technology (53 per cent of boys, 14 per cent of girls), home economics (5 per cent of boys, 34 per cent of girls) and any modern language (64 per cent of boys, 84 per cent of girls) (Department for Education 1993a: table 5).

In the 1960s and early 1970s, A-levels for girls tended to be in arts subjects, while boys studied sciences. With the rise of the social sciences, popular with both sexes, the gender divide became less stark, although still evident. In 1981, 70 per cent of English A-levels gained by school leavers went to girls; girls also gained the majority of French A-levels (72 per cent) and biology A-levels (56 per cent). In contrast, they received only 20 per cent of physics A-levels and 27 per cent of those in mathematics (Equal Opportunities Commission 1983). Results for 18-year-olds (in schools and colleges) in 1991–92 are similarly patterned: girls gained 70 per cent of English and 71 per cent of French A-levels. Their proportion of biology A-levels increased to 62 per cent. Their share of mathematics A-levels went up to 36 per cent and physics went up very slightly to 22 per cent (Department for Education 1993a: table 14).

Subject divisions persisted in higher education, too. In 1991–92:

> For UK domiciled full-time undergraduates, male students outnumbered female students in engineering and technology (in the ratio 6:1), mathematical sciences, and architecture and related studies (approximately in the ratio 3:1) and, in physical sciences (approximately in the ratio 2:1). In contrast, female students outnumbered male students in education (in the ratio 4:1) and in studies allied to medicine, languages and related studies and, librarianship and information sciences (approximately in the ratio 2:1).
> (Universities Funding Council 1993: 8)

However, in universities, as in schools, subject divisions are less stark than in the past. In an analysis of patterns of class and gender inequality in access to higher education from 1938 to 1990, Blackburn and Jarman (1993: 207) indicate that the early 1970s mark a turning point when women began to enter non-traditional subject fields in noticeable numbers.

Gender issues: Still with us?

The figures presented above suggest that women have benefited from the expansion of educational opportunities in Britain and that their performance belies any facile generalizations about under-achievement. Perhaps the most startling changes are occurring at university level. Subject differentiation is rather persistent, however, and men tend to dominate in the management roles in educational institutions. But statements from the mid-1970s, such as the following no longer ring true:

> Girls on average leave school earlier than boys though there has been some narrowing of the gap. After school the proportion of girls going on to study for a university degree is much smaller and fewer of them study technical or applied scientific subjects.
>
> (Central Statistical Office 1974: 25)

Interestingly, however, there seems to be a widespread perception that all the gender issues have been sorted out, at least those affecting girls. A recent editorial in the *Times Educational Supplement* (8 October 1993), commenting on a plan to teach the sexes separately in a secondary school, which appears to have been devised mainly to attract parents to choose that school rather than others, states:

> There has also been a big change since the early 1980s, when the first wave of feminist educational research showed boys dominating class-rooms and monopolising the attention of their teachers. Today, girls are outperforming boys in virtually every subject up to A-level . . . A big success for the radical feminists, 10 years later, is that – true or not – the idea that girls do better without boys has sunk deep into the parental psyche.

The editorial ignores another article in the same issue about widespread sexual harassment in schools (albeit in the United States: Myers 1993) that might suggest tempering any generalizations about 'big success'.

Some researchers see gender equality as steadily evolving:

> Generally, in the past, women have been disadvantaged in a similar way to students from less privileged class backgrounds. Fewer of them gained access to university, more of them took their degrees in colleges, and more of them qualified as mature students. However, this disadvantage seems to be disappearing and it seems likely that women's educational achievement will soon be on a par with that of men.
>
> (Egerton and Halsey 1993: 192)

Those of us who write about gender and schooling need to ponder whether we have succeeded or failed. To have such issues discussed in a serious way suggests success; but it seems that only certain issues have caught the public eye.

A persistent theme in this book is the extent to which gender has been integrated into scholarship, especially in the sociology of education. Compared to its place in 1970 (see Chapters 1 and 2), the study of gender could be said to have entered the sociology of education mainstream. Textbooks of the 1980s such as Burgess (1986) discussed issues of gender and race as well as class. A number of members of the *BJSE* editorial board have the sociology of women's education as their specialty, and articles on gender issues appear fairly frequently.

To see just how frequently such themes surfaced, I looked over the eight issues of the *British Journal of Sociology of Education (BJSE)* from 1991 and 1992, the most recent complete volumes available at the time of writing. Without considering book reviews or review essays, there were 44 articles, with 57 authors. Just over half (24) of the articles were from the UK; of the other 20, 10 were from Australia. I tried to classify the articles into those containing gender as a major theme, a minor one, and not at all (apart from perhaps a sentence or two). The count for both years was gender as a major theme in 10 articles, a minor theme in 9 articles, and neither a major nor minor theme in 25 articles. The 'minor theme' category was made up of articles that either brought gender into the analysis of data, had a sample that was primarily female and noted that fact, or devoted at least several paragraphs to the relevance of gender issues to the topic. A more restrictive categorization might have reduced this number, as several of the articles included were only peripherally concerned with gender.

There are a few other interesting observations to come out of this exercise. First, the categorization could only be done with at least a quick reading of the article; neither the title nor abstract would guarantee the content. Second, there appeared to be fluctuations from issue to issue, and year to year. Of the 10 articles logged as containing gender as a central theme, only one came from 1992. This article (Burgess and Carter 1992) explored the 'mumsy theme' in discourses about primary school teachers. Neither women nor gender appeared in the title or the abstract. The other 9 were from 1991, including 4 in one issue.

Third, there was a clear association between sex of author(s) and inclusion of gender as central. Of the articles with gender as a central theme, 7 were written by women, one by a woman and a man, and one by a man. Of the 25 without gender as a theme, 20 were written by men, 3 by women, one by a man and a woman, and one could not be classified by name alone. The minor theme category included 5 articles written by women, 3 by men and one that could not be classified.

Without conducting a more comprehensive study, looking at this journal over a longer time period and at other sociology journals, texts and so forth, I cannot advance firm conclusions about the influence of feminist work on sociology of education. However, while it is clear that we have moved on from the days of my 'No-woman's-land' analysis (Chapter 2), gender did not feature as strongly as I expected it would. And, although there is now clearly a place for work on gender in the sociology of education, many authors, especially male authors, are not integrating gender issues into their work. Of the 24 articles that could be classified as written by men alone, 20 had no gender themes and only 3 had minor themes. These findings suggest that gender issues have not become fully integrated into sociology of education, but remain the near-exclusive concern of women and more specifically feminists within the field.

New directions

My observations above suggest that one task for feminists is to consider how to convince their colleagues that gender is not a topic of interest only to women, but a fundamental organizing principle of social life. In Chapter 4, I pointed to the consequences for my own career of widely held, but limited, notions about research on gender. For those who would rather not spend their time reasoning with the unconvinced, there are also areas where feminist research could be extended.

We might, for example, take up the point suggested in the editorial quoted above, that 'there has been a big change since the early 1980s' (*TES*, 8 October 1993) in classroom dynamics. As indicated in Chapters 3 and 6, results of research in the 1970s and 1980s generally supported accusations of biased curriculum materials, teacher favouritism towards boys, and routine gender differentiation in many aspects of school functioning. With our more sophisticated theories of the 1990s (Jones 1993), we might return to some of these questions and find out which ones, under what conditions, still hold true. Schools mirror society, and it is unlikely that internal inequity and differentiation will disappear before that of the wider community. More could be done to relate gendered school practices to their social and economic setting, as, for example, Riddell (1992) does in her study of two rural comprehensive schools.

We could also consider when, how and why 'reform' efforts alter practice or belief (Chapter 6). From studies such as Weiler (1988) and Gilbert and Taylor (1991), we are beginning to understand why it is so difficult to introduce feminist ideas into the classroom. But there are efforts made to improve matters and we need to study their fate. Reviewing the literature on gender and science and technology education (Acker and Oakley 1993), it was clear that many projects intended to improve access for girls were not being evaluated or compared, and that their feminist theoretical underpinnings were narrow.

Another goal might be to put a sociological gloss on theories so far mainly employed by psychologists, concerning women's ways of knowing and learning (e.g. Gilligan 1982; Belenky *et al.* 1986). In Chapter 4, I described some results from a study of graduate students where women, especially, often displayed a sense of low confidence and entitlement. We could explain such findings in several ways; for example, as the result of gender-based socialization or of a mismatch between women's preferred 'ways' and university practices. These ideas need further development so that they can be firmly located in structures as well as, or instead of, being 'all in the mind', while retaining a notion of human agency (Wolffensperger 1993). I would also like to see more critical exploration of the university practices that have been so resistant to women's advancement and alternative forms of receiving and creating knowledge (Chapter 9).

My interest in teachers as an occupational group, evident for school teachers in Part 2 of this book, and for academics in Part 3, leads me to argue for a greater emphasis on the gendered nature of teaching. I do not mean that we should assume, simplistically, that the sexes teach or manage schools differently according to biology or even socialization. I do mean that topics such as teacher careers, collegiality and cultures need to be examined for the ways in which women and men have had different typical experiences and questions asked about why this happens.

Certainly, we need to continue questioning the utility of the concept of 'women' as a homogeneous group. For example, discussions of access to higher education require better information on the combined effects of class, gender and ethnicity. The many official statistics cited earlier in this chapter generalize about 'women'. Recent government statistical compilations are more likely to give information for different ethnic groups, so that it is possible to look at ethnic trends in, for example, level of education of the general public or likelihood of women being economically active. But most of the information I have summarized above has simply been presented as divided by sex.

It appears that social-class inequality in access to higher education is evident for both sexes and that earlier tendencies for class disadvantage to be greater for women are no longer being reported (Blackburn and Jarman 1993; Egerton and Halsey 1993). Modood's (1993a) research, mentioned earlier in Chapter 9, suggests that ethnicity and class interact in complex ways. Not all of the data he uses are available cross-tabulated by gender, so he ends up with statements like 'one can guess' (p. 171) at interactions of ethnicity and gender. He also argues that social-class effects are quite different for different ethnic groups:

> . . . groups with more disadvantaged class profiles than whites . . . pro-
> duce much larger proportions of applicants and admissions in the national
> higher education system . . . despite all of the social and institutional (not
> to mention cultural) disadvantages stacked against them.
>
> (Modood 1993a: 179)

Maynard (1990) makes a similar point about class and gender, the focus of considerable debate within sociology. The contortions required either to fit women into the existing conceptualizations of the class system, or, alter-natively, to create a new sex-class category, cast real doubt on all of the ways in which sociologists have approached stratification. In the study of education, gender needs to be maintained as a significant focus but without losing sight of the diversity of women and the dangers of generalization.

Conclusion

Educational trends, such as those described in this chapter, are bound up with economic, demographic, technological and political ones. Women are more likely to be in the labour force, and less likely to live in nuclear families, than they were a few years ago. The manual jobs that once made up the mainstay of male working-class life have declined dramatically; part-time jobs in the service industries, many traditionally female, account for increases in job positions (Webb 1989). In fact, such changes in the economy, Blackburn and Jarman (1993: 210) speculate, may be the driving force behind the increase in women's participation in higher education. Too much reliance on the state of the economy might be unwise, for economic forecasts are often unreliable; but on the bright side, a record number of women (60 of 651) entered the House of Commons in the 1992 election (Butler and Kavanagh 1992).

The news is not all bad. The chapters in this book tend towards the pessimistic, which may simply indicate my impatience with the *status quo*. Feminists like myself who started thinking and writing about feminist issues in the late 1960s have had to learn that change comes slowly. But even as one bemoans the sexism in one's department, or the unwillingness of the government to put 'women's issues' to the forefront, we do see the increase in women in universities, feminist studies in the curriculum and women in the House of Commons.

Our scholarship is becoming more sophisticated, a source both of pride and of frustration as we realize how our generalizations about women need modifying in the light of the many faces of women. We are still fighting to retain the independence and originality of women's studies and feminist pedagogy, and also to influence mainstream scholarship so that gender becomes integral. In my next collection of essays, which I imagine will be published around the year 2004, we shall see how far we have succeeded.

Note

1. Fulton (1993) advises booking a trip to the dentist to deal with the effects of frustrated teeth-grinding after trying to work out comparative statistics such as the ones I am presenting in this section: the country base (e.g. UK; Great Britain; England and Wales; England) and the details of collection and presentation change frequently through the years and in different sources. I had the same problem and have sometimes eliminated the country source where it made the statement impossibly convoluted; punctilious readers could consult the original reference.

References

Aaron, J. and Walby, S. (Eds) (1991) *Out of the Margins: Women's Studies in the Nineties.* London: Falmer Press.

Abramson, J. (1975) *The Invisible Woman: Discrimination in the Academic Profession.* San Francisco: Jossey-Bass.

Acker, S. (1981) No-woman's-land: British sociology of education 1960–1979. *Sociological Review, 29*(1): 77–104.

Acker, S. (1984a) Sociology, gender and education. In S. Acker, J. Megarry, S. Nisbet and E. Hoyle (Eds), *World Yearbook of Education 1984: Women and Education.* London: Kogan Page.

Acker, S. (1984b) Women in higher education: What is the problem? In S. Acker and D. Warren Piper (Eds), *Is Higher Education Fair to Women?* Guildford: Society for Research Into Higher Education.

Acker, S. (1986) What feminists want from education. In A. Hartnett and M. Naish (Eds), *Education and Society Today.* Lewes: Falmer Press.

Acker, S. (1987) Primary school teaching as an occupation. In S. Delamont (Ed.), *The Primary School Teacher.* Lewes: Falmer Press.

Acker, S. (1990a) Feminist critiques of educational practices and research. In T. Husen and T.N. Postlethwaite (Eds), *International Encyclopedia of Education*, Supplementary Vol. 2. Oxford: Pergamon Press.

Acker, S. (1990b) Managing the drama: The head teacher's work in an urban primary school. *Sociological Review, 38*: 247–71.

Acker, S. (1990c) Teachers' culture in an English primary school: Continuity and change. *British Journal of Sociology of Education, 11*(3): 257–73.

Acker, S. (1991) Teacher relationships and educational reform in England and Wales. *The Curriculum Journal, 2*(3): 301–316.

Acker, S. (1993) Women teachers working together. Unpublished paper. Toronto: Ontario Institute for Studies in Education.

Acker, S. (1994) The headteacher as career broker. In D. Dunlap and P. Schmuck (Eds), *Women Leading in Education.* Albany, NY: SUNY Press.

Acker, S. and Oakley, K. (1993) Gender issues in education for science and technology: Current situation and prospects for change. *Canadian Journal of Education,18*(3): 256–73.

Acker, S., Megarry, J., Nisbet, S. and Hoyle, E. (Eds) (1984) *World Book of Education 1984: Women and Education.* London: Kogan Page.

Acker, S., Hill, T. and Black, E. (1993) Thesis supervision: Managed or negotiated? Unpublished paper. Toronto: Ontario Institute for Studies in Education.

Adams, C. and Arnot, M. (1986) *Investigating Gender in Secondary Schools*. London: Inner London Education Authority.

Adler, N. (1976) Women students. In J. Katz and R. Hartnett (Eds), *Scholars in the Making*. Cambridge, MA: Ballinger.

Aiken, S., Anderson, K., Dinnerstein, M., Lensink, J. and MacCorquodale, P. (Eds) (1988) *Changing Our Minds: Feminist Transformations of Knowledge*. Albany, NY: SUNY Press.

Aisenberg, N. and Harrington, M. (1988) *Women of Academe*. Amherst, MA: University of Massachusetts Press.

Alcoff, L. (1988) Cultural feminism vs. post-structuralism. In E. Minnich, J. O'Barr and R. Rosenfeld (Eds), *Reconstructing the Academy*. Chicago, IL: University of Chicago Press.

Alexander, R.J. (1984) *Primary Teaching*. London: Holt, Rinehart and Winston.

Amos, V. and Parmar, P. (1981) Resistances and responses: The experiences of black girls in Britain. In A. McRobbie and T. McCabe (Eds), *Feminism for Girls*. London: Routledge and Kegan Paul.

Amos, V. and Parmar, P. (1984) Challenging imperial feminism. *Feminist Review 17*: 3–19.

Anon. (1989) 'Miss is a lesbian': The experience of a white lesbian teacher in a boys' school. In H. deLyon and F. Migniuolo (Eds), *Women Teachers*. Milton Keynes: Open University Press.

Anyon, J. (1983) Intersections of gender and class: Accommodation and resistance by working class and affluent females to contradictory sex-role ideologies. In S. Walker and L. Barton (Eds), *Gender, Class and Education*. Lewes: Falmer Press.

Apple, M. (1979) *Ideology and Curriculum*. Boston: Routledge and Kegan Paul.

Apple, M. (1986) *Teachers and Texts*. New York: Routledge and Kegan Paul.

Ardener, E. (1975) Belief and the problem of women. In S. Ardener (Ed.), *Perceiving Women*. London: Dent.

Ardener, S. (1975) Introduction. In S. Ardener (Ed.), *Perceiving Women*. London: Dent.

Arnot, M. (1981) Culture and political economy: Dual perspectives in the sociology of women's education. *Educational Analysis, 3*(1): 97–116.

Arnot, M. (1982) Male hegemony, social class and women's education. *Journal of Education, 164*(1): 64–89.

Arnot, M. (1985) Current developments in the sociology of women's education. *British Journal of Sociology of Education*, 6(1): 123–30.

Arnot, M. (1992) Feminism, education and the New Right. In M. Arnot and L. Barton (Eds), *Voicing Concerns: Sociological Perspectives on Contemporary Education Reforms*. Oxford: Triangle Books.

Arnot, M. (1993) A crisis in patriarchy? British feminist educational politics and state regulation of gender. In M. Arnot and K. Weiler (Eds), *Feminism and Social Justice in Education: International Perspectives*. London: Falmer Press.

Arnot, M. and Barton, L. (Eds) (1992) *Voicing Concerns: Sociological Perspectives on Contemporary Education Reforms*. Oxford: Triangle Books.

Arnot, M. and Weiler, K. (Eds) (1993) *Feminism and Social Justice in Education*. London: Falmer Press.

Arnot, M. and Weiner, G. (1987a) *Gender and Education Study Guide*. Milton Keynes: Open University.

Arnot, M. and Weiner, G. (Eds) (1987b) *Gender and the Politics of Schooling*. London: Hutchinson.

Arregger, C. (1966) *Graduate Women at Work*. Newcastle upon Tyne: Oriel.

Ås, B. (1975) On female culture: An attempt to formulate a theory of women's solidarity and action. *Acta Sociologica*, *18*: 142–61.

Aziz, A. (1990) Women in UK universities: The road to casualization? In S. Lie and V. O'Leary (Eds), *Storming the Tower: Women in the Academic World*. London: Kogan Page.

Baca Zinn, M., Cannon, L.W., Higginbotham, E. and Thornton Dill, B. (1986) The costs of exclusionary practices in women's studies. *Signs*, *11*(2): 290–303.

Bachrach, P. and Baratz, M. (1962) Two faces of power. *American Political Science Review*, *56*: 266–79.

Ball, S.J. (1981) *Beachside Comprehensive*. Cambridge: Cambridge University Press.

Ball, S.J. (1987) *The Micro-Politics of the School*. London: Methuen.

Ball, S.J. and Goodson, I. (Eds) (1985) *Teachers' Lives and Careers*. Lewes: Falmer Press.

Banks, O. (1976) *The Sociology of Education*. London: Batsford.

Banks, O. (1977) *Sociology of Education: A Bibliography*. London: Frances Pinter.

Bannerji, H., Carty, L., Dehli, K., Heald, S. and McKenna, K. (1991) *Unsettling Relations: The University as a Site of Feminist Struggle*. Toronto: Women's Press.

Barton, L. and Walker, S. (Eds) (1983) *Gender, Class and Education*. Lewes: Falmer Press.

Becker, H.S. and Geer, B. (1960) Latent culture: A note on the theory of latent social roles. *Administrative Science Quarterly*, *5*: 304–313.

Belenky, M., Clinchy, B., Goldberger, N. and Tarule, J. (1986) *Women's Ways of Knowing: The Development of Self, Voice and Mind*. New York: Basic Books.

Bernard, J. (1972) *The Future of Marriage*. New York: World.

Bernard, J. (1973) My four revolutions. In J. Huber (Ed.), *Changing Women in a Changing Society*. Chicago, IL: University of Chicago Press.

Bernbaum, G. (1977) *Knowledge and Ideology in the Sociology of Education*. London: Macmillan.

Bernstein, B. (1960) Language and social class. *British Journal of Sociology*, *11*: 271–6.

Bernstein, B. (1972) Education cannot compensate for society. In D. Rubenstein and C. Stoneman (Eds), *Education for Democracy*. Harmondsworth: Penguin.

Biklen, S.K. (1985) Can elementary school teaching be a career? *Issues in Education*, *3*: 215–31.

Biklen, S.K. (in press) *School Work: Gender and the Cultural Construction of Teaching*. New York: Teachers College Press.

Bird, L. (1992) Girls and positions of authority at primary school. In S. Middleton and A. Jones (Eds), *Women and Education in Aotearoa*, Vol. 2. Wellington: Bridget Williams Books.

Blackburn, R.M. and Jarman, J. (1993) Changing inequalities in access to British universities. *Oxford Review of Education*, *19*(2): 197–215.

Blair, M. and Maylor, U. (1993) Issues and concerns for black women teachers in training. In I. Siraj-Blatchford (Ed.), *'Race', Gender and the Education of Teachers*. Buckingham: Open University Press.

Bledstein, B.J. (1976) *The Culture of Professionalism*. New York: Norton.

Bowe, R. and Ball, S.J., with Gold, A. (1992) *Reforming Education and Changing Schools*. London: Routledge.

Bowles, G. and Klein, R. (Eds) (1983) *Theories of Women's Studies*. London: Routledge and Kegan Paul.

Bowles, S. and Gintis, H. (1976) *Schooling in Capitalist America*. London: Routledge and Kegan Paul.

Brah, A. and Deem, R. (1986) Towards anti-sexist and anti-racist schooling. *Critical Social Policy*, 6(1): 66–79.

Brah, A. and Minhas, R. (1985) Structural racism or cultural difference: Schooling for Asian girls. In G. Weiner (Ed.), *Just a Bunch of Girls*. Milton Keynes: Open University Press.

Brehony, K. (1990) Neither rhyme nor reason: Primary schooling and the national curriculum. In M. Flude and M. Hammer (Eds), *The Education Reform Act, 1988: Its Origins and Implications*. London: Falmer Press.

Breslauer, H. and Gordon, J. (1990) Redressing the Imbalance: The Public Policy Agenda and Academic Women. Paper presented at the *Annual Meeting of the Canadian Society for the Study of Higher Education*, Victoria, BC, June.

Briskin, L. and Coulter, R.P. (Eds) (1992) Special issue on feminist pedagogy. *Canadian Journal of Education*, 17(3): 247–389.

Britzman, D. (1991) *Practice Makes Practice*. Albany, NY: SUNY Press.

Broadfoot, P. and Osborn, M. (1987) Teachers' conceptions of their professional responsibility: Some international comparisons. *Comparative Education*, 23(3): 287–301.

Broadfoot, P. and Abbott, D., with Croll, P., Osborn, M. and Pollard, A. (1991) Look back in anger? Findings from the PACE project concerning primary teachers' experiences of SATs. Unpublished paper. Bristol: School of Education, University of Bristol.

Brookman, J. (1991) Graceful coming of age for women. *Times Higher Education Supplement*, 2 February, p. 4.

Bryan, B., Dadzie, S. and Scafe, S. (1985) *The Heart of the Race: Black Women's Lives in Britain*. London: Virago.

Buchan, L. (1980) It's a good job for a girl (but an awful career for a woman) In D. Spender and E. Sarah (Eds), *Learning to Lose: Sexism and Education*. London: The Women's Press.

Buchbinder, H. and Newson, J. (1990) Corporate–university linkages in Canada: Transforming a public institution. *Higher Education*, 20(4): 355–79.

Bunch, C. and Pollack, S. (Eds) (1983) *Learning Our Way: Essays in Feminist Education*. Trumansberg, NY: Crossing Press.

Burgess, H. and Carter, B. (1992) 'Bringing out the best in people': Teacher training and the 'real' teacher. *British Journal of Sociology of Education*, 13(3): 349–59.

Burgess, R.W. (1983) *Experiencing Comprehensive Education*. London: Methuen.

Burgess, R.W. (1986) *Sociology, Education and Schools: An Introduction to the Sociology of Education*. London: Batsford.

Burton, L. and Weiner, G. (1993) From rhetoric to reality: Strategies for developing a social justice approach to educational decision-making. In I. Siraj-Blatchford (Ed.), *'Race', Gender and the Education of Teachers*. Buckingham: Open University Press.

Buswell, C. (1981) Sexism in school routines and classroom practices. *Durham and Newcastle Research Review*, 9: 195–200.

Buswell C. vs. Newcastle City Council (1989) *Decision Document Folio Ref: 9/213/179. 6 February, 1989*. (Available from Regional Office of Industrial Tribunals, Newcastle upon Tyne, NE1 6NT, England.)

Butler, D. and Kavanagh, D. (1992) *The British General Election of 1992*. London: Macmillan.

Byrne, E. (1978) *Women and Education*. London: Tavistock.

Byrne, D., Williamson, B. and Fletcher, B. (1975) *The Poverty of Education*. London: Martin Robertson.

Canadian Association of University Teachers (1991) *Status of Women Supplement*. Ottawa: CAUT.

Carby, H. (1982) White woman listen! Black feminism and the boundaries of sister-hood. In Centre for Contemporary Cultural Studies, University of Birmingham, *The Empire Strikes Back*. London: Hutchinson.

Carlson, R. and Schmuck, P. (1981) The sex dimension of careers in educational management: Overview and synthesis. In P. Schmuck, W.W. Charters and R. Carlson (Eds), *Educational Policy and Management: Sex Differentials*. New York: Academic Press.

Carrington, B. and Short, G. (1987) Breakthrough to political literacy: Political education, antiracist teaching and the primary school. *Journal of Education Policy*, 2: 1–13.

Casey, K. and Apple, M. (1989) Gender and the conditions of teachers' work: The development of understanding in America. In S. Acker (Ed.), *Teachers, Gender and Careers*. Lewes: Falmer Press.

Central Statistical Office (1970) *Social Trends 1*. London: HMSO.

Central Statistical Office (1974) *Social Trends 5*. London: HMSO.

Central Statistical Office (1991) *Social Trends 21*. London: HMSO.

Central Statistical Office (1992) *Social Trends 22*. London: HMSO.

Central Statistical Office (1993) *Social Trends 23*. London: HMSO.

Chessum, L. (1989) *The Part-time Nobody: Part-time Women Teachers in West Yorkshire*. Bradford: WYCROW, University of Bradford.

Clance, P. and O'Toole, M. (1988) The imposter phenomenon: An internal barrier to empowerment and achievement. In E. Rothblum and E. Cole (Eds), *Treating Women's Fear of Failure*. New York: Harrington Press.

Clarricoates, K. (1978) Dinosaurs in the classroom: A re-examination of some aspects of the 'hidden curriculum' in primary schools. *Women's Studies International Quarterly*, 1: 353–64.

Clarricoates, K. (1980a) All in a day's work. In D. Spender and E. Sarah (Eds), *Learning to Lose*. London: The Women's Press.

Clarricoates, K. (1980b) The importance of being Ernest . . . Tom . . . Jane: The perception and categorization of gender conformity and gender deviation in primary schools. In R. Deem (Ed.), *Schooling for Women's Work*. London: Routledge and Kegan Paul.

Coffey, A. and Acker, S. (1991) 'Girlies on the warpath': Addressing gender in initial teacher education. *Gender and Education*, 3(3): 249–61.

Cogger, D. (1985) 'Women teachers on low scales.' Unpublished MEd thesis. Cardiff: University of Wales.

Coleman, J.S. (1961) *The Adolescent Society*. New York: Free Press of Glencoe.

Coleman, J.S. (1968) The concept of equal opportunity. *Harvard Educational Review*, 38(1): 7–22.

Collins, P.H. (1990) *Black Feminist Thought*. Boston, MA: Unwin Hyman.

Collison, P. and Millen, J. (1969) University chancellors, vice chancellors and college principals: A social profile. *Sociology*, 3: 77–109.

Committee of Vice-Chancellors and Principals of the Universities of the United Kingdon (1972) *Report of an Enquiry into the Use of Academic Staff Time*. London: CVCP.

Connell, R.W. (1985) Theorizing gender. *Sociology*, 19(2): 250–72.

Connell, R.W., Ashenden, D.J., Kessler, S. and Dowsett, G. (1982) *Making the Difference: Schools, Families and Social Division*. Sydney: Allen and Unwin.

Connelly, F.M. and Clandinin, D.J. (1988) *Teachers as Curriculum Planners*. Toronto: OISE Press.

Cook, J. and Fonow, M. (1986) Knowledge and women's interests: Issues of epistemology and methodology in feminist sociological research. *Sociological Inquiry*, *56*(1): 2–29.

Coser, L. (1974) *Greedy Institutions: Patterns of Undivided Commitment*. New York: The Free Press.

Cott, N. (1986) Feminist theory and feminist movements: The past before us. In J. Mitchell and A. Oakley (Eds), *What is Feminism*? Oxford: Basil Blackwell.

Crozier, G. and Menter, I. (1993) The heart of the matter? Student teachers' experiences in school. In I. Siraj-Blatchford (Ed.), *'Race', Gender and the Education of Teachers*. Buckingham: Open University Press.

Culley, L. and Demaine, J. (1983) Social theory, social relations and education. In S. Walker and L. Barton (Eds), *Gender, Class and Education*. Lewes: Falmer Press.

Cunnison, S. (1985) Making it in a man's world: Women teachers in a senior high school. *Occasional Paper No. 1*. Hull: University of Hull, Department of Sociology and Social Anthropology.

Cunnison, S. (1989) Gender joking in the staffroom. In S. Acker (Ed.), *Teachers, Gender and Careers*. Lewes: Falmer Press.

Dale, R. (1992) Recovering from a pyrrhic victory? Quality, relevance and impact in the sociology of education. In M. Arnot and L. Barton (Eds), *Voicing Concerns: Sociological Perspectives on Contemporary Education Reforms*. Oxford: Triangle Books.

David, M.E. (1980) *The State, the Family and Education*. London: Routledge and Kegan Paul.

David, M.E. (1984) Women, family and education. In S. Acker *et al.* (Eds), *World Yearbook of Education 1984: Women in Education*. London: Kogan Page.

David, M.E. (1989) Prima donna inter pares? Women in academic management. In S. Acker (Ed.), *Teachers, Gender and Careers*. London: Falmer Press.

David, M.E. (1993) *Parents, Gender and Education Reform*. Cambridge: Polity Press.

Davies, B. (1989a) The discursive production of male/female dualism in school settings. *Oxford Review of Education*, *15*(3): 229–41.

Davies, B. (1989b) *Frogs and Snails and Feminist Tales: Preschool Children and Gender*. Sydney: Allen and Unwin.

Davies, L. (1979) Deadlier than the male? Girls' conformity and deviance in school. In L. Barton and R. Meighan (Eds), *Schools, Pupils and Deviance*. Nafferton: Driffield.

Davies, L. (1987) Racism and sexism. In S. Delamont (Ed.), *The Primary School Teacher*. Lewes: Falmer Press.

Davies, L. (1990) *Equity and Efficiency? School Management in an International Context*. Lewes: Falmer Press.

Davies, L. and Meighan, R. (1975) A review of schooling and sex roles with particular reference to the experience of girls in secondary schools. *Educational Review*, *27*: 165–78.

Davis, D. and Astin, H. (1990) Life cycle, career patterns and gender stratification in academe: Breaking myths and exposing truths. In S. Lie and V. O'Leary (Eds), *Storming the Tower: Women in the Academic World*. London: Kogan Page.

de Beauvoir, S. (1949/1972) *The Second Sex*. Harmondsworth: Penguin.

Deem, R. (1978) *Women and Schooling*. London: Routledge and Kegan Paul.

Deem, R. (Ed.) (1980) *Schooling for Women's Work*. London: Routledge and Kegan Paul.

Delamont, S. (1978) The domestic ideology and women's education. In S. Delamont and L. Duffin (Eds), *The Nineteenth Century Woman: Her Cultural and Physical World*. London: Croom Helm.

Delamont, S. (1980) *Sex Roles and the School*. London: Methuen.

Delamont, S. (1989) Gender and British postgraduate funding policy: A critique of the Winfield Report. *Gender and Education*, 1: 51–7.

Delmar, R. (1986) What is feminism? In J. Mitchell and A. Oakley (Eds), *What is Feminism?* Oxford: Basil Blackwell.

Department of Education and Science, University Grants Committee (1979) *Statistics of Education 1976, vol. 6, Universities*. London: HMSO.

Department of Education and Science (1987) *Statistics of Education: Teachers in Service, England and Wales*. London: DES.

Department of Education and Science (1991) *Statistics of Education: Teachers in Service, England and Wales, 1988*. London: DES.

Department of Education and Science (1992) *Statistics of Education: Teachers in Service, England and Wales, 1989 and 1990*. London: DES.

Department for Education (1993a) *GCSE and A/AS Examination Results 1991/92*. Statistical Bulletin Issue No. 15/93. London: DFE.

Department for Education (1993b) *Statistics of Education: School Examinations, GCSE and GCE 1991*. London: DFE.

Department for Education (1993c) *Statistics of Schools, January 1992*. London: DFE.

Department for Education (1993d) *Student Numbers in Higher Education, Great Britain 1981/82 to 1991/92*. Statistical Bulletin Issue No. 17/93. London: DFE.

Desjardins, C. (1989) The meaning of Gilligan's concept of 'different voice' for the learning environment. In C. Pearson, D. Shavlik and J. Touchton (Eds), *Educating the Majority: Women Challenge Tradition in Higher Education*. New York: Macmillan.

Douglas, J.W.B. (1964) *The Home and the School*. London: MacGibbon and Kee.

Dove, L. (1986) *Teachers and Teacher Education in Developing Countries*. London: Croom Helm.

Doyle, W. and Ponder, G.A. (1977) The practicality ethic in teacher decision-making. *Interchange*, 8: 1–12.

Drakich, J., Smith, D.E., Stewart, P., Fox, B. and Griffith, A. (1991) *Status of Women in Ontario Universities: Final Report, Vol. 1: Overview*. Toronto: Ministry of Colleges and Universities, Government of Ontario.

DuBois, E.C., Kelly, G.P., Kennedy, E.L., Korsmeyer, C.W. and Robinson, L.S. (1985) *Feminist Scholarship: Kindling in the Groves of Academe*. Urbana, IL: University of Illinois Press.

Durkheim, E. (1895/1938) *The Rules of Sociological Method*. London: Collier-Macmillan.

Durkheim, E. (1897/1952) *Suicide*. London: Routledge and Kegan Paul.

Dyhouse, C. (1977) Good wives and little mothers: Social anxieties and schoolgirls' curriculum 1890–1920. *Oxford Review of Education*, 3: 21–36.

Economic and Social Research Council (1988) Research programme on research training in the social sciences. Briefing Paper. Swindon: ESRC.

Edwards, R. (1993) *Mature Women Students*. London: Taylor and Francis.

Egerton, M. and Halsey, A.H. (1993) Trends by social class and gender in access to higher education in Britain. *Oxford Review of Education*, 19(2): 183–95.

Eisenstein, H. (1984) *Contemporary Feminist Thought*. London: Unwin.

Eisenstein, H. (1991) *Gender Shock: Practicing Feminism on Two Continents*. Boston, MA: Beacon Press.

Epstein, C.F. (1970) *Woman's Place: Options and Limits in Professional Careers.* Berkeley: University of California Press.

Equal Opportunities Commission (1983) *Eighth Annual Report 1983. Appendix: Men and Women: A Statistical Digest.* London: HMSO.

Esland, G. and Cathcart, H. (1981) *Education and the Corporate Economy.* Unit 2 of Course E353, 'Society, Education and the State'. Milton Keynes: Open University Press.

Etzioni, A. (Ed.) (1969) *The Semi-Professions and their Organization.* New York: Free Press.

Evans, M. (1993) A faculty for prejudice. *The Times Higher,* 12 November, p. 20.

Evans, T. (1979) Creativity, sex-role socialization and pupil–teacher interactions in early schooling. *Sociological Review, 27*: 139–55.

Evans, T. (1982) Being and becoming: Teachers' perceptions of sex-roles and actions toward their male and female pupils. *British Journal of Sociology of Education, 3*: 127–43.

Evetts, J. (1986) Teachers' careers: The objective dimension. *Educational Studies, 12*: 225–44.

Evetts, J. (1989) The internal labour market for primary teachers. In S. Acker (Ed.), *Teachers, Gender and Careers.* Lewes: Falmer Press.

Evetts, J. (1990) *Women in Primary Teaching.* London: Unwin Hyman.

Farley, J., Brewer, J.H. and Fine, S.W. (1977) Women's values: Changing faster than men's? *Sociology of Education, 50*: 151.

Feiman-Nemser, S. and Floden, R. (1986) The cultures of teaching. In M.C. Wittrock (Ed.), *Handbook of Research on Teaching.* New York: Macmillan.

Ferber, M. and Huber, J. (1975) Sex of students and sex of instructor: A study of student bias. *American Journal of Sociology, 80*: 949–63.

Filteau, C. (Ed.) (1989) *Proceedings of a Conference on Women in Graduate Studies in Ontario.* Toronto: Ontario Council on Graduate Studies.

Flude, M. and Hammer, M. (Eds) (1990) *The Education Reform Act 1988.* Lewes: Falmer Press.

Fogarty, M., Rapoport, R. and Rapoport, R. (1971) *Sex, Career and Family.* London: Allen and Unwin.

Fonda, N. and Moss, P. (Eds) (1976) *Mothers in Employment.* Uxbridge: Brunel University Management Programme and Thomas Coram Research Unit.

Fraser, N. and Nicholson, L. (1990) Social criticism without philosophy: An encounter between feminism and postmodernism. In L. Nicholson (Ed.), *Feminism/Postmodernism.* London: Routledge and Kegan Paul.

Freeman, B.C. (1977) Faculty women in the American university. In P. Altbach (Ed.), *Comparative Perspectives on the Academic Profession.* New York: Praeger.

French, J. and French, P. (1984) Gender imbalances in the primary classroom. *Educational Research, 26*: 127–36.

Friedan, B. (1963) *The Feminine Mystique.* New York: Norton.

Fullan, M. (1982) Research into educational innovation. In H.L. Gray (Ed.), *The Management of Educational Institutions.* Lewes: Falmer Press.

Fuller, M. (1978) 'Dimensions of Gender in a School.' Unpublished PhD thesis, University of Bristol.

Fuller, M. (1983) Qualified criticism, critical qualifications. In L. Barton and S. Walker (Eds), *Race, Class and Education.* London: Croom Helm.

Fulton, O. (1993) Women catch up. *The Times Higher,* Synthesis: Higher Education Trends, 16 July, pp. ii–iii.

Furlong, J. (1992) Reconstructing professionalism: Ideological struggle in initial teacher education. In M. Arnot and L. Barton (Eds), *Voicing Concerns: Sociological Perspectives on Contemporary Education Reforms*. Oxford: Triangle Books.

Gaskell, J. (1986) Conceptions of skill and the work of women: Some historical and political issues. In R. Hamilton and M. Barrett (Eds), *The Politics of Diversity*. London: Verso.

Gaskell, J. (1992) *Gender Matters from School to Work*. Milton Keynes: Open University Press.

Gaskell, J. and McLaren, A. (Eds) (1991) *Women and Education: A Canadian Perspective*. Calgary: Detselig.

Gearhart, S.M. (1983) If the mortarboard fits . . . radical feminism in academia. In C. Bunch and S. Pollack (Eds), *Learning Our Way*. Trumansburg, NY: Crossing Press.

Gelb, J. (1989) *Feminism and Politics*. Berkeley, CA: University of California Press.

Gilbert, P. and Taylor, S. (1991) *Fashioning the Feminine: Girls, Popular Culture and Schooling*. Sydney: Allen and Unwin.

Gilligan, C. (1982) *In a Different Voice*. Cambridge, MA: Harvard University Press.

Gluck, S.B. and Patai, D. (Eds) (1991) *Women's Words: The Feminist Practice of Oral History*. New York: Routledge.

Goffman, E. (1961) *Encounters*. Indianapolis, IN: Bobbs-Merrill.

Goodson, I. (1991) Sponsoring the teacher's voice: Teachers' lives and teacher development. *Cambridge Journal of Education*, 21(1): 35–45.

Gosden, P.H.J.H. (1972) *The Evolution of a Profession*. Oxford: Basil Blackwell.

Grafton, T., Miller, H., Smith, L., Vegoda, M. and Whitfield, R. (1987) Gender and curriculum choice: A case study. In M. Arnot and G. Weiner (Eds), *Gender and the Politics of Schooling*. London: Hutchinson.

Grant, C. and Sleeter, C. (1985) Who determines teacher work: The teacher, the organization, or both? *Teaching and Teacher Education*, 1: 209–220.

Grant, L. (1992) Race and the schooling of young girls. In J. Wrigley (Ed.), *Education and Gender Equality*. Washington, DC: Falmer Press.

Grant, L., Ward, K. and Forshner, C. (1993) Mentoring, gender, and careers of academic scientists. Paper presented at the *Annual Meeting of the American Educational Research Association*, Atlanta, GA, April.

Grant, R. (1987) A career in teaching: A survey of middle school teachers' perceptions with particular reference to the careers of women teachers. *British Educational Research Journal*, 13: 227–39.

Grant, R. (1989) Women teachers' career pathways: Towards an alternative model of 'career'. In S. Acker (Ed.), *Teachers, Gender and Careers*. Lewes: Falmer Press.

Gray, E. (1989) The culture of separated desks. In C. Pearson, D. Shavlik and J. Touchton (Eds), *Educating the Majority: Women Challenge Tradition in Higher Education*. New York: Macmillan.

Gray, J. (1981) From policy to practice – some problems and paradoxes. In B. Simon and W. Taylor (Eds), *Education in the Eighties: The Central Issues*. London: Batsford.

Greed, C. (1991) *Surveying Sisters: Women in a Traditional Male Profession*. London: Routledge

Griffin, C. (1985) *Typical Girls?* London: Routledge and Kegan Paul.

Grumet, M. (1981) Pedagogy for patriarchy: The feminization of teaching. *Interchange*, 12(2–3): 165–84.

Grumet, M. (1988) *Bitter Milk: Women and Teaching*. Amherst, MA: University of Massachusetts Press.

Grumet, M. (1990) Voice: The search for a feminist rhetoric for educational studies. *Cambridge Journal of Education*, *20*(3): 277–82.

Gumport, P. (1990) Feminist scholarship as a vocation. *Higher Education*, *20*: 231–43.

Halsey, A.H., Heath, A.F. and Ridge, J.M. (1980) *Origins and Destinations: Family, Class and Education in Modern Britain*. Oxford: Clarendon Press.

Hanmer, J. and Leonard, D. (1980) Men and culture: The sociological intelligentsia and the maintenance of male domination, or superman meets the invisible women. Paper presented at the *British Sociological Association Annual Conference*, Lancaster, April.

Harding, S. (1986) *The Science Question in Feminism*. Ithaca, NY: Cornell University Press.

Harding, S. (1991) *Whose Science? Whose Knowledge?* Ithaca, NY: Cornell University Press.

Hare-Mustin, R. and Marecek, J. (1990) Gender and the meaning of difference: Postmodernism and psychology. In R. Hare-Mustin and J. Marecek (Eds), *Making a Difference: Psychology and the Construction of Gender*. New Haven, CT: Yale University Press.

Hargreaves, A. (1982) Resistance and relative autonomy theories: Problems of distortion and incoherence in recent Marxist analyses of education. *British Journal of Sociology of Education*, *3*(2): 107–126.

Hargreaves, A. (1984) Experience counts, theory doesn't: How teachers talk about their work. *Sociology of Education*, *57*: 244–54.

Hargreaves, A. (1994) *Changing Teachers, Changing Times: Teachers' Work and Culture in the Post-Modern Age*. London: Cassell/New York: Teachers College Press/Toronto: OISE Press.

Hargreaves, D. (1978) Whatever happened to symbolic interactionism? In L. Barton and R. Meighan (Eds), *Sociological Interpretations of Schooling and Classrooms: A Reappraisal*. Driffield: Nafferton.

Hartnett, A. and Naish, M. (Eds) (1986) *Education and Society Today*. Lewes: Falmer Press.

Hatton, E. (1987) Determinants of teacher work: Some causal complications. *Teaching and Teacher Education*, *3*: 55–60.

Hennig, M. and Jardim, A. (1979) *The Managerial Woman*. London: Pan.

Hey, V. (1993) Review of *Gender and Schools*. *Gender and Education*, *5*(3): 329–31.

Hill, T., Acker, S. and Black, E. (1994) Research students and their supervisors in education and psychology. In R. Burgess (Ed.), *Postgraduate Education and Training in the Social Sciences*. London: Jessica Kingsley.

Hilsum, S. and Start, K.B. (1974) *Promotion and Careers in Teaching*. Slough: National Foundation for Educational Research.

Hirsch, M. and Keller, E.F. (Eds) (1990) *Conflicts of Feminism*. New York: Routledge.

Hochschild, A. (1975a) Inside the clockwork of male careers. In F. Howe (Ed.), *Women and the Power to Change*. New York: McGraw-Hill.

Hochschild, A. (1975b) The sociology of feeling and emotion: Selected possibilities. In M. Millman and R.M. Kanter (Eds), *Another Voice: Feminist Perspectives on Social Life and Social Science*. Garden City, NY: Anchor.

Holly, D.N. (1965) Profiting from a comprehensive school: Class, sex and ability. *British Journal of Sociology*, *16*: 150–58.

Holmstrom, L.L. (1973) *The Two-Career Family*. Cambridge, MA: Schenkman.

hooks, b. (1988) *Talking Back*. Toronto: Between the Lines.

Hoyle, E. (1986) *The Politics of School Management*. London: Hodder and Stoughton.

Hughes, E.C. (1958) *Men and Their Work*. New York: Free Press.

Hustler, D. and Cuff, T. (1986) Teachers' perceptions of the GIST project: An independent evaluation. In D. Hustler, T. Cassidy and T. Cuff (Eds), *Action Research in Classrooms and Schools*. London: Allen and Unwin.

Ingleby, J.D. and Cooper, E. (1974) How teachers perceive first-year school-children: Sex and ethnic differences. *Sociology*, 8: 463–73.

Interim Advisory Committee on School Teachers' Pay and Conditions (1990) *Third Report*. London: HMSO.

Jackson, D. (1988) *Fellowship Scheme for Women Returners to Science and Engineering: Personal Experiences of Returners*. Guildford: University of Surrey.

Jackson, D. (1989) Women returners. Paper presented at the *Conference on Women and Higher Education*, King's College, Cambridge, April.

Jackson, J. (Ed.) (1970) *Professions and Professionalization*. Cambridge: Cambridge University Press.

Jackson, P. (1968) *Life in Classrooms*. New York: Holt, Rinehart and Winston.

Jayawardena, K. (1986) *Feminism and Nationalism in the Third World*. London: Zed Books.

Jencks, C. *et al.* (1972) *Inequality: A Reassessment of the Effect of Family and Schooling in America*. New York: Basic Books.

Johnson, J. (1990) Behind the bastion. *Times Higher Education Supplement*, 20 April, p. 14.

Jones, A. (1993) Becoming a 'girl': Post-structuralist suggestions for educational research. *Gender and Education*, 5(2): 157–66.

Jones, C. (1985) Sexual tyranny: Male violence in a mixed secondary school. In G. Weiner (Ed.), *Just a Bunch of Girls*. Milton Keynes: Open University Press.

Joseph, J. (1961) A research note on attitudes to work and marriage of six hundred adolescent girls. *British Journal of Sociology*, 12: 176–83.

Joyce, M. (1987) Being a feminist teacher. In M. Lawn and G. Grace (Eds), *Teachers: The Culture and Politics of Work*. Lewes: Falmer Press.

Kandiyoti, D. (1988) Bargaining with patriarchy. *Gender and Society*, 2(3): 274–90.

Kanter, R.M. (1975) Women and the structure of organizations: Explorations in theory and behavior. In M. Millman and R. Kanter (Eds), *Another Voice*. Garden City, NY: Anchor.

Kanter, R.M. (1977) *Men and Women of the Corporation*. New York: Basic Books.

Karabel, J. and Halsey, A.H. (1977) Educational research: A review and an interpretation. In J. Karabel and A.H. Halsey (Eds), *Power and Ideology in Education*. New York: Oxford University Press.

Kay, C.Y. (1990) At the Palace: Researching gender and ethnicity in a Chinese restaurant. In L. Stanley (Ed.), *Feminist Praxis*. London: Routledge.

Kelly, A. (1985) The construction of masculine science. *British Journal of Sociology of Education*, 6: 133–54.

Kelly, A. (1986) Gender differences in teacher–pupil interaction: A meta-analytical review. Paper presented at the *British Educational Research Association Annual Conference*, Bristol, September.

Kelly, A. *et al.* (1985) Traditionalists and trendies: Teachers' attitudes to educational issues. *British Educational Research Journal*, 11: 91–104.

Kelsall, R.K. (1963) *Women and Teaching*. London: HMSO.

Kelsall, R.K. and Kelsall, H.M. (1970) The status, role and future of teachers. In E.J. King (Ed.), *The Teacher and the Needs of Society in Evolution*. Oxford: Pergamon Press.

Kelsall, R.K., Poole, A. and Kuhn, A. (1972) *Graduates: The Sociology of an Elite*. London: Tavistock.

Kenway, J. (1990) *Gender and Education Policy*. Geelong, Victoria: Deakin University Press.

Kenway, J. and Modra, H. (1992) Feminist pedagogy and emancipatory possibilities. In C. Luke and J. Gore (Eds), *Feminisms and Critical Pedagogy*. New York: Routledge.

Kenway, J. and Willis, S. (Eds) (1990) *Hearts and Minds: Self-esteem and the Schooling of Girls*. London: Falmer Press.

Kessler, S., Ashenden, D., Connell, R.W. and Dowsett, G. W. (1985) Gender relations in secondary schooling. *Sociology of Education*, 58: 34–48.

Khayatt, M.D. (1990) Lesbian teachers: An invisible presence. In F. Forman *et al.*, *Feminism and Education: A Canadian Perspective*. Toronto: Centre for Women's Studies in Education, Ontario Institute for Studies in Education.

Khayatt, M.D. (1992) *Lesbian Teachers*. Albany, NY: SUNY Press.

King, R. (1978) *All Things Bright and Beautiful? A Sociological Study of Infants' Classrooms*. Chichester: John Wiley.

King, R. (1982) Organisational change in secondary schools: An action approach. *British Journal of Sociology of Education*, 3: 3–18.

Kitzinger, C. (1990) Beyond the boundaries: Lesbians in academe. In S. Lie and V. O'Leary (Eds), *Storming the Tower: Women in the Academic World*. London: Kogan Page.

Klein, S. (Ed.) (1985) *Handbook for Achieving Sex Equity Through Education*. Baltimore, Md: Johns Hopkins University Press.

Lacey, C. (1977) *The Socialization of Teachers*. London: Methuen.

Laird, S. (1988) Reforming 'women's true profession': A case for 'feminist pedagogy' in teacher education? *Harvard Educational Review*, 58(4): 449–63.

Lane, M. (1972) Explaining educational choice. *Sociology*, 6: 255–66.

Langeveld, M.J. (1963) The psychology of teachers and the teaching profession. In G.Z.F. Bereday and J.A. Lauwerys (Eds), *The Yearbook of Education 1963: The Education and Training of Teachers*. London: Evans Brothers.

Lather, P. (1991) *Getting Smart: Feminist Research and Pedagogy With/In the Postmodern*. New York: Routledge.

Lee, D.J. (1968) Class differentials in educational opportunity and promotions from the ranks. *Sociology*, 2: 293–312.

Lee, P.C. (1973) Male and female teachers in elementary schools: An ecological analysis. *Teachers College Record*, 75(1): 79–98.

Leggatt, T. (1970) Teaching as a profession. In J. Jackson (Ed.), *Professions and Professionalization*. Cambridge: Cambridge University Press.

Leicester, M. (1993) *Race for a Change in Continuing and Higher Education*. Buckingham: Open University Press.

Levine, A. and Crumrine, J. (1975) Women and fear of success: A problem in replication. *American Journal of Sociology*, 80: 964–74.

Lewin, E. and Olesen, V. (1981) Lateralness in women's work: New views on success. *Sex Roles*, 6: 619–30.

Lewis, L. (1975) *Scaling the Ivory Tower: Merit and its Limits in Academic Careers*. Baltimore, Md.: Johns Hopkins University Press.

Lie, S. (1990) The juggling act: Work and family in Norway. In S. Lie and V. O'Leary (Eds), *Storming the Tower: Women in the Academic World*. London: Kogan Page.

Lieberman, M. (1956) *Education as a Profession*. Englewood Cliffs, NJ: Prentice-Hall.

Lightfoot, S.L. (1983) The lives of teachers. In L.S. Shulman and G. Sykes (Eds), *Handbook of Teaching and Policy*. New York: Longman.

Littlewood, M. (1989) The 'wise married woman' and the teaching unions. In H. DeLyon and F. Migniuolo (Eds), *Women Teachers: Issues and Opportunities*. Milton Keynes: Open University Press.

Liversidge, W. (1962) Life chances. *Sociological Review*, 10: 17–34.

Llewellyn, M. (1980) Studying girls at school: The implications of confusion. In R. Deem (Ed.), *Schooling for Women's Work*. London: Routledge and Kegan Paul.

Lobban, G. (1975) Sex roles in reading schemes. *Educational Review*, 27: 202–210.

Lofland, L. (1975) The 'thereness' of women: A selective review of urban sociology. In M. Millman and R.M. Kanter (Eds), *Another Voice: Feminist Perspectives on Social Life and Social Science*. Garden City, NY: Anchor.

Lortie, D.C. (1975) *Schoolteacher: A Sociological Study*. Chicago, IL: University of Chicago Press.

Luke, C. and Gore, J. (1992a) Women in the academy: Strategy, struggle and survival. In C. Luke and J. Gore (Eds), *Feminisms and Critical Pedagogy*. New York: Routledge.

Luke, C. and Gore, J. (Eds), (1992b) *Feminisms and Critical Pedagogy*. New York: Routledge.

Lyons, G. (1980) *Teacher Careers and Career Perceptions*. Windsor: NFER-Nelson.

Lyons, G. and McCleary, L. (1980) Careers in teaching. In E. Hoyle and J. Megarry (Eds), *World Yearbook of Education 1980: Professional Development of Teachers*. London: Kogan Page.

MacDonald, M. (1980a) Schooling in the reproduction of class and gender relations. In L. Barton, R. Meighan and S. Walker (Eds), *Schooling, Ideology and the Curriculum*. Lewes: Falmer Press.

MacDonald, M. (1980b) Socio-cultural reproduction and women's education. In R. Deem (Ed.), *Schooling for Women's Work*. London: Routledge and Kegan Paul.

Mackie, M. (1977) On congenial truths: A perspective on women's studies. *Canadian Review of Sociology and Anthropology*, 14: 117–28.

MacKinnon, C. (1982) Feminism, marxism, method and the state: An agenda for theory. *Signs*, 7(3): 515–44.

Maher, F. and Tetreault, M.K.T. (1993) Doing feminist ethnography: Lessons from feminist classrooms. *Qualitative Studies in Education*, 6(1): 19–32.

Mahony, P. (1985) *Schools for the boys? Co-education Reassessed*. London: Hutchinson.

Manicom, A. (1992) Feminist pedagogy: Transformations, standpoints, and politics. *Canadian Journal of Education*, 17(3): 365–89.

Marks, P. (1976) Femininity in the classroom: An account of changing attitudes. In J. Mitchell and A. Oakley (Eds), *The Rights and Wrongs of Women*, pp. 176–98. Harmondsworth: Penguin.

Marland, M. (1983) Staffing for sexism: Educational leadership and role models. In M. Marland (Ed.), *Sex Differentiation and Schooling*. London: Heinemann.

Maynard, M. (1990) The re-shaping of sociology? Trends in the study of gender. *Sociology*, 24(2): 269–90.

Maynard, M. (1993) Feminism and the possibilities of a postmodern research practice. *British Journal of Sociology of Education*, 14(3): 327–31.

McKellar, B. (1989) Only the fittest of the fittest will survive: Black women and education. In S. Acker (Ed.), *Teachers, Gender and Careers*. Lewes: Falmer Press.

McLaren, P. (1989) *Life in Schools*. White Plains, NY: Longman.

McNamara, D. (1976) On returning to the chalk face: Theory not into practice. *British Journal of Teacher Education*, 2: 147–60.

McPherson, G. (1972) *Small Town Teacher*. Cambridge, MA: Harvard University Press.

McRobbie, A. (1978) Working class girls and the culture of femininity. In Women's Studies Group, Centre for Contemporary Cultural Studies, University of Birmingham, *Women Take Issue*. London: Hutchinson.

McRobbie, A. (1982) The politics of feminist research: Between talk, text and action. *Feminist Review*, 12: 46–57.

Measor, L. (1983) Gender and the sciences: Pupils' gender-based conceptions of school subjects. In M. Hammersley and A. Hargreaves (Eds), *Curriculum Practice*. Lewes: Falmer Press.

Measor, L. and Sikes, P. (1992) *Gender and Schools*. London: Cassell.

Meighan, R. (1986) *A Sociology of Educating*, 2nd edn. London: Holt, Rinehart and Winston.

Metz, M. (1989) Teachers' pride in craft, school subcultures, and societal pressures. In L. Weis *et al*. (Eds), *Crisis in Teaching*. Albany, NY: SUNY Press.

Middleton, S. (1984) The sociology of women's education as a field of academic study. *Discourse*, 5(1): 42–62.

Middleton, S. (1989) Educating feminists: A life-history study. In S. Acker (Ed.), *Teachers, Gender and Careers*. Lewes: Falmer Press.

Middleton, S. (1993) A post-modern pedagogy for the sociology of women's education. In M. Arnot and K. Weiler (Eds), *Feminism and Social Justice in Education*. London: Falmer Press.

Middleton, S. and Jones, A. (Eds) (1992) *Women and Education in Aotearoa*, Vol. 2. Wellington: Bridget Williams Books.

Miles, S. and Middleton, C. (1990) Girls' education in the balance: the ERA and inequality. In M. Flude and M. Hammer (Eds), *The Educational Reform Act, 1988: Its Origins and Implications*. London: Falmer Press.

Miller, C. and Swift, K. (1977) *Words and Women*. Harmondsworth: Penguin.

Miller, J.B. (1991) The development of women's sense of self. In J. Jordan, A. Kaplan, J.B. Miller, I. Stiver and J. Surrey (Eds), *Women's Growth in Connection: Writings from the Stone Center*. New York: Guilford Press.

Millerson, G.L. (1963) *The Qualifying Associations*. London: Routledge and Kegan Paul.

Mills, C.W. (1959) *The Sociological Imagination*. New York: Grove Press.

Mirza, H.S. (1992) *Young, Female and Black*. London: Routledge.

Mitchell, J. and Oakley, A. (Eds) (1986) *What is Feminism?* Oxford: Basil Blackwell.

Modood, T. (1993a) The number of ethnic minority students in British higher education: Some grounds for optimism. *Oxford Review of Education*, 19(2): 167–82.

Modood, T. (1993b) Subtle shades of student distinction. *The Times Higher*, Synthesis: Higher Education Trends, 16 July, p. iv.

Moore, K.M. (1987) Women's access and opportunity in higher education: Towards the twenty-first century. *Comparative Education*, 23(1): 23–34.

Morrell, C. (1991) Uncommon knowledge: Women in science and women's studies at the University of Saskatchewan. In T. Wotherspoon (Ed.), *Hitting the Books: The Politics of Educational Retrenchment*. Toronto: Garamond.

Morrish, I. (1978) *The Sociology of Education*. London: Allen and Unwin.

Mortimore, J. and Blackstone, T. (1982) *Disadvantage and Education*. London: Heinemann.

Mulford, W. (1982) Consulting with education systems about the facilitation of co-ordinated effort. In H.L. Gray (Ed.), *The Management of Educational Institutions*. Lewes: Falmer Press.

Murphy, J. (1981) Disparity and inequality in education: The crippling legacy of Coleman. *British Journal of Sociology of Education*, 2(1): 61–70.

Murphy, L. and Livingstone, J. (1985) Racism and the limits of radical feminism. *Race and Class*, *26*: 61–70.

Musgrave, P. (1979) *The Sociology of Education*. London: Methuen.

Myers, K. (1993) Unwelcome touches of student life. *Times Educational Supplement*, 8 October, Section 2, p. 6.

Nash, R. (1973) Clique formation among primary and secondary school children. *British Journal of Sociology*, *24*: 303–313.

National Union of Teachers (1980) *Promotion and the Woman Teacher*. London: NUT.

Ng, R. (1991) Teaching against the grain: Contradictions for minority teachers. In J. Gaskell and A. McLaren (Eds), *Women and Education*. Calgary: Detselig.

Nias, J. (1981a) 'Commitment' and motivation in primary school teachers. *Education Review*, *33*(3): 181–90.

Nias, J. (1981b) Teacher satisfaction and dissatisfaction: Herzberg's 'two factor' hypothesis revisited. *British Journal of Sociology of Education*, *2*(3): 235–46.

Nias, J. (1986) What is it 'to feel like a teacher'? Paper presented at the *British Educational Research Association Annual Conference*, Bristol, September.

Nias, J. (1989) *Primary Teachers Talking*. London: Routledge and Kegan Paul.

Nias, J., Southworth, G. and Yeomans, R. (1989) *Staff Relationships in the Primary School*. London: Cassell.

Nicholson, L. (1990) Introduction. In L. Nicholson (Ed.), *Feminism/Postmodernism*. London: Routledge.

Nielsen, J. (Ed.) (1990) *Feminist Research Methods*. Boulder, CO: Westview Press.

Norquay, N. (1990) Life history research: Memory, schooling and social difference. *Cambridge Journal of Education*, *20*(3): 291–300.

Oakley, A. (1974) *The Sociology of Housework*. London: Martin Robertson.

O'Brien, M. (1983) Feminism and education: A critical review essay. *Resources for Feminist Research*, *12*(3): 3–16.

Olesen, V. and Whittaker, E. (1968) *The Silent Dialogue: A Study in the Social Psychology of Professional Socialization*. San Francisco, CA: Jossey-Bass.

Ollerenshaw, K. and Flude, C. (1974) *Returning to Teaching*. Lancaster: University of Lancaster.

Oram, A. (1989) A master should not serve under a mistress: Women and men teachers 1900–1970. In S. Acker (Ed.), *Teachers, Gender and Careers*. Lewes: Falmer Press.

Orr, P. (1985) Sex bias in schools: National perspectives. In J. Whyte, R. Deem, L. Kant and M. Cruickshank (Eds), *Girl Friendly Schooling*. London: Methuen.

Ortner, S.B. (1974) Is female to male as nature is to culture? In M.Z. Rosaldo and L. Lamphere (Eds), *Woman, Culture, and Society*. Stanford: Stanford University Press.

Ozga, J. and Lawn, M. (1988) Schoolwork: Interpreting the labour process of teaching. *British Journal of Sociology of Education*, *9*(3): 323–36.

Pagano, J. (1990) *Exiles and Communities: Teaching in the Patriarchal Wilderness*. Albany, NY: SUNY Press.

Papanek, H. (1973) Men, women and work: Reflections on the two-person career. In J. Huber (Ed.), *Changing Women in a Changing Society*. Chicago: University of Chicago Press.

Parry, N. and Parry, J. (1974) The teachers and professionalism: The failure of an occupational strategy. In M. Flude and J. Ahier (Eds), *Educability, Schools and Ideology*. London: Croom Helm.

Parsons, T. (1961) The school class as a social system. In A.H. Halsey, J. Floud and C.A. Anderson (Eds), *Education, Economy, and Society*. New York: Free Press.

Partington, G. (1976) *Women Teachers in the Twentieth Century in England and Wales*. Windsor: National Foundation for Educational Research.

Pearson, C., Shavlik, D. and Touchton, J. (Eds) (1989) *Educating the Majority: Women Challenge Tradition in Higher Education*. New York: Macmillan.

Peshkin, A. (1993) The goodness of qualitative research. *Educational Researcher, 22*(2): 23–9.

Pollard, A. (1985) *The Social World of the Primary School*. London: Holt, Rinehart and Winston.

Powney, J. and Weiner, G. (1991) *'Outside of the Norm': Equity and Management in Educational Institutions: Project Report*. London: South Bank Polytechnic.

Pratt, J. (1985) The attitudes of teachers. In J. Whyte, R. Deem, L. Kant and M. Cruickshank (Eds), *Girl Friendly Schooling*. London: Methuen.

Pratt, J., Bloomfield, J. and Seale, C. (1984) *Option Choice: A Question of Equal Opportunity*. Windsor: NFER-Nelson.

Prentice, A. and Theobold, M. (Eds) (1991) *Women Who Taught: Perspectives on the History of Women and Teaching*. Toronto: University of Toronto Press.

Purvis, J. (1973) School teaching as a professional career. *British Journal of Sociology, 24*: 43–57.

Purvis, J. (1981) Women and teaching in the nineteenth century. In R. Dale *et al.* (Eds), *Education and the State*, Vol. II. Lewes: Falmer Press.

Purvis, J. and Hales, M. (Eds) (1983) *Achievement and Inequality in Education*. London: Routledge and Kegan Paul.

Randall, G. (1987) Gender differences in pupil–teacher interaction in workshops and laboratories. In G. Weiner and M. Arnot (Eds), *Gender Under Scrutiny*. London: Hutchinson.

Rees, R. (1990) *Women and Men in Education*. Toronto: Canadian Education Association.

Rees, T. (1989) Contract research: A new career structure? *AUT Woman, 16*(1): 4.

Reid, I. (1978) *Sociological Perspectives on School and Education*. London: Open Books.

Reid, I. (1986) *The Sociology of School and Education*. London: Fontana.

Reid, I. (1989) *Social Class Differences in Britain*, 3rd edn. London: Fontana.

Reinharz, S. (1992) *Feminist Methods in Social Research*. New York: Oxford University Press.

Rendel, M. (1980) How many women academics 1912–1976? In R. Deem (Ed.), *Schooling for Women's Work*. London: Routledge and Kegan Paul.

Rendel, M. (1984) Women academics in the seventies. In S. Acker and D. Warren Piper (Eds), *Is Higher Education Fair to Women?* Guildford: Society for Research into Higher Education.

Reynolds, C. (1990) Too limiting a liberation: Discourse and actuality in the case of married women teachers in Canada. In F. Forman *et al.*, *Feminism and Education: A Canadian Perspective*. Toronto: Centre for Women's Studies in Education, Ontario Institute for Studies in Education.

Reynolds, P.A. (1990) How long is a piece of string? Reflections on British higher education since 1945. *Higher Education, 20*: 211–21.

Rich, A. (1979) *On Lies, Secrets, and Silence*. New York: Norton.

Richards, J.R. (1980) *The Sceptical Feminist*. London: Routledge and Kegan Paul.

Richardson, E. (1973) *The Teacher, the School and the Task of Management*. London: Heinemann.

Riddell, S. (1988) 'Gender and subject option choice in two rural comprehensive schools.' Unpublished PhD dissertation, University of Bristol.

Riddell, S. (1992) *Gender and the Politics of the Curriculum*. London: Routledge.

Roberts, H. (Ed.) (1981) *Doing Feminist Research*. London: Routledge and Kegan Paul.

Roberts, K. (1968) The entry into employment: An approach towards a general theory. *Sociological Review*, 16: 165–84.

Robertson, A. and Kapur, R.L. (1972) Social change, emotional distress, and the world view of students: An empirical study of the existentialist ethic and the spirit of suffering. *British Journal of Sociology*, 23: 462–77.

Robinson, W.P. and Rackstraw, S.J. (1978) Social class differences in posing questions for answers. *Sociology*, 12: 265–80.

Rogers, R. (Ed.) (1986) *Education and Social Class*. Lewes: Falmer Press.

Rosaldo, M.Z. (1974) Woman, culture and society: A theoretical overview. In M.Z. Rosaldo and L. Lamphere (Eds), *Women, Culture and Society*. Stanford, CA, Stanford University Press..

Rosenberg, M. (1968) *The Logic of Survey Analysis*. New York: Basic Books.

Rossi, A.S. and Calderwood, A. (Eds) (1973) *Academic Women on the Move*. New York: Russell Sage.

Rowbotham, S. (1973) *Woman's Consciousness, Man's World*. Harmondsworth: Penguin.

Russell, S. (1986) The hidden curriculum of school: Reproducing gender and class hierarchies. In R. Hamilton and M. Barrett (Eds), *The Politics of Diversity*. London: Verso.

Rutter, M. and Madge, N. (1976) *Cycles of Disadvantage: A Review of Research*. London: Heinemann.

Sadker, M., Sadker, D. and Klein, S. (1991) The issue of gender in elementary and secondary education. In G. Grant (Ed.), *Review of Research in Education 17*. Washington, DC: American Educational Research Association.

Sandford, L. and Donovan, M.E. (1985) *Women and Self-esteem*. New York: Penguin.

School Teachers' Review Body (1993) *Second Report 1993*. London: HMSO.

Schutz, A. and Luckmann, T. (1974) *The Structures of the Life World*. London: Heinemann.

Segal, L. (1987) *Is the Future Female?* London: Virago.

Serbin, L., O'Leary, K.D., Kent, R. and Tonick, I. (1973) A comparison of teacher response to the pre-academic and problem behaviour of boys and girls. *Child Development*, 44: 796–804.

Sexton, P. (1969) *The Feminized Male: Classrooms, White Collars, and the Decline of Manliness*. New York: Vintage.

Sharp, R. and Green, A. (1975) *Education and Social Control*. London: Routledge and Kegan Paul.

Sharpe, S. (1976) *Just Like a Girl*. Harmondsworth: Penguin.

Shaw, J. (1976) Finishing school: Some implications of sex-segregated education. In D.L. Barker and S. Allen (Eds), *Sexual Divisions and Society: Process and Change*. London: Tavistock.

Shilling, C. (1993) The demise of sociology of education in Britain? *British Journal of Sociology of Education*, 14(1): 105–112.

Sikes, P., Measor, L. and Woods, P. (1985) *Teacher Careers: Crises and Continuities*. Lewes: Falmer Press.

Simeone, A. (1987) *Academic Women: Working Towards Equality*. South Hadley, MA: Bergin and Garvey.

Simon, R. and Dippo, D. (1986) On critical ethnographic work. *Anthropology and Education Quarterly*, 17: 195–202.

Simpson, R.L. and Simpson, I.H. (1969) Women and bureaucracy in the semi-professions. In A. Etzioni (Ed.), *The Semi-professions and Their Organization*. New York: Free Press.

Siraj-Blatchford, I. (1990) Positive discrimination: The underachievement of initial teacher education. *Multicultural Teaching*, 8(2): 14–19.

Skelton, C. (1985) 'Gender issues in a PGCE primary teacher training programme.' Unpublished MA dissertation, University of York.

Skelton, C. and Hanson, J. (1989) Schooling the teachers: Gender and initial teacher education. In S. Acker (Ed.), *Teachers, Gender and Careers*. Lewes: Falmer Press.

Smith, D.E. (1974) Women's perspective as a radical critique of sociology. *Sociological Inquiry*, 44: 7-13.

Smith, D.E. (1975) An analysis of ideological structures and how women are excluded: Considerations for academic women. *Canadian Review of Sociology and Anthropology*, 12: 353–69.

Smith, D.E. (1979) A sociology for women. In J. Sherman and E. T. Beck (Eds), *The Prism of Sex*. Madison, WI: University of Wisconsin Press.

Smith, D.E. (1987) *The Everyday World as Problematic: A Feminist Sociology*. Boston, MA: Northeastern University Press.

Smith, M.L. (1991) Put to the test: The effects of external testing on teachers. *Educational Researcher*, 20(5): 8–11.

Sparkes, A. (1987) Strategic rhetoric: A constraint in changing the practice of teachers. *British Journal of Sociology of Education*, 8: 37–54.

Spencer, D.A. (1986) *Contemporary Women Teachers: Balancing School and Home*. New York: Longman.

Spender, D. (1978) Educational research and the feminist perspective. Paper presented at the *British Educational Research Association Conference on Women, Education and Research*, Loughborough, April.

Spender, D. (1980) *Man Made Language*. London: Routledge and Kegan Paul.

Spender, D. (Ed.) (1981) *Men's Studies Modified: The Impact of Feminism on the Academic Disciplines*. Oxford: Pergamon Press.

Spender, D. (1982) *Invisible Women: The Schooling Scandal*. London: Writers and Readers.

Spender, D. and Sarah, E. (Eds) (1980) *Learning to Lose: Sexism and Education*. London: The Women's Press.

Spurling, A. (1990) *Report of the Women in Higher Education Research Project*. Cambridge: King's College.

Squirrell, G. (1989) In passing . . . teachers and sexual orientation. In S. Acker (Ed.), *Teachers, Gender and Careers*. Lewes: Falmer Press.

Stacey, J. (1991) Can there be a feminist ethnography? In S.B. Gluck and D. Patai (Eds), *Women's Words: The Feminist Practice of Oral History*. New York: Routledge.

Stanley, L. (1984) How the social science research process discriminates against women. In S. Acker and D. Warren Piper (Eds), *Is Higher Education Fair to Women?* Guildford: Society for Research into Higher Education.

Stanley, L. (1990) Feminist praxis and the academic mode of production: An editorial introduction. In L. Stanley (Ed.), *Feminist Praxis*. London: Routledge.

Stanley, L. and Wise, S. (1983) *Breaking Out: Feminist Consciousness and Feminist Research*. London: Routledge and Kegan Paul.

Stanley, L. and Wise, S. (1990) Method, methodology and epistemology in feminist research processes. In L. Stanley (Ed.), *Feminist Praxis*. London: Routledge.

Startup, R. (1972) How students see the role of university lecturer. *Sociology*, 6: 237–54.

Statham, J. and Mackinnon, D., with Cathcart, H. (1989) *The Education Fact File*. London: Hodder and Stoughton.

Statistics Canada (1992) *Teachers in Universities 1988/89*. Ottawa: Minister of Industry, Science and Technology.

Stewart, J. (1986) *The Making of the Primary School*. Milton Keynes: Open University Press.

Stiver, I. (1991) The meaning of 'dependency' in female–male relationships. In J. Jordan, A. Kaplan, J.B. Miller, I. Stiver and J. Surrey, *Women's Growth in Connection: Writings from the Stone Center*. New York: Guilford Press.

Strober, M. and Tyack, D. (1980) Why do women teach and men manage? A report on research on schools. *Signs*, 5(3): 494–503.

Suleiman, L. and Suleiman, S. (1985) 'Mixed blood – That explains a lot of things': An education in racism and sexism. In G. Weiner (Ed.), *Just a Bunch of Girls*. Milton Keynes: Open University Press.

Sutherland, M. (1985) *Women Who Teach in Universities*. Stoke-on-Trent: Trentham.

Synge, J. (1973) Scottish regional and sex differences in school achievement and entry to further education. *Sociology*, 7: 107–116.

Synge, J. (1993) Inequality as a theme in sociology of Canadian education: An overview of two decades of research. Paper presented at the *Annual Meeting of the Canadian Sociology and Anthropology Association*, Ottawa, June.

Taylor, H. (1985) INSET for equal opportunities in the London borough of Brent. In J. Whyte, R. Deem, L. Kant and M. Cruickshank (Eds), *Girl Friendly Schooling*. London: Methuen.

Taylorson, D. (1984) The professional socialization, integration and identity of women PhD candidates. In S. Acker and D. Warren Piper (Eds), *Is Higher Education Fair to Women?* Guildford: Society for Research into Higher Education.

ten Dam, G.T.M. and Volman, M.M.L. (1991) Conceptualising gender differences in educational research: The case of the Netherlands. *British Journal of Sociology of Education*, 12(3): 309–321.

The Higher (1991) MA pioneer charges Kent with sexism. *The Higher*, 29 November, p.6.

Theodore, A. (Ed.) (1971) *The Professional Woman*. Cambridge, MA: Schenkman.

Thomas, K. (1990) *Gender and Subject in Higher Education*. Guildford: Society for Research into Higher Education/Milton Keynes: Open University Press.

Thompson, J. (1983) *Learning Liberation: Women's Response to Men's Education*. London: Croom Helm.

Thorne, B. and Henley, N. (Eds) (1975) *Language and Sex: Difference and Dominance*. Rowley, MA: Newbury House.

Thurston, G.J. (1981) 'Women teachers and maternity leave.' Unpublished MEd dissertation, University College, Cardiff.

Times Educational Supplement (1993) What about the boys? *TES*, 8 October, p. 18.

Timperley, S.R. and Gregory, A. (1971) Some factors affecting the career choice and career perceptions of sixth form school leavers. *Sociological Review*, 19: 95–114.

Tomlinson, S. (1983) Black women in higher education: Case studies of university women in Britain. In L. Barton and S. Walker (Eds), *Race, Class and Education*. London: Croom Helm.

Toren, N. (1993) The temporal dimension of gender inequality in academia. *Higher Education*, 25: 439–55.

Tropp, A. (1957) *The School Teachers*. London: Heinemann.

Trown, E.A. and Needham, G. (1980) *Reduction in Part-time Teaching: Implications For Schools and Women Teachers*. Manchester: Equal Opportunities Commission.

Trown, E.A. and Needham, G. (1981) Headships for women: Long-term effects of the re-entry problem. *Educational Studies*, 7(1): 41–5.

Universities Funding Council (1993) *University Statistics 1991–92, Vol. 1: Students and Staff*. Cheltenham: Universities' Statistical Record.

Utley, A. (1991) Blacks fare badly in entry stakes. *Times Higher Education Supplement*, 21 June, p. 1.

Valentine, C.A. (1968) *Culture and Poverty: Critique and Counter-Proposals*. Chicago: University of Chicago Press.

Vartuli, S. (Ed.) (1982) *The PhD Experience: A Woman's Point of View*. New York: Praeger.

Walford, G. (1992) The reform of higher education. In M. Arnot and L. Barton (Eds), *Voicing Concerns: Sociological Perspectives on Contemporary Education Reforms*. Oxford: Triangle Books.

Walker, B. (1981) 'Women and the N.U.T.' Unpublished MEd dissertation, University of Bristol.

Walker, S. and Barton, L. (Eds) (1983) *Race, Class and Education*. London: Croom Helm.

Walkerdine, V. (1981) Sex, power and pedagogy. *Screen Education*, *38*: 14–24.

Walkerdine, V. (1986a) Post-structuralist theory and everyday social practices: The family and the school. In S. Wilkinson (Ed.), *Feminist Social Psychology: Developing Theory and Practice*. Milton Keynes: Open University Press.

Walkerdine, V. (1986b) Progressive pedagogy and political struggle. *Screen*, *27*(5): 54–60.

Waller, W. (1932/1965) *The Sociology of Teaching*. New York: John Wiley.

Warnock, M. (1985) Teacher, teach thyself. *The Listener*, *28*: 10–14.

Webb, M. (1989) Sex and gender in the labour market. In I. Reid and E. Stratta (Eds), *Sex Differences in Britain*, 2nd edn. Aldershot: Gower.

Weber, M. (1946) On science as a vocation. In H. Gerth and C.W. Mills (Trans. and Eds), *From Max Weber: Essays in Sociology*. New York: Oxford University Press.

Wedge, P. and Prosser, N. (1973) *Born to Fail?* London: Arrow Books.

Weedon, C. (1987) *Feminist Practice and Poststructuralist Theory*. Oxford: Basil Blackwell.

Weiler, K. (1988) *Women Teaching for Change*. South Hadley, MA: Bergin and Garvey.

Weiner, G. (Ed.) (1985) *Just a Bunch of Girls*. Milton Keynes: Open University Press.

Weiner, G. (1986) Feminist education and equal opportunities: Unity or discord? *British Journal of Sociology of Education*, 7(3): 265–74.

Weiner, G. and Arnot, M. (Eds) (1987) *Gender Under Scrutiny*. London: Hutchinson.

Weinshank, A.B., Trumbull, E.S. and Daly, P.L. (1983) The role of the teacher in school change. In L.S. Shulman and G. Sykes (Eds), *Handbook of Teaching and Policy*. New York: Longman.

Welch, L.B. (Ed.) (1992) *Perspectives on Minority Women in Higher Education*. New York: Praeger.

Wells, J.H. (1985) 'Humberside goes neuter': An example of LEA intervention for equal opportunities. In J. Whyte, R. Deem, L. Kant and M. Cruickshank (Eds), *Girl Friendly Schooling*. London: Methuen.

West, C. and Zimmerman, D. (1977) Women's place in everyday talk. *Social Problems*, *24*: 521–29.

Westcott, M. (1979) Feminist criticism of the social sciences. *Harvard Education Review*, *49*(4): 422–30.

Wetherell, M. (1986) Linguistic repertoire and literary criticism: New directions for a social psychology of gender. In S. Wilkinson (Ed.), *Feminist Social Psychology: Developing Theory and Practice*. Milton Keynes: Open University Press.

Whitbread, A. (1980) Female teachers are women first: Sexual harassment at work. In D. Spender and E. Sarah (Eds), *Learning to Lose: Sexism and Education*. London: The Women's Press.

Whyte, J. (1986) *Girls into Science and Technology: The Story of a Project*. London: Routledge and Kegan Paul.

Whyte, J., Deem, R., Kant, L. and Cruickshank, M. (Eds) (1985) *Girl Friendly Schooling*. London: Methuen.

Wilkinson, S. (1991) Why psychology (badly) needs feminism. In J. Aaron and S. Walby (Eds), *Out of the Margins: Women's Studies in the Nineties*. London: Falmer Press.

Williams, G., Blackstone, T. and Metcalf, D. (1974) *The Academic Labour Market: Economic and Social Aspects of a Profession*. Amsterdam: Elsevier.

Williams, J. (1987) The construction of women and black students as educational problems: Re-evaluating policy on gender and 'race'. In M. Arnot and G. Weiner (Eds), *Gender and the Politics of Schooling*. London: Hutchinson.

Williams, J., Cocking, J. and Davies, L. (1989) *Words or Deeds: A Review of Equal Opportunities Policies in Higher Education*. London: Commission for Racial Equality.

Willis, P. (1977) *Learning to Labour*. Farnborough: Saxon House.

Wine, J. (1989) Gynocentric values and feminist psychology. In A. Miles and G. Finn (Eds), *Feminism: From Pressure to Politics*. Montreal: Black Rose Books.

Witkin, R. (1971) Social class influence on the amount and type of positive evaluation of school lessons. *Sociology*, 5: 169–89.

Wolffensperger, J. (1993) 'Science is truly a male world'. The interconnectedness of knowledge, gender and power within university education. *Gender and Education*. 5(1): 37–54.

Wolpe, A.M. (1977) *Some Processes in Sexist Education*. London: Women's Research and Resources Centre.

Woods, P. (1979) *The Divided School*. London: Routledge and Kegan Paul.

Woods, P. (1983) *Sociology and the School*. London: Routledge and Kegan Paul.

Wright, C. (1987) The relations between teachers and Afro-Caribbean pupils: Observing multiracial classrooms. In G. Weiner and M. Arnot (Eds), *Gender Under Scrutiny*. London: Hutchinson.

Wrigley, J. (Ed.) (1992) *Education and Gender Equality*. Washington, DC: Falmer Press.

Yates, L. (1986) Theorising inequality today. *British Journal of Sociology of Education*, 7(2): 119–34.

Yates, L. (1987) Australian research on girls and schooling 1975–1985. In J.P. Keeves (Ed.), *Australian Education: Review of Recent Research*. Sydney: Allen and Unwin.

Young, M.F.D. (Ed.) (1971) *Knowledge and Control: New Directions for the Sociology of Education*. London: Collier-Macmillan.

Name Index

Subject Index

academics, feminist, 2–3, 13, 128–9,
132–3, 148, 149–50
'as managers, 6
academics, men, 64, 127–9, 137, 138,
143, 148
feminist scholarship and, 57, 58
university ranks of, 135, 136
academics, women, 41–2, 59–61, 62–4,
125–33, 158–9
as tokens, 41, 127–9, 132
differences among, 134–5
family-work conflict, 126–7, 138, 140
in Canada, 14, 64–7, 70, 147, 151
in Great Britain, 9, 14, 59–61, 62–4,
125, 134–50, 151
in philosophy, 58
in psychology, 59, 63, 65–6
knowledge of women and, 130–2
marginalization of, 9, 13–14, 58–9, 148
promotional discrimination and,
139–41, 148
university ranks of, 135, 136
see also research, feminist
Acker, Sandra
educational biography of, 2, 12–14,
59–61
feminist theory of, 1–2, 4–10
study of graduate students, 61–7,
69–71
study of teachers, 110–20
ageism, 140
anti-sexist initiatives
resistance to, 93–8, 103

Asian girls, 145
Association of University Teachers
(AUT), 137, 139
Australia, 19, 43, 45, 46, 96, 147
gender equality initiatives in, 96

backlash, 3, 96, 152
'Beyond the Glass Ceiling', 6
black girls, 21, 145
black women, 45, 50
in academe, 134
in higher education, 145
boys
education of, 31, 39–40, 90–1, 152–3
entry into higher education, 142, 153
socialization of, 52
sociological studies of, 3–7
subject differentiation and, 154, 155
teacher interaction and, 91–2
British Journal of Sociology of Education, 16,
18, 156
British Journal of Sociology, gender analysis
of, 30–5
British Psychological Society, 59
British Sociological Association (BSA),
18
Southwest Women's Caucus, 14, 19

Cambridge University, 138
Canada, 19, 43, 48, 121
sociology of education in, 16
women academics in, 14, 64–7, 70,
147, 150

sex differences, 19, 44
    as terminology, 42
    in education, 46, 51
    in feminist methodology, 67–9
    in sociology, 28–37
    in sociology of education texts, 35–7
    in teaching, 76–88
    see also gender
sex discrimination, 46, 47
    against academic women, 139–41
    anti-sexist strategies, 51–2
    in feminist scholarship, 58
    in teaching careers, 77–80
Sex Discrimination Act, 139
sex inequality, 34, 41
sex-role socialization, 46–7, 48, 52, 138
sexist bias
    in language, 32–3
    in schools, 38–40
sexual division of labour, 48
    in academe, 142
    in teaching, 76–88
sexual harassment, 51, 144
sexual orientation, 59, 143
sexual politics, 51–2
    in higher education, 44
skills, socialization for, 48
social-class, in education, 142, 151–2
    see also class
socialist feminism, 134
    academic analysis of, 141–3, 149
    educational theories of, 10, 44–5, 45–7
    scholarship, 144–5
sociological journals
    gender analysis of, 4–5, 30–5, 156
    women's research in, 40–1
Sociological Review, gender analysis of,
    30–5
sociologists, feminist, 28–9, 42, 70
sociology
    feminist, 28–9
    sex bias in, 28–9
sociology of education, 15
    decline of, 17–18
    feminist, 37–41
    gender and, 15, 155
    in Britain, 15–18, 27–42
    in Canada, 16
    in the United States, 16
    methodology, 16

neo-Marxism and, 15
right-wing influence, 17
sexist bias in, 30–7
texts
    gender analysis of, 35–7, 42
women in, 29–37
sociology of women's education, 14,
    18–22, 24
    scholarship of, 19–20, 40–1
Sociology
    gender analysis of, 30–5
Statistics Canada, 147

teacher education
    control over, 17
    entry of girls into, 153
    gender issues and, 94
    ideologies, 98–100
teachers
    anti-racist initiatives and, 98
    anti-sexist initiatives and, 96–8, 103
    classroom equality and, 100–1
    feminism, resistance to, 95
    gay and lesbian, 104
    gender issues, resistance to, 93–7
    interaction with pupils, 91–2
    isolation of, 81, 101
    micropolitics and, 101–2
    teaching ideologies and, 98–100
    workplace cultures of, 120
    see also men teachers; women teachers
teaching
    as women's profession, 7–8
    career development, 8–9, 22
    sexual division of labour in, 76–88, 89
    women's place in, 114–17
teaching careers
    advancement in, 107–9, 111–12,
        113–20, 121
    in England and Wales, 107–9
    influences on, 106–7
    re-entry into, 112–13
    senior positions in, 108, 109
    structures of, 107–9, 121
teenage girls, 7, 34
    femininity and, 20–1
    see also girls

United States, 19, 21, 43, 46, 60, 107, 121
    anti-sexist initiatives in, 96–7

GENDER MATTERS FROM SCHOOL TO WORK

Jane Gaskell

During the last ten years, there has been a great deal of concern about the linkages between school and work. Sociologists have explored the organization of schooling in relation to work; policy makers have tried to 'improve' the linkages with a variety of new programmes in the schools and the labour market.

Most of the research, the policy and the theorizing on school and work has only peripherally considered the impact of gender relations. This is despite a burgeoning feminist scholarship in the academy, dramatic changes in the way young women are approaching school and work, and the demonstrably different ways in which young men and young women enter the labour market.

This book makes gender a central concern in the analysis of work and schooling. Gender relations are power relations that have shaped and continue to shape both school and work. The book explores the way young men and women experience and account for the relations between school and work, and it analyses the way schooling and work have been organized by historical and continuing patterns of gender and class inequality.

Contents

INNOVATION AND CHANGE
DEVELOPING INVOLVEMENT AND UNDERSTANDING

Jean Rudduck

Jean Rudduck argues that we must involve classroom teachers and students in the processes of innovation and change in our schools. It is the right of teachers and pupils as partners in the daily life of the classroom to understand what they are doing and why they are doing it; to recognize the areas where they can influence and improve the experience of learning and teaching; and to appreciate, each in their own ways, that the goal always is to extend the possibilities of control over one's own working environment and over one's life chances through deeper professional and personal understanding. Throughout she emphasizes the significance of co-operative work, of who 'owns' the new ideas and the innovations, and of the meaning as well as the management of change.

Contents

RACISM AND EDUCATION
RESEARCH PERSPECTIVES

Barry Troyna

The dilemma facing educational systems in culturally diverse societies is both real and demanding. Too much allowance for diversity can lead to fragmentation and loss of control; too little, to alienation, unrest and loss of control.

Over the past decade or so, Barry Troyna has been involved actively in research aimed at illuminating the role played by educational policy and provision in the legitimation and reproduction of racial inequalities. In the first part of *Racism and Education: Research Perspectives* he draws on his research into educational policy at both state and institutional level to argue that policy makers and practitioners have avoided getting to grips with one of the central impulses of culturally and ethnically mixed societies: racism.

In the second part he focuses on the research enterprise itself. He highlights some of the methodological limitations of existing research on multicultural and antiracist education – research, that is, which has played a powerful role in the framing of educational policy and practice. In the final chapter of the book Troyna provides a vigorous and provocative defence of antiracist education against the criticisms mounted by those of the New Right, multiculturalists and 'critical revisionists'.

Contents